Jim Seymour's

PC Productivity Bible

BY

JIM SEYMOUR

EDITED BY

NORA SEYMOUR

Brady Publishing

New York   London   Toronto   Sydney   Tokyo   Singapore

Brady Publishing

Simon & Schuster, Inc.
15 Columbus Circle
New York, NY 10023

Manufactured in the United States of America

10 9 8 7 6 5 4 3 2

Library of Congress Cataloging-in-Publication Data

Seymour, Jim.
    [PC productivity bible]
    Jim Seymour's PC productivity bible/by Jim Seymour: edited by
Nora Seymour.
       p. cm.
    Includes index.
    1. Microcomputers—Programming.   I. Seymour, Nora. II. Title.
III. Title: PC productivity bible.
QA76.6.S473 1991
005.265—dc20
ISBN 0-13-511080-7

91-437
CIP

Dedication

For Mary Anne and Nora.

Trademarks

All brand and product names mentioned herein are trademarks or registered trademarks of their respective holders.

Limits of Liability and Disclaimer of Warranty

Table of Contents

Introduction

This book had its genesis about four years ago, when a good friend and long-time client told me he was fed up with buying computer books that he invariably found were out of touch with the realities of the business world. "I'm tired of computer books," he said. "What I want is a *business* book that talks about computers."

That was, I realized, what I'd been writing and speaking about for years. I know, understand, and enjoy using PCs. I don't want to trot out the false modesty here: I enjoy being thought of in some circles as a "computer expert." But I enjoy a lot more being thought of in wider circles as a business expert who focuses on productivity issues . . . and who understands something about how personal computers fit into that process.

For years I vowed I'd never write a "computer book." They were hard, sometimes painfully hard, to read. They often didn't sound like they'd been written by writers, but by the computers themselves. And if I didn't like reading books like that, I surely wasn't going to foist another one off on innocent bystanders.

But over the years, a great many people approached me about doing a book. They asked about a compilation of my columns from *PC Week, PC Magazine, PC/Computing,* and other magazines. They told me I should publish my speeches to executive and trade groups in a book. They flattered me a lot. The idea was certainly appealing: I liked the thought of giving those columns and speeches some permanence and a new and different audience by gathering the best of them into a book.

But compilation books don't work in this business. It's great for Art Buchwald to put out collections of his droll columns every year and a half, and for Jim Davis to collect his Garfield cartoon strips into books. Those columns and cartoons have a timelessness I enjoy and envy. But writing about business, and especially about the use of computers in business, demands currency. If it's three or four years old, it's dead. Who wants to hear about Intertec Super-Brains, NorthStar Horizons, PC-XTs? Or, for that matter, about 1989 forecasts for the coming business year, or storm clouds on the S&L industry's horizon?

So a collection of past columns and speeches was out.

But the more people asked about a book, and the more I thought about one, the more I saw that there were some enduring themes, some ideas of lasting value in that intersection between business and computing. What's really interesting, after all, is never the new hardware or software, but *how people work with that hardware and software:* the human factors. What's really useful isn't tips for using specific software packages but tips on *bringing these tools to bear on business problems.* And what's really important is not how much a business tool costs, but *how much it pays back.*

That's what I wanted to write about; and on a blank page, informed by the past but not held captive by it.

Over the years my firm's consulting practice has changed phenomenally. Those changes reflected the continuing evolution of American business's love affair with, and understanding of the power of, personal computers. Early on, we helped companies buy mainframes and minis. With the advent of the PC, the practice turned to helping companies choose, install, and support PCs and software—and, especially, to helping the users of those PCs see how these new tools could become *power* tools, personal-productivity enhancements, not frustrating impediments to getting their jobs done.

Then the practice shifted into connectivity-related issues. As the truth of Sun Microsystems' Chairman Scott McNealy's line became evident—"The network *is* the computer"—we helped companies plan local-area networks and choose network applications. We got in the middle of theological wars over network cabling *("Twisted-pair is the only way to go!" "Co-ax is what we need!" "Only a fool would install anything but fiber optics!")* and topologies and protocols *("Ethernet is the answer to this company's needs!" "Unless we go with an IBM Token Ring this thing is never going to work!")* and tried to mediate the arguments. And we looked hard, in studies after those networks were installed, at what newly connected LAN users liked and didn't like about working in a connected environment.

Over time, the practice shifted again to its present focus: developing so-called strategic systems, precisely targeted computer-based systems designed to exploit opportunities to gain strategic advantage. That work remains challenging, because in it I function as a connecting point—and sometimes as a lightning rod—between the technical sides and business sides of client companies.

We sit down in that work not, to paraphrase George Bernard Shaw, to do that which has been done before, but to dream that which has *never* been done . . . and ask "why not?"

This book reflects that perspective, and grows out of that evolution. If I bring a strength to that strategic-systems creation process, it's not as inventor but as synthesizer: bringing together strands of work from finance, marketing, and administrative people, from electronic engineers and systems designers, from psychologists and human-factors analysts. The result, in both strategic-systems development and in this book, works best when it is both provocative and evocative, and when it addresses the world of ideas as directly as it does the world of things.

In constructing this book, I shamelessly adapted a model created 20 years ago by Robert Townsend, the man who turned Avis from also-ran to an industry leader. In his 1970 book, *Up the Organization,* Townsend put together a series of many relatively short chapters, creating a hybrid form drawn from both the essay and the manifesto. Each chapter, or topic, was like a BBC TV program: exactly as long as it needed to be; neither long nor short; and certainly not of any fixed length, but *right.* That makes for difficult broadcast scheduling but delightful reading, for it means a reader can dip into the book at almost any point, read all Townsend has to say on a subject, and then put the book down, to return at another time.

I cannot claim to have mastered Townsend's model, but it is useful for the reader to know how much I admire it, and that I have tried to follow it here. This is a distinctly nonlinear book: there is no particular advantage to beginning with the first chapter and reading straight through to the one hundred and fifth. And while I certainly hope you'll read every chapter, I know that most readers will pick and choose, reading a few chapters of immediate importance to them and some others from simple curiosity, returning to the book again later for another tour. That's fine with me.

One fundamental premise behind this approach is to acknowledge plainly that the book hardly covers every possible personal-computer topic. And my intention has not been to say all there is to say, even all *I* have to say, about the topics that are covered, but rather to address what I hope are the most interesting and useful points in each area.

Finding the right aim and voice for a book such as this one can be difficult. One dimension of that aim, for example, is the average reader's level of technical sophistication about PCs. I resist the notion that there is such a thing as an "average" reader of a book like this; I see its audience as consisting of people who fall at many points on a line between neophyte and expert. When I have been unsure of the amount of detail to bring to a subject—whether to begin halfway into the topic, assuming a substantial level of technical background and interest, or to begin at the beginning, so as not to lose readers less interested in the technical side—I have tried to err on the side of the latter.

This is certainly not a beginner's book, nor is it necessarily an expert's book. I'm convinced even the most savvy PC technical wizards will find a lot here of value; but since my goal was to write about *computers in business, for businesspeople,* I have often taken paths that do not fall along a technical/nontechnical axis, but that approach the subject from other directions. My hope is that people all along the spectrum of technical knowledge and interest will find this approach congenial and rewarding.

As I was organizing the book, I found that most of the material I wanted to cover fell naturally into several familiar areas, along the lines of traditional personal computer applications. Thus there is a spreadsheet section, a word-processing section, and so on. But there were other, important side streets I wanted to walk with the reader. Often, those journeys veered away from a strict focus on PCs and productivity, and into management issues or human-relations issues.

So I reorganized the book to accommodate those side trips without confusing the reader bent on digging right into the *what's* and *how's* of the tips on using PC hardware and software. Those side journeys are gathered into sections called *Time Out,* which appear four places in the book. If some readers are not much interested in these diversions, they won't get in the way; but I'm confident that, for many readers, these little lateral arabesques will be among the most valuable parts of the book.

This book was written during the last half of 1990, and thus both benefits from and suffers from the state of the art of PCs, and the state of my own understanding of how PCs can be used, at that point. If a reader wonders why products that came to market later do not march through the pages of this book, it is because I can only write about what I have used with my own hands; books based on product specifications, press releases, and Real Soon Now upgrades are not very useful.

Similarly, if you should see something here that contradicts something I have said in print in the past, know that I'm well aware of those contradictions, and am not much worried by them. Products change, how we use them changes, and certainly my own understanding of both has changed over time. If I think I now see things more clearly than I did when I wrote a column a year or three years or ten years ago, I count that as a gain, and trust that you will not tar me with the errors of columns past.

I should add that prices quoted here are so-called "street prices," or the prices a reasonably well-informed buyer will pay to a typical retailer or direct-marketer. Computer-industry "list" pricing is odd at best, infuriating at worst.

Mixing both list prices and typical actual selling prices makes comparisons confusing, so I have stayed with the latter throughout the book.

One other convention should be noted. When I speak of various releases of software, I use the common computer-industry form of inserting an "x" to mean "any." So references to "MS-DOS 3.3x" includes all versions of MS-DOS from 3.30 through 3.39 (though only Versions 3.30, 3.31, 3.32, and 3.33 really exist). References to Lotus *1-2-3* Release 2.x includes 2.01, 2.1, 2.2, and so on.

Finally, I cannot close these notes without acknowledging two people who fundamentally shaped this book, and several million more whose profound role in drawing up its agenda may be less obvious.

Burt Gabriel, then a new staff editor at Simon & Schuster's Brady Books division and now a Senior Editor, was present at the creation of this book. The form of the book changed dramatically over the years, and Burt did heroic duty fending off a series of management teams and sales forces eager to sell a book I did not yet know how to write. Burt's courage and belief in the book opened the way for us both to see how it should be written—and also to see that it could not have been written before now. He made it a much better book, for which those managers and sales forces—and now, the readers—should thank him.

The largest force in shaping this book has been my editor, mentor and task-master—in every way, the book's co-creator—Nora Seymour. Simply the finest editor I have known in 30 years in publishing, she is also much more than an editor. She understood before I did the path this book should take, and has kept it civilized and focused when I have attempted to stray into self-indulgence and obscurity. I am proud beyond my ability to say that she is also now my wife. If I can contribute to her own books a fraction of the insight and support she brought to this one, I will be surprised but very pleased.

Finally, the several million readers of *PC Magazine, PC Week, PC/Computing, Today's Office, MacUser,* and other magazines in whose pages my work has appeared for so many years should know I am very conscious of the direct role they've played in shaping this book. Their often-fierce letters, their detailed and insightful comments when we've talked at trade shows and after speeches, and their incredible support throughout, have taught me about a lot more than computers. The loyalty and commitment they have shown to my work is at once both inspiring and humbling: because they take this so seriously, I must, too.

My profound thanks to all of them.

—Jim Seymour

I

SPREADSHEET STRATEGIES

Spreadsheets As Metaphors

People—especially those who haven't used a PC much—sometimes tell me they're amazed at the success of PC spreadsheet programs. They could understand, they say, if what really put PCs on the map in business was word processing, because . . . well, there are *so* many uses for word processing software. Or if it was the idea of having powerful but easy-to-use databases on a PC. That's what computers are all about, anyway, isn't it . . . databases?

I've never been surprised that it was spreadsheet software that brought PCs into business. I was one of those giddy early users of *Visicalc* on an Apple II, and I remember as if it happened only last week the incredible feeling of . . . *POWER* . . . that combination delivered. It didn't matter a bit that I still had to use a terminal to go hunting for data in the Big Blue Ice Palace downstairs. It didn't matter that *Visicalc* printouts looked terrible, that the Apple's disk drive was slow, that its screen was hard to read. This was a power tool, a lever for the mind, the likes of which I'd never gotten my hands on before.

The genius of Dan Bricklin and Bob Frankston, the technical wizards behind *Visicalc,* and Dan Fylstra, the entrepreneur who brought *Visicalc* to market, was that together they hit on one of those incredibly rare *exactly-right* metaphors: the two-dimensional matrix of a spreadsheet's rows and columns.

The essence of solving numbers problems in business is *money over time.* How you deal with, raise, spend, earn, keep, and manage money over time determines whether your efforts will succeed or fail. Sure, you need products—goods or services. But you need to produce those products, distribute them, sell them to people, get paid for them, invest in the capacity to make more of them.

You need to manage *money over time.*

And a two-dimensional array of rows and columns is the perfect way to visualize that progression. That you can get the columns and rows added up, the percentages calculated, and the rest of the arithmetic done for you is the icing on the cake. What really counts is the power to visualize that management of money over time . . . and then to be able to start playing what-if games.

What if you increase sales 10 percent a month for the next two years? What if you accelerate payments from distributors, reducing average receivables by seven days? By 15 days? What if you delay payments on the license for the new process for 90 days? What if you increase production by 20 percent but only increase production costs by 10 percent?

What if . . . ?

I wasn't at all surprised that spreadsheets were the foundation upon which the success of PCs in business was built. Computer word processing was convenient. Computer graphics were clever. Computer communications was fascinating. Computer databases were useful. But spreadsheets were *powerful . . .* and they put that power right in our hands.

The UnLotus
Alternatives

Three or four years ago, any talk about serious business use of spreadsheet software began and ended with *1-2-3*. Lotus's hottest product so dominated the PC business that the terms "Lotus" and "*1-2-3*" became synonymous with "spreadsheet software." Other software publishers had been in the MS-DOS spreadsheet market for years, beginning with *SuperCalc,* a DOS version of which was introduced not long after IBM rolled out its first PC in late 1981. But none of those products—indeed, not even all of them taken together—had made much of a dent. The DOS spreadsheet market was a *1-2-3* market.

Today, that's changed. Though Lotus's litigation against other software publishers who have allegedly trodden on its legal rights to the look and feel of the *1-2-3* interface has discouraged some new entries, there are good alternatives to *1-2-3*. And, for many businesses, good reasons to buy them.

There have been at least four keys to the survival, and in a few cases the prosperity, of these "unLotus" spreadsheet programs. First, *1-2-3* compatibility: Spreadsheet packages that cannot read from and write to *1-2-3* file formats have little chance of success. It's also helpful if they're keystroke-compatible with *1-2-3*, so users can follow familiar habits, and can also run existing *1-2-3* macros.

Second, improved performance and/or more features: There has to be a good reason to buy something other than the overwhelming standard. Microsoft *Excel* and Borland's *Quattro Professional* are the clear winners here. Both are better products than any current version of *1-2-3*.

Excel requires Microsoft *Windows,* of course, and for the first couple of years of the product's life that was an impediment: versions of *Windows* before 3.0 were slow, clumsy, and demanded a lot of computing power, which translated into expensive upgrades. Which in turn translated into relatively slow sales for *Excel. Windows* 3.0 reversed that, though, and the elegance and functionality it adds to *Excel* moves the program even further ahead of *1-2-3.*

Quattro Pro is also a superior product; not needing *Windows,* it has the advantage of running on almost every PC ever made—though like virtually every other PC program, it performs much better on 80286-, 80386-, and 80486-based PCs. *Quattro Pro* gives users much of the look and feel—the *responsiveness*—of a graphical-environment product such as *Excel,* but without the performance penalties and overhead of a true graphical environment. Like *Excel, Quattro's* strengths, and its edge over *1-2-3,* lie in its superior interface and longer list of better-executed features.

Third, price: Even if a product is as good as *1-2-3,* it had still better compete strongly on price, or people will simply choose the old standard. Paperback Software's *VP/Planner Plus* did this with a lower street price than *1-2-3;* Computer Associates' *SuperCalc 5* does it with "site license" pricing for large corporations, which makes it cheap to put *SuperCalc* on every PC in a company.

Fourth, combination with other kinds of programs: Man does not live by spreadsheets alone. One reason so-called "integrated software" has survived in the market is that buyers can get Lotus-like spreadsheet functions in programs that also include modules for word processing, graphics, database management, and, sometimes, communications. Microsoft *Works* is king of the hill here: speed, ease-of-use, a good mix of features and a $99 street price is a powerful combination. Other, less well-known entries, such as *Enable,* Lotus's own *Symphony, Smart, First Choice, AlphaWorks,* and a few more have been able to hold on in part because they give buyers a taste of spreadsheet power—if rarely on the *1-2-3* level—along with other useful functions.

I make the point that your PC spreadsheet-software choice doesn't *have* to be *1-2-3* because so many PC users have fallen into the trap of simply assuming that *1-2-3* is the only choice. That blinds you to better products from other sources, and by limiting your range of choices to the Lotus universe cuts you off from important advances in spreadsheet-software design. As good an idea as the original *1-2-3* was for its time, Lotus hardly has a corner on good ideas.

In fact, competition has *improved 1-2-3*: Lotus is making some smart moves again these days. By dividing the *1-2-3* line for PCs into four versions— the plain-DOS 2.2, a *Windows* version, 3.1 for high-end DOS and the (largely obsolete) character-oriented OS/2 1.1, and a true graphical-interface *OS/2-Presentation Manager* product *(1-2-3/G)*—Lotus is trying to position itself as offering all the spreadsheet power any PC user needs. By developing other versions of *1-2-3* that run on the Macintosh, Unix workstations, VAX mini-computers, and even mainframes, Lotus is extending that franchise to all the important non-PC platforms as well.

So *1-2-3* in one form or another may still be a good choice for you. But remember: It's not the *only* choice.

Start with Paper
And Pencil?

One of the great pleasures of working with a PC spreadsheet program is the ease of making changes in a worksheet. While you're building a worksheet you can always "open up" the grid to insert rows or columns. You can move at will all or part of a row, column, or rectangular range of cells. You can, in fact, completely rearrange the spreadsheet, even transposing rows into columns and columns into rows.

So why would any sane person start by sketching out on paper how a spreadsheet should look? Why not just jump into it at the computer, using the much-publicized *interactive* nature of PCs and PC software to figure out how it should fit together as you go, rearranging on the fly?

Because that's exactly how most new spreadsheet users get into trouble. And how experienced hands find themselves destroying existing and often invaluable worksheets.

Thinking Ahead

Before you start building a worksheet, ask yourself some questions. Are you going to print the spreadsheet, so you can pass it on to others for review and comment, or as part of a typed report? Or maybe just take that printout with you on the train tonight, so you can think about what it really means away from the distractions of the office . . . and the computer? Wouldn't it help then to give a little thought *now* to how it will look when it's printed, whether it should be tall or wide, how many columns of type you can get on a page from your printer?

Are you going to use macros in the spreadsheet? If so, you'll certainly want a "safe" zone to keep them in, an area you won't accidentally copy a few rows into, wiping out your carefully built macros. What about a data table? You won't want to overwrite that, either.

A few minutes' thought and scribbling on a pad can avoid those problems. As with many of the tricks in this section on building better spreadsheets, not every worksheet you construct needs elaborate planning on paper before going to the computer. But for those worksheets likely to be kept and used for some time—business models that will inevitably be modified, updated, perhaps passed on to others for further modification and updating—a coherent plan is essential.

And that begins with pencil and paper.

Thumbnail Sketches

It certainly isn't necessary to plan out your spreadsheet on a cell-by-cell basis. (There are, curiously, printed "spreadsheet pads" available for just that purpose. The idea is that you're supposed to fill in every cell with the text, numbers, or formula you want in the worksheet, then simply type in the results at the PC. That's going overboard. *Way* overboard.) What's needed is a kind of block diagram, showing in a general way what will go where in the finished worksheet.

Consider the logic behind the positioning of some of those blocks. The ID Block (see *WHAZZIS? Identify Your Spreadsheets!*) and the P Block (see *Parameterize with a P Block*), should be tucked safely up near the top, out of harm's way (read: out of danger of being accidentally overwritten). The "working" data-entry, and repeated-recalculation part of the spreadsheet come next. Tucked down below is a safe space for footnotes documenting what the spreadsheet does, and off to the right is a space for macros.

Why not put the macros down below, too? There is the danger of overwriting them by copying existing rows over them when opening a space for the insertion of new material. Doesn't that leave the documentation at similar risk? Yes, but while documentation is important, and should be zealously guarded against accidental overwriting, macros are even more important for some spreadsheet mavens, because their worksheets virtually will not run without them. If you're seriously concerned about losing your worksheet's annotation, move the notes over to the right, as well.

When Worksheets Dictate Their Own Style

Some kinds of spreadsheets almost demand strongly horizontal or strongly vertical layouts. Unfortunately, we too often recognize those demands only after we've set up the spreadsheet in the opposite direction. Preplanning on paper can really help when laying out and entering the data for these format-specific worksheets.

For example, financial *pro formas* tend to reach out to the right, across the top, or near the top, of the worksheet. No matter how many rows deep they may be, they're almost always wider than they are tall.

Conversely, database lists, such as name and telephone-number lists of business contacts, needn't be very wide, but do tend to grow downwards. (Which is a good thing, since those lists often grow much longer than expected; with one entry to a row, you'll welcome modern spreadsheet packages' generous maximum-potential vertical-size limits—commonly 8,192 rows—versus their much-more-limited maximum horizontal dimensions.) Thus database lists are candidates from the very beginning for strongly vertical layouts.

Also consider the kinds of changes you're likely to want to make in your spreadsheet as it grows. If you're going to be adding additional data-entry areas to the right of the original sheet's data area, it will soon become very difficult, or even impossible, to insert additional rows in the spreadsheet without destroying what you've already built to the left—since spreadsheet rows must, of course, extend the full width of the worksheet.

Similarly, if you're likely to have to insert columns, and perhaps change the width of columns, you'll probably wreck anything above or below the area you're working on in a strongly vertical spreadsheet.

Planning in Three Dimensions

If you're using one of the newer spreadsheet packages that support one form or another of three-dimensional worksheets, your job is much easier . . . but planning first how you'll *use* those three dimensions is even more important. When you're working with 3-D 'sheets, you'll typically break out into separate worksheets, or into separate "pages" of single master worksheets, what would otherwise be discrete zones or patches on a much larger (and harder to plan, and to use) 2-D spreadsheet.

That division of the model into logical subsections makes for spreadsheets that are a lot easier to understand, explain, print, and revise—*if* you make good use of that three-dimensionality.

There's more on managing the third dimension in *There's 3-D and Then There's* 3-D, later in this section of the book. If you're new to 3-D worksheets—or if you know your spreadsheet program supports multipage worksheets, but you've never gotten around to using them because you're not sure just exactly how they work—that chapter is must-reading before laying out your next major spreadsheet model . . . on paper or at the computer!

Little quick-and-dirty 10×20-matrix worksheets rarely involve considerations of the sort discussed here, and thus require little preplanning. Going directly to the computer when you're building them makes more sense: that kind of interactivity is a large part of why we find PCs and PC software so congenial.

But if you're sitting down to build a worksheet you think may be in use for some time—which almost certainly means one that will be modified time and again—or if you're planning a very large model (whether 2-D or 3-D), scribbling a structural "map" of that worksheet before you ever touch a key is likely to produce a better result, one that's easier to build, use, and revise.

With a lot less frustration.

WHAZZIS? Identify
Your Spreadsheets!

Ever have an orphan spreadsheet land in your IN box? One of unknown parentage and origin?

Or worse still—and this one can really destroy working relationships—have you ever gotten a spreadsheet from a colleague for review, spent some time massaging the figures, saved it as a new version, printed out the fruits of your labor, then returned both that electronic file and maybe a printout to the author—only to learn the version you'd slaved over wasn't the *current* version? That it had been superseded by a later iteration, and all your work was in vain?

That used to happen to me, too. But not lately. Because I've learned to simply refuse to work on any spreadsheet that doesn't have proper identification on it: who created it, the filenames and versions of any electronic and paper copies I've been given, the date the spreadsheet was created and the date it was most recently updated, and enough of a title to accurately identify its purpose.

Name, Rank, and Serial Number

Of course, you don't need that much detail on every spreadsheet. But it's not hard to develop a routine of writing at least some of that kind of information into the upper-left-hand corner of every worksheet as you begin setting it up. At minimum, your name or initials, the date of creation, a word or two about what the worksheet is supposed to do, and the filename will help. Then every printout or electronic copy will carry enough information to help that piece of paper or file stand on its own. So if you *do* go through multiple iterations, and *do* save and print out several copies, and *do* file them away, you won't wonder several months later what that worksheet was all about, and where on your hard disk you can find the electronic copy of a given version of it.

A two-line identifier block should handle almost all of your needs. The first line includes the name of the worksheet (*Q4/91 Inventory-Management Analysis*); the second, the filename, your name, and the version and revision-date numbers (*Q4INVANL.WK1-Graham Gordon-v. 3B-rev. Jan 16, 1992*). Note that all entries in both lines are simply plain text (or labels, in spreadsheet parlance), so in *1-2-3*, for example, they must be preceded by an apostrophe (which does not print) to tell the program they're just text. The entries reside entirely in cells A1 and B1, and will automatically spill over into as many adjacent columns as necessary, up to the number-of-characters-per-cell limit of the program you're using, which in the case of *1-2-3* is 40.

ID Overkill

You can get fancier with ID blocks, but don't go so far overboard that building them becomes so burdensome and time-consuming that you start skipping them on those spreadsheets you're not sure will endure for the ages. It's human nature to succumb to that kind of excess in making revisions—and that's subtly encouraged by the PC software industry, which regularly hurls itself into fits of "featuritis," bulking-up new versions of established programs so grossly that we long for the svelte releases of earlier days. With that subliminal nudge, many PC users overdo such civilized and useful touches as ID blocks: with every revision, they get bigger, fancier, and more complex, until finally they're so bloated that the ID blocks take longer to build than the spreadsheet itself.

Resist that temptation. Please.

Not every spreadsheet needs complex identification data. But every spreadsheet needs *some* indication of its source, version, and currency—and if you don't get into the habit of inserting that information when you begin building the worksheet, you're going to wind up with a lot of orphan spreadsheets on your desk and in your files.

And before long, a lot of those orphan spreadsheets will have been inflicted on others.

Parameterize With A
P Block

For several years I taught day-long Lotus *1-2-3* workshops for corporate users. Without fail, participants came up at the end of the day to talk for awhile about how they used Lotus, about their own special problems with the program and how they'd worked around those problems. And almost always, to talk about what they liked best (and sometimes, least!) about the day's presentation. A constant among these comments was one that began *"You know, the thing that really made today worthwhile was. . . ."*

And the last half of that sentence was very often something like: *". . . that thing about using a little box where you set out the variables you're going to use in the spreadsheet and then you keep referring to 'em all the time."*

It's a powerful idea, and I understand those responses. Separating variables from the body—the "logic," strictly speaking—of the worksheet, makes worksheets far easier to construct, use, and maintain. That's especially so for *what-if* spreadsheets, where you're not building a records-maintenance tool or an information-reporting form, but instead are going to be wrestling with the complex effects of changes in several variables. With the variables safely off to one side, you can use the program's ability to repeatedly reference them and, in effect, to rebuild the worksheet automatically for you around *new* variables.

Separating the important assumptions made in a spreadsheet from the logic, or cell-by-cell calculation instructions of that model, also makes it easy for newcomers to the worksheet to understand what the model is about and how it works. And it makes it easy for the spreadsheet's creator (or anyone else) to play "what if?" quickly and safely, in an organized way, without destroying the underlying logic. Finally, it makes for good discipline when you're *planning* a model to have to identify first the fundamental assumptions the model will test.

Parameterizing a Spreadsheet

I groped around uncomfortably for a name for this process for years, until I came across a book by Dick Heiser: *Real Managers Use Personal Computers!* (Que Corporation, Indianapolis, 1983). In that book, Heiser, one of the pioneers in the personal computer industry—he opened and ran The Computer Store, the very first consumer-goods-style storefront computer shop, back in 1975, when that kind of retailing was considered something akin to lunacy— coined an ugly yet wonderful non-word to describe the idea of pulling critical variables out of a spreadsheet, then referring to them repeatedly in formulas, rather than typing in the same values over and over again.

Dick calls the process "parameterizing" a spreadsheet.

I immediately adopted his term, and while I offer an apology to the grammarians who will shrink from that construction and accuse me (and Heiser) of having tin ears, I offer no apology whatsoever for using a word that so accurately describes what we do when we break out the parameters we're going to adjust in successive iterations of a spreadsheet.

In fact, I've taken Dick's term a step further. I like to refer to that little patch in the upper-left-hand corner of a spreadsheet, where we post those variables on a bulletin board for everyone to see, as the "parameter block," or "P Block," of the worksheet.

The idea behind a P Block is simple: If you're going to be testing an idea with repeated adjustments of one or more variables, why subject yourself to the trouble (and potential for mistakes) of having to type in those variables over and over? Why not instead set them out in a special area of the worksheet, then use your program's capacity to reference those cells to insert the new values each time you run a *what-if* on the 'sheet.

Thanks to spreadsheet programs' capacity to create absolute references —single-cell addresses, such as A13 or F17, which are not adjusted for position when other cells referring to them are copied or moved—we can construct a core of values for the spreadsheet in one place, then set up a series of logical statements in another, and let the program do the work for us each time we want to try another iteration.

Simple P Blocks

Here's a quick example. Say you've built a simple three-years-by-months cash-flow model to analyze the impact of various rent levels on a proposed business venture's fixed costs. You know that in your area, you can expect annual rent increases of 25 percent at the end of the first and second years—but of course, since this is a start-up, you don't know what the actual starting rent will be. Indeed, that's one of the functions of the model: You want to run several iterations, testing the effect of various rent levels, to see how much you can afford to pay.

One way to set up the model is to enter your first proposed rent figure in the 12 RENT cells for the first year; then enter a figure 25 percent higher into the next 12 cells, representing the second year; then enter yet another figure, 25 percent higher than *that,* in the next 12 cells, for the third year.

That's not a very smart spreadsheet. Because not only did you have to enter data in 36 separate cells—granted, you could have entered the three base figures into the RENT cells in the columns for the first month of each year, then copied those cells across the remainder of each year, easing the workload somewhat—but when you now want to play what-if with various monthly rent levels, you have to go back and reenter all those figures for each new proposed starting rent figure.

Why not instead write a little P Block in the upper-left corner of the worksheet, and insert a BASE RENT figure as one parameter in that P Block? Then you can write simple formulas referencing that BASE RENT cell, times the appropriate rent-increase percentage, into the RENT cells in the body of the worksheet. If the BASE RENT-value cell is D8, for example, the formula (in a *1-2-3* model) for the first 12 months is (D8*1.0), then (D8*1.25) for the following 12 months, then (D8*1.5) [or if you want the second increase compounded on the base of the first, ((D8*1.25)*1.25)] for the next 12 months.

To test different rent levels? Just change that one BASE RENT value in cell D8. Instantly the spreadsheet ripples the new values throughout the model and you have your answers.

Ping-Ponging among Several Variables

Of course, you're not limited to just one base value, or assumption, in a P Block; you can use several.

Say we're forecasting break-even for a retail store in a large shopping mall. In most shopping center leases, monthly lease payments are based not only on the number of square feet involved, but also on a percentage of the previous month's gross sales (or sometimes, on the average of monthly sales for the previous quarter, or on other, similar, bases). Thus while the owner of the property enjoys participation in the profits of the lessee (but, perversely, suffers no absorption of his losses), the lessee not only finds himself giving up part of his gross revenues to the lessor, but also now finds forecasting net income more difficult, since each month's lease payment is no longer a fixed sum, knowable in advance. (Equitable? Not necessarily . . . but a good illustration of the leverage held in negotiations by the owner of a desirable property: You can have it their way, or not at all.)

A spreadsheet model can't help solve the problem of fairness for the lessee, but setting out both the base lease payment and also the percentage-of-gross-sales kicker in a P Block can make the job of preparing income forecasts a great deal easier.

The real point here should be evident: Use as few absolute values, and as many formulas, as possible in your worksheets. That's exactly the opposite of how most people work with spreadsheets—in large part, I'm convinced, because they're uncomfortable writing formulas, which recall for them the dark days of high school algebra classes.

The logic required for most worksheet formulas is incredibly simple . . . and the payoff for using formulas instead of absolute values in the body of the worksheet is enormous.

Don't Overdo P Blocks

P Blocks can become complicated, with many entries. That's not a problem, so long as the number and complexity of those entries really do reflect the nature and complexity of the problem addressed in the model.

I once worked with a *1-2-3*-based foreign-currency-movements model that was used by a large multinational corporation taking forward positions in the exchange market to buffer losses due to fluctuations in Western European and Asian currencies. The model had more than *60* variables set out in its P Block. As much as the client (and I) wanted to simplify that model and reduce the number of variables, it proved irreducible; the econometricians really needed all those factors. The P Block had itself become not only a listing of variables to be manipulated, but had grown to become a minimodel itself.

But as a rule, you should be wary of going overboard and making the P Block into a model within a model. It's perfectly possible for P Blocks to include derived (calculated) values assembled from the arithmetic manipulation of other cells (including some, perhaps, outside the P Block—but watch out for circular references!), or to draw in data from a look-up table (applying range and limits tests to the data). That's almost certainly overkill, adding needless complexity, wasting time in building and using the model, and locking others who use the worksheet into a bizarre and forbidding environment they may misunderstand and distrust.

I've often been told, sometimes heatedly and occasionally in the same post-workshop circles where I've just been told what a profound revelation P Blocks are, that this is a perfectly self-evident idea that any reasonably sharp spreadsheet user tumbles onto in the first week.

Maybe. But even more people have told me that not only had the idea never occurred to them, but that learning such a powerful trick was by itself worth the time and expense of attending my *1-2-3* seminar.

Though I like to think you'll pick up lots of great tips from this book, the notion of using P Blocks might just be that one trick that immediately pays the freight for buying the book.

Patch Spreadsheets:
Poor Man's 3-D

When you're sitting there with pencil and paper, blocking out your worksheet-to-be, focus on the inherent structure, relationships, and logic within it. Is data grouped naturally, for example, into clusters of information of the sort you're used to dealing with?

What's going to happen when you print the worksheet? Assuming you've organized the various sections of the spreadsheet on a functional basis, are those sections going to be printable in a reasonably coherent fashion? Are you going to be on your hands and knees on the floor of your office, cutting and pasting together long strips of printout into functionally related pages?

One easy path to grouping data logically, and formatting it so that comprehensible printouts are easy to produce, is to use one of the so-called 3-D spreadsheet programs. These allow you to break information into several discrete worksheets, or at least several discrete worksheet "pages," then (if you wish) summarize those 'sheets' data onto one roll-up, or consolidation sheet. Since the individual pages of 3-D spreadsheets are inevitably smaller than one big "flat" model containing all the data, 3-D 'sheets can be easier and faster to build, understand, use, revise, and print.

But what if you don't have a 3-D spreadsheet program? Or what if you use a spreadsheet so infrequently that upgrading to one just isn't worth the cost and the time spent climbing up its learning curve? Since the very first personal computer spreadsheet packages were created, savvy businesspeople have been getting around the limitations of flat, 2-D models by constructing them in carefully separated pages, or patches. When you lay out those separate zones of the worksheet so as to gather related material in blocks, and perhaps then summarize each of those related blocks in one overall cover sheet, they can be very powerful business tools.

Don't miss *There's 3-D, and Then There's* 3-D, later in this section. But keep reading, because even if you *can* afford a snazzy new 3-D worksheet program, you may find that using what you have makes more sense . . . once you start building "patch" worksheets.

Defining Spreadsheet Pages

I find it easiest to think about the layout of large, flat, patch worksheet models in terms of allowing easy printouts. Visualizing a large flat workspace in terms of related printed "pages" makes the job easier for most of us. And even if you think you won't need to print that model, long experience suggests that you will—if only to help debug it as you construct it. Sooner or later, a paper copy of almost *every* spreadsheet is needed. Whether those pages of printout are easy or difficult to print and collate depends on how well the worksheet was designed. In fact, that isn't a bad test for the quality of the layout in terms of grouping datasets logically.

I approach multiple-page worksheets constructed in flat, 2-D spreadsheet programs by deciding in advance what size paper and what size type will be used to print them, then designing those output "pages" into the spreadsheet structure itself. For example, if you're going to be using standard 8½ × 11 inch cut-sheet paper in the usual vertical (now often called "portrait") orientation in a printer that prints 16 characters per inch (cpi) type in its compressed mode, with 6 lines to the vertical inch, and you're going to want 1-inch margins left and right, top and bottom, you'll have 54 lines with 120 characters in each line to work with.

So why not organize the various parts of your spreadsheet in a way that causes each part to exactly fill one of those predefined "print pages?"

A nice trick that extends the usefulness of this organization is to then use your spreadsheet's range-naming command to name each "page" for printing purposes, so that at print time, you need only specify a range name such as *P1*, for example, to print page one of the worksheet. There's more on this trick in a page or two, and more on range-naming in general later in this section.

Reporting Cash Flow

Let's look at a practical example. Say you're building a model that will produce monthly cash-flow statements, plus a year-to-date roll-up. You don't want to go through several linked worksheets (which would require a true 3-D spreadsheet program or an add-on product such as Intex Solutions' *XYZ: Consolidate*), and you *do* want all the data in one place, on one spreadsheet. Your monthly statements aren't automatically extracting that data from separate accounting-data source files (whether in an accounting program or as separate worksheets); you'll be entering the new figures in the cash-flow model each month yourself, relying on the spreadsheet program to get the numbers added-up correctly and the formatting consistent from one month to the next—and to carry data forward to that year-to-date summary page.

By sketching out the layout on paper, you've decided you'll need six vertical columns, of greatly varying widths, for each report. For a 12-month fiscal year, plus a year-end summary, you'll need 13 groups of 6 columns each, for a 78-column-wide worksheet. And from your current cash-flow statements, you know you'll need 48 rows, or lines, per page to present the data.

So you set aside the first five rows of your worksheet for the ID block (see *WHAZZIS? Identify Your Spreadsheets!*) and a little space after it, then assign the next 48 rows—rows 6–53—for the reporting lines in each statement. Columns A–F are assigned to January's statement, columns G–L to February's, on across the spreadsheet through columns BU–BZ for the "thirteenth month," or end-of-year summary.

When you're planning any wide spreadsheet model—and especially these "paged worksheets"—it's often tricky to calculate the names of the columns past the first 26: that is, columns A–Z. Most spreadsheet programs' row-naming conventions identify columns 27 through 52 as AA–AZ, columns 53–78 as BA–BZ, etc. That makes sense . . . to the people who wrote the software. But figuring out the "names" of those columns well off to the right of the first 26 does get tedious.

Years ago I made up a little cheat sheet to help me quickly look up the correct names of those extended columns. I've included that information on the cheat sheet bound into the back of this book. It can save your time as well as your sanity when you're planning big models!

This plan creates a "patch" worksheet, which will let you easily specify and print any month's cash flow statement—and will also let you format the cash flow statement to look as if it were typed or prepared in a word-processing program. Moreover, because you've planned the worksheet as a series of separate entities, connected by their ties to the annual summary, you've designed a well integrated whole, consisting of separate but linked parts that will be easy to build, use, explain, and maintain.

And maybe best of all, once you have the formatting just right for the range A6..F53, it's easy to copy that range across the spreadsheet 12 more times to build the model, confident that you've got a consistent, accurate format for each month.

Printing Patch Spreadsheets

Let's take the idea a step further, to make printing those monthly statements, and the year-to-date summary, really easy. Assign to each of the 12 monthly cash-flow patches a descriptive range name (such as *JAN, FEB, MAR*, etc.), and assign one to the year-end summary, as well (such as *1992 CASH FLOW*).

Now other people who use the model won't need to know cell references for the respective patches to print the results they need, and they won't need to use a GO TO command to jump to those areas on-screen; they just specify the month of the year, and the program shows or prints their cash flow statement.

Another helpful step involves adding a separate documentation "patch" beneath the body of the worksheet—occupying, say, cells A53 through F73 or so—where you provide printing instructions for these patches. That patch itself gets a range name, of course—how about *INSTRUCTIONS*?—and reminds users how to print the various zones, or pages, of the spreadsheet.

What About Vertical Patch Worksheets?

Don't think the trick of breaking up large models into easily visualized, easily printed pages, or patches, of information is useful only for those models that get strung across the top of the huge virtual (or potential) worksheet you're working with in most spreadsheet programs. It works just as well for vertical-format worksheets. In fact, before beginning your model it's worth thinking a bit about which dimension offers greater flexibility for the kind of worksheet you're building—and especially for the kinds of changes you may have to make.

If you lay out your multiple-patch worksheet as a series of side-by-side pages (across the top of the screen, so to speak), and you want consistent formatting from one "page" to the next, you'll wreak havoc with the model if you later have to squeeze in an extra row here or there in one of the pages. Add a row in any of them and you're adding it in *all* of them, of course.

If instead you lay out that model as a series of pages stacked vertically in the worksheet (down the left edge of the computer's display, to continue the analogy), you'll find it easy to adjust any or all of them by adding or deleting new rows as needed. And if you add or delete those rows after range-names are assigned, the ranges covered by those names will expand or contract properly to include the addition. *(Be careful: If a newly added row is at the very top or bottom of a range, you'll need to reassign the range name to cover the whole block of cells.)*

But now, instead of having trouble adding horizontal rows, you'll have trouble adding *vertical* columns—since a column you add to *any* of the pages of this long, skinny vertical worksheet will, of course, cut down through all the pages of the matrix. And a column deleted from any of the pages will be deleted from all of them, too.

Patch Strategies

Which formatting approach to use? Constant-format worksheets that are unlikely to be changed work well when constructed as horizontal arrays, while those that will probably have lines added are better handled vertically.

But if you think there's a good chance you'll have to insert both rows *and* columns in the model over time, the only answer is a stair-stepped arrangement of individual worksheet pages. This kind of model seems wasteful of space within the worksheet matrix (and in Versions 1a and 1a* of *1-2-3* would have caused serious memory problems). Spreadsheet veterans recoil from layouts like this, having been burned too often by "low memory" and "out of memory" problems.

But with the vastly improved memory management model introduced by Lotus beginning with *1-2-3* 2.0, and the generally superior memory management of most other modern spreadsheet programs—which reserve memory only for active, or working cells, and can also usually swap very large files back and forth to disk, using what's called "virtual memory"—this kind of stair-stepping has become a functional (if inelegant) answer to the need for frequent layout revisions of complex models built in two-dimensional spreadsheet programs.

Let me underscore that word *inelegant*. This stair-stepping idea is not one I suggest with great enthusiasm, as a widely useful answer to everyone's needs. I find building a checkerboard worksheet a nuisance, and prefer to avoid it where necessary . . . but I've used it when I had to. It's a quick, effective trick to keep in your bag of worksheet-management tools.

For more conventional worksheets, once the overall design is stable and I'm entering real data, I find myself adding rows, typically used for additional levels of detail, far more often than I add new columns, for new *categories* of information. So I build many more vertically arrayed worksheets than I do wide, shallow horizontal worksheets. Even in areas such as financial *pro formas,* where the likelihood of someone saying "Let's see what happens if we carry this out another year" seems great, my experience has been that far more often someone says "But what if we add . . . ," and we have to open up a new row or two for that additional level of detail.

Thus my preference for vertical arrays.

The specifics of each model you build will determine whether a horizontal or vertical "patch" approach is best. And some worksheets, of course, won't lend themselves to clever page-at-a-time printing layouts, but will still benefit greatly in terms of internal logic and your ability to explain them to others—and perhaps, in their *usability* by others.

If all this sounds pretty convoluted, and you think there simply has to be a better way—well, there is: Use a 3-D spreadsheet package, about which you'll find much more in *There's 3-D and Then There's* 3-D.

☙

There's 3-D and Then There's 3-D

Few new software options have garnered so much attention in the last couple of years as the idea of "three-dimensional" spreadsheets. Lotus promised, and with *1-2-3* Release 3.0 delivered, true 3-D worksheets—a first in the character-based world of DOS spreadsheet programs. Now, 3-D and 3-D-like features are claimed by many spreadsheets. How these multidimensional worksheets operate varies greatly; and choosing the right one requires some understanding of the different ways these products function.

First the good news: Three-dimensionality by whatever name and to whatever degree can boost your productivity—and, probably, your mental health as well.

From the first days of PC spreadsheets, we've been building ever bigger and bigger models. When we started complaining about running out of memory, Lotus egged us on in our bad habits by improving *1-2-3's* memory-management, ending the madness of Releases 1, 1a, and 1a*, which reserved memory space for every cell within the boundary formed by the cell farthest to the right and down from cell A1. Then, when that proved not to be enough for our habit and we started complaining again, Lotus encouraged our craziness even more by codeveloping the Lotus-Intel-Microsoft Expanded Memory Specification ("LIM EMS," or just "EMS"). Suddenly we could use as much as four megabytes of EMS RAM for worksheets—which meant that those worksheets could grow far beyond most *1-2-3* users' ability to build, debug, maintain, or even *understand* them.

Those huge "flat" models always sounded good in the planning stages: they seemed so powerful and could, at least in theory, offer such superb, big-computer-level decision support. But in practice they were often disasters. Too big for all but the most doggedly persistent to debug, they often collapsed around the ears of those who tried building them. An in-house auditor at a client company of mine finally gave up and threw away a three-megabyte *1-2-3* model he'd been working on, more or less full-time, for more than four months. It didn't do what he expected—the answers were erratic, and often demonstrably wrong—but the sheer size of the worksheet, which had something like 10,000 active cells, had outgrown his ability to track down and fix its hidden mistakes.

With 3-D-style worksheets, though, we can replace those mega-spreads with a stack of much smaller, easier-to-build, easier-to-debug, easier-to-*understand* 'sheets. If the final calculations of that stack of worksheets are rolled up to a cover sheet, with separate areas for both the fundamental variables being tested and also for the answers delivered by the stack's calculations, almost anyone can understand, update, and use the model.

Using 3-D Concepts

There are several fundamentally different approaches to 3-D spreadsheet work.

One involves constructing what I sometimes call a "spreadsheet pad": a stack of absolutely identical-format pages, probably summed up on the topmost sheet. This is a great way to build spreadsheet models that use identical sets of input from many sources. One example: collecting next-fiscal-year budget requests from each of many departmental managers, then rolling those budget plans up into a single budget-forecast summary on the top sheet of the "pad." You still have each manager's work available as a discrete sheet, or page, within the stack, so you can quickly flip to any one department's projections, then back to the summary sheet.

Another example: gathering scientific data from many reporting stations, then summing and averaging (or otherwise manipulating) those data points by cross-station categories in the top sheet.

Envisioning how a spreadsheet program works with these pads is easy. Since the worksheet layout for each sheet is the same, you use a kind of electronic knitting needle to stab down through the stack at any given point, then pull it back out, gathering the calculated results of those same-position cells into a summary cell on the topmost sheet. The summing formulas are easy to construct; it's quick and easy to build this style of 3-D spreadsheet.

A second, related approach is to have a stack of pages in which every sheet *except* the topmost one is identical. This is helpful when you're gathering same-format information from many sources, but want to perform more complex analyses on the summed results. The topmost page then becomes both a data-summary and data-analysis tool, while the underlying pages represent the separate data sources. Once again, these spreadsheet "pads" are easy to construct, and the formulas are not difficult to write.

Using 3-D in the Real World

A final approach is to build a series of completely *dis*similar spreadsheet pages, with many kinds of references and links bouncing back and forth among them. This takes more time to plan, and a lot more time to build . . . but it also often reflects much more accurately how things work.

An example: In the corporate world, it may be possible to enforce upon division heads an absolutely constant spreadsheet-based reporting format. I emphasize the *may be* in that, because if you succeed, it will have been at great effort and probably at some cost to your personal relationships with those managers. But don't be surprised if, when each of those filled-in spreadsheet templates arrives—their agreement to your plan notwithstanding—you find they've each made "just a few little changes."

Because no matter how cleverly you construct the reporting model, you'll never know enough about the real-world exigencies of those managers to be able to cover all their *if's* and *and's*. So by insisting upon absolute standardization, you run a substantial risk of turning that budget-reporting system into a very blunt tool, indeed. Those division managers will understand that immediately, and will do everything they can to protect themselves from your excessive simplification.

A tough-minded CFO might get away with demanding that kind of reporting structure. You may not be able to.

Which can make assembling those results into a tidy, single model a bear, as you keep running into little alterations in the model, and are forced to somehow reconcile them with your fixed form. *(If you really do want to force people into a fixed reporting form, consider running the worksheet reporting-template you develop for them through a spreadsheet compiler, to eliminate the possibility of changes at their end. See* Canned Worksheets: Spreadsheet Compilers, *in this section.)*

All of this suggests that often it may be best to start with a stack of similar-format data-assembly worksheet pages in a 3-D model . . . but to accept and integrate into that stack the ultimately very dissimilar pages that you'll develop as you work with the model.

Choosing a Tool

Here's a quick look at how each of the major PC spreadsheet packages approaches 3-D functions.

In the DOS environment, only *1-2-3* Release 3.x offers true 3-D multisheet worksheet files. By "true 3-D" I mean the ability to have more than one worksheet in memory at a time, in addition to the ability to construct links among worksheets. Release 3.x worksheet files can contain up to 250 separate 'sheets (the actual number will depend on how much memory is available, of course), each of which can be a fully functioning, independent worksheet. To insert each additional worksheet after the first, just use *1-2-3's* /Worksheet Insert Sheet command. To view the worksheets in a diagonally displaced form, like a stack of index cards with each moved down and to the side a bit from the one underneath, use *1-2-3's* /Worksheet Window Perspective command. If you want a stack of same-format worksheets with Release 3.x, and want the commands you issue on the topmost sheet to be carried through the whole stack, use the /Worksheet Global Group Enable command.

Worksheets in Release 3.x stacks don't need to be identical in format, of course; you can make each one different, and you'll still be able to construct links among them.

But using *1-2-3* Release 3.0 quickly shows the limitations of a character-based environment in managing 3-D spreadsheet files. While I find it incredibly easy to roll through a stack of same-format 3.0 worksheets in a multiple-sheet file, I find navigating among a stack of differently formatted 'sheets in a 3.0 file a mess. Lotus's own *1-2-3/G* program, a graphical-interface extension of Release 3 that runs under OS/2-*Presentation Manager,* quickly confirms that: It's far easier to keep your bearings when you're flipping through a series of differently formatted windowed worksheets in *1-2-3/G* than in *1-2-3* 3.x.

Using Microsoft *Excel* on the PC, under *Windows* or OS/2-*PM,* also confirms the superiority of the graphical interface for managing three-dimensionality. Of course, since *Excel* under *Windows* (or *Presentation Manager*) allows you to have more than one worksheet available at once (all easily manageable through *Excel's* "workspace" command), it offers easy-to-learn, easy-to-use three-dimensional worksheet functions, too.

Borland's *Quattro Professional* offers some three-dimensional capabilities through its own proprietary windowing system, though since it must do so under character-based DOS, it can't approach the convenience and functionality of a graphical-interface program.

Finally, users of *1-2-3* 2.x shouldn't feel completely left out. Though 2.x can only accommodate one spreadsheet in memory at a time, it can use external linking to other spreadsheets not currently in memory to gain some of the advantages of true 3-D worksheet packages. Those external-reference formulas aren't hard to write—in effect, you simply write a formula including the full pathname of the other file, plus the appropriate cell references, as well as the function to be performed—though the inconvenience of using a system that allows only one of several linked 'sheets to be in memory at once does make this a circuitous way to getting three-dimensional power into your models.

The Hidden Keypad

Entering data in a spreadsheet is different from most other work we do at the PC. The emphasis on numeric entries—but still with a few alphabetical and other characters mixed in—means that to be really efficient, we need to change our way of working with the PC's keyboard.

The simplest answer is to use the NUMLOCK key to lock the combination numeric keypad/cursor keypad on your PC's keyboard into a strictly numeric mode. Use it, not the numeric keys strung across the top of the keyboard, for numeric entries. Your fingers can really fly over that numeric keypad as if it were a ten-key adding machine; just reach out to the adjacent cursor keys (or the ENTER key) to load the data into each cell and move to the next one.

But there's a little problem here: Many of us find it faster and more efficient to leave NUMLOCK off, and keep our right hand in one place over those numeric keys, using them for both numeric entry and also for cursor movements. Toggling in and out of NUMLOCK mode, to switch back and forth between numeric entry and cursor movements from those keys, will drive you crazy; it isn't a serious option.

There's a wonderful, easy-to-learn shortcut built into the PC's keyboard—in effect, a hidden dual-purpose keypad—that very few spreadsheet users know exists. Just let your left hand rest at the left end of the keyboard, your right hand on the numeric keypad at the right end. When you want those numeric-keypad keys to enter numbers, hold down the left-hand SHIFT key. Release the SHIFT key and those numeric-keypad keys revert to cursor-movement keys.

It's so much easier and faster to enter large volumes of data this way—just holding down the SHIFT key when you need direct entry of numbers from the numeric keypad—that I'm amazed more PC users don't use this trick. Almost certainly, I'm convinced, because they don't know about it.

But now you do.

☙

Save, Save, Save

Here is perhaps the single most useful and important piece of advice I can give you for working with spreadsheets: *save, save, save your work frequently.* You've heard that before, of course, usually applied across the board for work at your PC. And I agree that saving the current version to disk frequently is a great idea when you're working with word-processing programs, graphics programs, database programs, and so on.

But the exhortation to *save, save, save* has special importance with spreadsheets.

When you're building a worksheet, you're usually dealing with its structure *and* its content at the same time. Unless you're simply filling in a template, you're not only entering data, but also entering formulas and probably doing structural tune-ups (such as changing a column width to accommodate the longer numbers you've just realized it will hold, or transposing columns, or inserting a new block of rows) as you go.

The chance of making a major mistake when you're making changes on that level is sufficiently great that the safe, smart thing to do is to save the file very frequently—and not to simply save it under its last name, so that with each save you overwrite the previous version, but to keep making *incremental saves,* each successive file a snapshot of the worksheet in slightly more developed form.

For example, the first time you save that spreadsheet model on the effects of changing your accounts payable cycle to a longer hold-period, call it something like APHOLD01.WK1. Then with the next save, a few minutes later, save it as APHOLD02.WK1. And next time, as APHOLD03.WK1. And keep saving in that pattern—literally saving a new, slightly expanded version every minute or two, perhaps five minutes at the most—until you finish.

You'll wind up with something like APHOLD35.WK1 as your last version . . . and 34 more files, each an incremental step towards your final version. Don't worry about all those files on your disk: when you're sure you have a version you like, go back and erase all but the last two or three. But always keep at least the last couple of iterations before the one you consider final: You won't know if the "final" one has a fatal flaw until you've worked with it for awhile.

If you're worried that keeping several versions on disk may mean you accidentally load the wrong one and start working with it—putting new data into a version that's one or two generations old—change the filenames of those last, not-quite-there versions to something like APHOLDX.WK1, APHOLDY.WK1, and APHOLDZ.WK1. But don't erase them!

The obvious reason for stacking up these incremental saves on your hard disk is that it gives you wonderful, cheap protection against a power outage taking away your most recent work, and also some protection against a hard-disk failure that damages a part of the disk's surface. Those benefits alone would certainly be sufficient to make it worth using this notion of repeated file-saves.

But the real advantage is that this scheme can save you from *yourself:* for example, when you accidentally overwrite a row or column by moving a new one into its place—but forget to first open up a space for the one you're moving, and so destroy the existing row or column. It also spares you from having to backtrack to find and correct a circular reference that you just created as you changed the model. Or from a hundred other everyday, perfectly ordinary spreadsheet disasters.

To use this trick, you'll also want to devise a rational, consistent naming convention for your spreadsheet files: a few rules for yourself on how you name the first version of each new worksheet, both to make it easy to find when you scan through the files on your disk, and also to make certain there's room in those filenames for the critical trailing digits that let you identify incremental saves of work in progress.

Keep reading. Naming conventions are covered in detail in the next chapter, *For Lack of a Name, The Worksheet Was Lost.*

For Lack of a Name,
The Worksheet Was Lost

How do you decide how to name files when you save them?

I've asked that question of hundreds, maybe thousands, of corporate PC users. I've almost always gotten an answer something like this: *"Well, I . . . uhh . . . you know . . . I mean, I try to figure out some way to abbreviate what it's about . . . some way to fit it into eight characters. I don't know. . . ."*

But maybe every 50 times I ask that, I get a much more thoughtful answer, from someone who's obviously worked out a personal system for naming files in an organized way. Sometimes these answers go into incredible detail; sometimes they even stray into a bizarre and goofy kind of "metaphysics of file-naming." But even when the answers are long and elliptical, it's clear these PC users know they're onto something important: a simple, easy-to-remember, easy-to-apply strategy for naming files in ways that make them easy to identify later, and avoids disasters such as inadvertent overwriting of important files by saving a later file under the same name.

MS-DOS, the operating system used by most of us for business PC work, doesn't help. The eight-character limitation on DOS filenames makes it awfully difficult to construct meaningful, recognizable filenames. The optional three-letter filename extension DOS allows helps, but only indirectly. While we usually can't use that extension ourselves with PC applications, which appropriate it for themselves, adding a standardized filename extension to every file created by the program (*e.g., 1-2-3's* .WKS, .WK1, and .WK3 extensions), those application-linked filename extensions do help us tell at a glance what kind of file SHHAYHSZ.WK1 is when we see it in a directory listing.

So if DOS won't help—if nice, informative 40-character filenames still lie in the future for most of us—then we've got to use the eight measly file-naming characters we have very carefully.

Though in this chapter we'll look at naming worksheet files, meaningful filenames are important in all the work you do at the PC. Start using a simple, logical system of naming your worksheet files and you'll soon find yourself doing the same thing for word-processing documents, graphs, and other kinds of computer files.

Your Personal File-Naming Convention

It's not hard to figure out such a system for your own use. You get to write all the rules: It doesn't matter what I like, nor what that overbearing PC Power User who sits three cubes down from your desk likes. But to get you started, here's a checklist of ideas that work for me, and that I've found others using with great success:

- **Use largely alphabetical filenames, rather than an all-numeric file-naming convention.** In some rare cases, it may be useful to use an all-digit form. For example, I save my columns that appear in *PC Week* on disk under filenames based on the date those columns appear—using the form 90-07-12.DOC for the column that appeared on July 12, 1990. But generally, filenames that are alphabetical, or that at least begin with letters rather than numbers, are more meaningful and thus easier to figure out six weeks or six months later.

- **Develop groups of filenames.** Use filename conventions that naturally cluster related material. You might, for example, save each of your quarterly *1-2-3* worksheets analyzing transaction volume as 91Q1TRAN.WK1, 91Q2TRAN.WK1, and so on. Or you could name your separate, state-by-state *Excel* name-address-telephone-number databases as NAMES-CA.XLS, NAMESNY.XLS, NAMESTX.XLS, etc.

- **Leave one or two character positions at the end of filenames to allow for one or two digits to identify successive saves of the file.** For example, as you're building a *1-2-3* model on interest-rate fluctuations, you might save each successive iteration as INTRAT01.WK3, INTRAT02.WK3, and so on. If you then want to make clear which is the current "final" version—remember that you're probably still going to be tinkering with that model six months from now, so "final" is only a relative term!—call the current working version INTRATES.WK3. By scrubbing the incremental-saves digits out of the "real" version's filename, you'll never mistake one of those partial, tentative models for the current one.

- **Use subdirectories on your hard disk to group files.** This isn't exactly a file-naming convention, I'll concede, but it's closely related. While using related filenames to group files into naturally sorted directory displays can help, go a step further and gather groups of related files logically into subdirectories. Most people don't make very effective use of subdirectories, but organizing your files in this way can really make a difference when it comes to finding a certain file quickly—and not accidentally overwriting important files. The combination of grouping by filename and then grouping within subdirectories is an effective way of organizing your work.

Spreadsheet Publishing: Using Print-Formatting Tools

When spreadsheets first came into use, most of us saw them as something like large-array adding machines. We used them to construct little grids of numbers that could automatically, and fairly quickly, be added up, with some assurance of accuracy. The huge analytical models of today were far beyond our vision of what was possible with spreadsheets.

The printouts from those early spreadsheets didn't get much thought, either. We considered ourselves lucky enough to get something, *anything*, on paper, let alone a good-looking printout. Most of the time devoted to worrying about printed copies of worksheets was spent on hands and knees on the floor, scissors and Scotch tape at hand, as we tried to put together coherent hard copy from the strands of printout emerging from our dot-matrix printers.

Today almost everything about PC spreadsheets has changed, from the size and complexity of the programs to the size and complexity of the worksheets we build with them; from memory requirements to the amazing array of mathematical functions available; to . . . the attention paid to better-looking printouts. Where once even getting a printout was distinctly secondary to getting those rows and columns added up, and *any* printed copy was *good* printed copy, and the notion of turning those printed pages into something that looked like a typeset printed page was undreamt of, today many uses of spreadsheet programs are specifically print-focused.

On one level, better-looking printouts are simply a reflection of the times: PC users and those who work with their results have gotten accustomed to good-looking output. But on another level, there is substantial interest today in what some call "annual-report quality" output: pages that really do look as if they came from a well-designed annual report, not from a PC printer driven by a spreadsheet program. And finally, some PC users are using the print formatting tools built into the best of the current group of spreadsheet programs to construct worksheets that, when printed, look nothing at all like a worksheet printout . . . but appear to be perfectly normal invoices, purchase orders, statements, and other standard office forms.

Wherever you fall on that spectrum—whether you simply want to turn out cleaner-looking spreadsheet reports that catch your boss's attention, or whether you're designing an invoicing system that uses a program such as *Excel* as its computational and printing engine—the range and depth of spreadsheet print-formatting tools available today is amazing.

In fact, that interest in more attractive spreadsheet printouts, and the range of tools designed to produce them, have led to the coining of a new phrase: "spreadsheet publishing."

Better Tools

Early spreadsheet printing utilities focused on tricks such as turning pages sideways on dot-matrix printers, so you had fewer long strands to glue together to assemble a printout of a complete worksheet. Paul Funk's *Sideways* was the champ at that trick (and remains a big-selling tool in its current, far more sophisticated version). Now these tools focus primarily on the use of varying type styles to dress up printouts, on dropping in shaded backgrounds over part of the worksheet, on drawing boxes around regions of the spreadsheet, and on subtle little touches like adding true double-underscoring beneath a grand-total column footing, in lieu of the ugly PC convention of inserting a row of equals signs, as in =======, beneath the total.

Funk Software has one of the leading entries in the new generation of spreadsheet-publishing utilities, as well: *Allways.* A Lotus add-in, it works with *1-2-3* Release 2.x software, and offers several sizes and varieties of type, box-drawing, dot-patterns, and most of the other visual devices used to spice up worksheet printouts. It works so well, in fact, that Lotus bought the technology from Funk and includes it in *1-2-3* 2.2; Funk still sells *Allways* as an add-on for Releases 2.0, 2.01 and 2.1.

Lotus also bought the rights to another, very different dress-for-success package for *1-2-3* spreadsheets, *Impress.* Its tools are now provided in the box with *1-2-3* Release 3.1; *Impress's* developer, PC Publishing, sells the package separately for users of Releases 2.x of *1-2-3.*

Borland's *Quattro Professional* also has good print-formatting tools, and includes (as do *Allways, Impress,* and their offspring packaged with *1-2-3*) a range of attractive downloadable fonts from Bitstream.

Lotus's decision to buy the rights to those products and add their features to *1-2-3* was no doubt spurred by Microsoft's success with *PC Excel,* which for the first time brought serious print-formatting tools to PC spreadsheets. Running under *Windows, Excel* can turn out astonishingly unspreadsheet-like results. Included in the *Excel* package are samples of such things as IRS Form 1040 printouts produced from the program on laser printers, to show how little an *Excel* printout need look like a computer-generated spreadsheet page.

Clearly, that's the future of spreadsheet publishing formatting tools and techniques: built-in controls that work seamlessly on the design of your spreadsheet, in the same way you work on constructing its logical structure. As useful as *Allways* and *Impress* are, once you've used *Excel's* integral formatting tools, you'll never want to go back to the add-in-module route.

A Checklist for Spreadsheet Publishers

Let's get down to some of the specifics of spreadsheet publishing techniques, to help turn your worksheet printouts into something more than "computer reports."

- **Margins** Perhaps because the margin-setting controls on programs such as *1-2-3* are so confusing and badly implemented, most spreadsheet users accept the programs' default margins at the left, right, top, and bottom of the page. If they do pay any attention to resetting the margin measurements, it's usually because they're trying to squeeze more columns onto the printout—and in the process, they go to even narrower and less attractive margins than their program normally uses.

  Graphic designers talk a lot about "white space," which refers, collectively, to all the unprinted areas on a page. While paying attention to white space is certainly important in terms of separating sections of a page from one another, and in floating headlines and subheadings down a bit from the previous section, white space is nowhere so important as in setting up page margins. Avoid those ugly, skinny half-inch margins so many people have gotten accustomed to using with spreadsheets— again, usually because their focus was on trying to squeeze more data onto the page.

  Left and right margins of about .75–.9 inches, a bottom margin of 1.2 inches and a top margin of 1.1 inches are about as small as you can use and still get a good-looking page. Much better, when the data format permits, are left and right margins of about 1–1.2 inches, a bottom margin of 1.3–1.5 inches and a top margin of 1.25–1.4 inches. Left and right margins should be equal; the bottom margin should always be a little deeper than the top, so the printed material doesn't seem to be sliding off the bottom of the page.

■ **Type** Though white space sets the frame for your printed spreadsheet, type is the most potent tool of the spreadsheet publisher. With earlier versions of spreadsheet programs, it was possible, if only with great effort, to insert different type sizes and effects (boldfacing, italics, etc.). But the use of type for worksheet printouts came into its own with the introduction of *Excel,* and was extended to the broad business spreadsheet market by *Allways* and *Impress* with various versions of *1-2-3*, and by *Quattro Professional.*

A boldface, centered heading across the top of a worksheet gives it a professional look. Using smaller boldface heads at the left margin, for each new group of rows, extends that look. You can also use small boldface or italic type at the top of each column heading.

One of the most important benefits of using typeset-look type in spreadsheet publishing is that you can choose a condensed typeface as the standard type font for your worksheet. The narrower letters and numbers of that condensed font will help you squeeze in more columns, when necessary. The greater variety of type sizes available with downloadable or printer-resident typeset-look fonts also means you can often sneak that standard typeface size down just a bit—say, from 10-point Helvetica Narrow to 9-point—when you're right on the edge of being able to get another column onto the page.

Be wary of going overboard on the small-type approach. Unless your primary goal is simply to squeeze a mass of data onto the printed page, too-small type will defeat your efforts to produce better-looking worksheet printouts. As a rule of thumb, consider these type sizes (in points) for most spreadsheet work:

ITEM	MINIMUM TYPE SIZE	NORMAL TYPE SIZE	MAXIMUM TYPE SIZE
Main Headline [1]	18	24–30	36
P Block, ID Block	10	11	12
Primary Subheadings [2]	12	14	18
Secondary Subheadings [2]	11	12	14
Standard Type	8	10–11	12
Column Headings [3]	7	9–10	11
Footnotes and Annotation	8	9	11
Page Headers and Footers [4]	8	9	10

all sizes in points

[1] boldface strongly recommended
[2] boldface recommended
[3] italic or boldface recommended
[4] italic recommended

One last caveat: Don't use underlining to accent type. Underlining is a hold-over from the days of typewriters, where it was used in manuscripts to indicate material that should be italicized when typeset. Underlining eventually became a necessary evil in typewritten originals, where options such as boldface and italic type were not available. But underlined typeset-look type looks awful, and marks the person who uses it as a neophyte in the world of desktop publishing, spreadsheet division.

Also eschew such unfortunate type effects available with some printers as drop shadows, outline type, and filled characters. And at all costs, avoid "combination-of-ingredients" type specs, such as boldface, italic, drop-shadow, underlined headlines. The idea is to produce *better*-looking worksheets, not uglier ones, isn't it?

- **Column Width and Height** Column-width settings take on a new importance when you move into the realm of spreadsheet publishing. And with more sophisticated programs, manual adjustment of row height provides a new kind of control.

  When you're using typeset-look typefaces, column widths should generally be set to narrower values than you're accustomed to with fixed-pitch 10- or 12-characters-to-the-inch typewriter type. Even for columns requiring as many as nine or ten digits, you'll probably want to set column widths down to seven or eight. Again, this helps get more columns on each printed page, and it looks better than widely spaced columns of relatively small type. Those rivers of white space running down the page between columns of figures not only waste space; they're unattractive and they make it difficult for the eye to jump from column to column when scanning across the worksheet.

  Programs that let you adjust type size usually also adjust row heights automatically, to provide the correct vertical spacing for the type size chosen. But you may well want greater vertical spacing in some lines, for effect; some programs provide this new formatting option. You might want to make rows that contain section headings at the left edge of the worksheet taller, for example, so a little extra white space appears before those rows.

  You'll also want to adjust the height of the row just under your column footings' grand totals to a very small setting, such as 2, so you can use the program's line- and box-drawing options to provide an attractive double-underscore beneath those grand totals. Keep reading for more on double-underscores.

- **Rules and Boxes** You can often make a spreadsheet printout more attractive and easier to read by drawing boxes around sections of the worksheet, or rules between those sections. Indeed, this kind of design tool is the key to producing invoices, purchase orders, packing lists, statements and other business forms that are really, underneath their attractive faces, worksheets, with all the calculation and other mathematical powers of a worksheet.

  Newcomers to the notion of spreadsheet publishing are often surprised to find that line-drawing is usually accomplished by running a rule around one or more sides of the invisible box that form a cell. It does seem odd at first, but soon you'll catch on to using a line across the bottom of a row of cells (or across the top of the row of cells beneath them) when you want a horizontal line.

Drawing lines at the top and bottom of a cell, in a row with its height adjusted to a very small value, provides a much more attractive double-underscore for the number in the cell just above the partially boxed cell, than the old trick of using a row of equal signs in the spreadsheet cell under the total.

Finally, a great trick to use if you're trying to duplicate the look of a conventional paper-and-pencil form is to adjust both a column's width and its height to small values—say, 3 or 4—then draw a rule around all four edges of a cell. Presto: you've got an instant check-off box.

- **Shading** Most spreadsheet-publishing add-on utilities, and programs such as *Excel* that have those tools built in, allow you to lay a gray dot-pattern over parts of your spreadsheet. This can be useful to highlight a section's subheading, for example, or to fill in areas outside the critical, boxed "answer" sections of a worksheet. But be careful: A little shading goes a long way.

Avoid using heavy shading, which can obscure the type beneath it. The lightest shading setting available in a program is usually the best choice.

- **Integral Graphs** Some newer spreadsheet-publishing-oriented packages make it easy to display a graph of the worksheet's data on the same page with the rows and columns. That kind of integral graph can be very effective: The same page then includes both the graph, as a quick summary of the numbers, and also the numbers themselves, for those who want to see the detail behind the graph.

Some programs can print more than one graph on a page. That can occasionally be useful, but watch out for the Swiss Army Knife syndrome: the all-things-to-all-people tool. If you need elaborate graphing options, you're probably better off with a separate, high-level graph-and-chart program, such as *Harvard Graphics* or *Charisma*.

- **Color** Spreadsheet software publishers love to show sample pages created with their products, then printed in color. Not only color graphs, but also color type often appears in these sample pages, which have become a staple of spreadsheet software advertising. And some of those software houses even tout the alleged advantages of color type onscreen.

Don't let these flashy ads fool you into investing in a color printer for spreadsheet publishing. Color type usually looks terrible, a classic example of doing something because you *can*, not because it makes any sense. Sure, color graphs are nice . . . but the black-and-white fill-patterns generated by spreadsheet programs can be just as effective as color. Someday we may all have come to expect color in most of what we read.

For now, nudging your worksheets into color is gilding the lily: Those who see your worksheets will pay more attention to the gee-whiz factor of color than to the analytical and decision-support insights of those worksheets.

For now, color just doesn't make much sense for most spreadsheet publishing.

When Tiny Type Is
Big Enough

Among the most useful, if also among the least-known, tools to become available in the past couple of years for spreadsheet mavens are small-type font cartridges for laser printers. Produced by several third-party suppliers—that is, from companies that don't make laser printers themselves—these cartridges offer very small type sizes that allow users to print much larger spreadsheets on a single page.

Especially when combined with legal-size paper, small type can make complex worksheets far easier to understand, if only because now you can *see* the whole 'sheet at a glance. Of course, they can also mean an end to those tacky sessions on your knees on the office floor, with Ms. Smerdley's huge scissors in hand and a roll of Scotch tape at your elbow, as you cut apart multiple-page worksheet printouts and try to fit them together into one messy but contiguous sheet.

The range of type sizes offered by small-type cartridges typically starts at 12-point/10-characters-per-inch, or about the size of the usual built-in laser-printer type font, and goes down to as small as about 3-point/30-characters-per-inch. JetWare, for example, provides 12-, 16.6-, 21.4-, and 30-CPI type fonts, in both portrait and landscape modes, in its 123 Cartridge.

Though including the largest of those type sizes may at first seem odd—why put in 12-point/10-CPI typefaces when that size is already found in most laser printers?—you'll discover that you use them often. First, because it's often effective to have large-type "headlines" across the top of the spreadsheet—and it's easy to change type sizes with the formatting controls built into most current spreadsheet programs. Second, since these larger faces match the look of the smaller ones, they produce a more attractive result than would mixing the 12-point/10-CPI Courier built into your laser printer with the cartridge's very different-looking smaller type on the small page. And third, because these typefaces are more legible than those built into laser printers.

Picking Small-Type Cartridges

I've used cartridges from JetWare, Pacific Data Products, and IQ Engineering. It's hard to choose a favorite here, because the results from all three companies' small-type cartridges are remarkably similar. But I especially like the Lotica typeface provided by JetWare; it reminds me of Optima (also called Zapf Humanist), a popular, attractive, and highly legible typeface created by one of this century's great masters of type design, Hermann Zapf.

In addition to using smaller type to squeeze in more characters horizontally across the page, you can also choose to print more lines per inch, vertically, to squeeze lines close together. That will further increase the "information density"—but perhaps also increase the squinty-eye problems—of your worksheets. The standard setting for most PC laser printers is 6 lines per inch; I usually use 8 LPI with these smaller type sizes, and have been known, if only rarely, to go as tight as 10 LPI with *very* small type.

But there's surely a point of diminishing returns here: When the spreadsheet gets hard to read, your colleagues aren't going to think you're such a hot spreadsheet jock. What's too small? My suggestion: Stop short of the very smallest type and very tightest lines-per-inch settings.

More for Your Money

If you're a little uneasy about spending $125–$175 for one of these small-type cartridges—worried that if you're only going to use it for spreadsheets, and then only once in a while, you'll hardly find it worth the cost—you may want to look at other font cartridges from these same firms that also offer a wide range of more standard typefaces and sizes, as well as the small type you want for printing spreadsheets.

IQ Engineering's Super Cartridge 2 and Super Cartridge 2L (the landscape version, which prints sideways, or the long way, across pages), for example, are the best LaserJet cartridges I've ever seen. In addition to a very wide range of typeset-look typefaces (Times Roman, Helvetica, and a few less-useful ones), they also offer "typewriter-type" faces such as Letter Gothic and Prestige Elite. In Letter Gothic, the IQ Engineering cartridges offer a truly tiny 4-point version, which produces 30 characters per inch. There's also a 7-point Prestige Elite, which delivers 17 CPI, and a 5-point Line Printer font that offers about 27 cpi (though I find the slightly smaller 4-point Letter Gothic more legible than the 5-point Line Printer, with an extra 3 CPI as a bonus). At $500 or so each, these two IQ Engineering cartridges are expensive, but they provide superb results.

JetWare and Pacific Data Products also offer multiple-font cartridges that combine several standard typefaces and sizes with very small monospaced fonts suitable for worksheet printouts. Pacific Data's well-known "25 in One!" cartridge, for example, claims to deliver all the typefaces and sizes in Hewlett-Packard's best-selling 25 LaserJet font cartridges for about $300—little more than the price of one H-P cartridge.

Make certain any font cartridge you buy mainly for spreadsheet use includes landscape-format character sets, since in most cases the spreadsheets you'll be printing will be wider than they are tall, and thus will be printed horizontally, across the page. (But note that if you have an H-P LaserJet III or other recent laser printer that includes automatic font rotation, you'll need only the portrait-format fonts, since the printer will, upon request, rotate them 90 degrees for sideways printing.)

A final tip for those who rely on these special small typefaces: If the letters begin to look a little heavy, and parts of the characters (such as the little loops inside lower-case *e*'s and *a*'s) start to fill in, adjust the print-darkness control on your laser printer to a lighter setting. Often I set a LaserJet II's darkness control all the way down to the lowest-density setting when printing with very small type. (But remember that, perversely, Canon laser-engine printers' darkness control produces the lightest type at its *highest* setting, 9; and its darkest density at the lowest setting, 1.)

❧

Quick-Squint
Spreadsheet Auditing

For all the time we spend building worksheets—in writing formulas, writing macros, formatting the final output, entering data—and then basing important business decisions on their calculations, most of us spend remarkably little time making sure those spreadsheets work the way we intend them to work.

In fact, the whole idea of formally debugging, or auditing, a spreadsheet still comes as news to too many corporate PC jocks. "I built it; I know what it does" is the prevailing attitude among some spreadsheet hotshots. Given the potential for disasters, both corporate and personal, lurking in a less-than-perfect spreadsheet model, that kind of hubris is appalling.

It's also surprising, since in so many other ways real PC power users are usually tough-minded realists who lean towards carefully considered business decisions, not by-guess-and-by-gosh flying blind.

For a few years after *1-2-3* appeared, I had a standing offer for companies I visited in my consulting practice. I told them I'd bet $100 that they could bring me any spreadsheet in use in the company, and I'd find flaws in it they didn't know existed. Not minor irritations, such as misspelled words, nor esthetic failings, such as columns formatted wrong or bad printouts. I meant serious stuff: columns footed with formulas that didn't add up all the rows in those columns, or cells that referenced other cells with the wrong data (or no data, which is the same thing) in them, or look-up tables that returned the wrong values, or relative cell references in formulas that demanded absolute references and thus folded the wrong numbers into the spreadsheet's results. If I couldn't find such a mistake, I'd give the guy who built the spreadsheet the hundred bucks.

It got to be a game; at company after company, people would bring me spreadsheet models that their hottest PC experts had constructed. They'd walk in with a disk, proud as could be, convinced that this time they were going to get me. *This* time it was a spreadsheet so thoroughly vetted that they used it every day, in support of critical business decisions. And then I'd find fatal, or at least frightening, flaws in it.

And over the course of the three or four years I played that game, I never had to pay up.

I wasn't trying to offend my clients, of course, and since there wasn't a $100 payoff to *me* when I found those mistakes, I wasn't in it for the money. But I was trying hard to make a point. And I succeeded: A lot of those companies now have formal policies about not using unaudited worksheets in everyday work; and even better, many of the people who went through that exercise with me are now outspoken advocates of testing new spreadsheet models thoroughly before they're loosed on a naive and trusting world.

Yet still the problem exists: *Too many companies put blind faith in unaudited spreadsheets, putting big money—and sometimes the company itself—on the line.*

Debugging Tools . . . and Attitudes

I had an unfair advantage when I sat down to test those worksheets, of course. Or actually, two unfair advantages.

First, I came to the table with skepticism. Unlike the people in those companies who used the flawed models, I didn't begin with the assumption that the model was right. In fact, I sat down with the opposite expectation: that like so many other worksheets, this one, too, hid serious problems beneath a benign face. And unlike the proud papas who built those time-bombs, I wasn't blinded by pride of authorship, the crippling disease that masks even the most egregious mistakes in our work.

The second advantage? I used a spreadsheet auditing kit. There's less to that phrase than meets the eye. I simply brought along the disks for a couple of clever spreadsheet-debugging utilities, *Spreadsheet Auditor* and the *Cambridge Spreadsheet Analyst*. Each program consisted of a suite of logical tests and probes it applied to the worksheet in question. They found hidden circular references, formulas that referenced cells without data, cells that contained values but were never used in calculations, and other less-than-evident but very suspicious, even dangerous, problems.

So I can't take much credit for busting those spreadsheets and saving the hundred bucks. The computer did the work. *But I knew enough to USE the computer to attack those worksheets' credibility* . . . which no one in those companies had thought, or bothered, to do.

Today, programs like *Spreadsheet Auditor* and the *Cambridge Spreadsheet Analyst* have pretty much disappeared from the market. In part, that's because spreadsheet software publishers have begun to build decent debugging tools into the current versions of their programs. But unfortunately, I think it's also because the idea of debugging spreadsheets has once again begun to slip into the oblivion of *nice-but-not-necessary.* And that worries me. A lot.

While the internal tools provided in the mainstream PC spreadsheet programs don't have the rigor and depth of those dear departed tools I used, they're good, and can be very helpful. Unfortunately, it's hard to find people who use them. I *know* they don't, because when I'm out on a consulting visit and the topic of verifying spreadsheets comes up, I often ask a simple question about the specifics of using one or another of those debugging features. The people I'm talking with give me blank stares: What feature? Where is it in the menu structure? They've been standing there with me, agreeing vociferously on the need to actively, even aggressively, challenge new worksheets . . . and yet when we start to talk about the tools they have on their PCs for that job, they don't know they exist. So how could they be using them?

The Big Squint

At minimum, let me suggest an extremely simple but powerful method for checking the validity of your new worksheets. It requires no tools whatsoever, not even those already on your PC's hard disk. But because it engages the human brain in checking a worksheet's logic—and once your mind catches one mistake, it will work on you subconsciously, nagging at you with the possibility that there may be more—it may get you into the regular habit of running at least basic checks on your new models.

I've long called this notion "quick-squint" spreadsheet auditing, because it can tell you at a glance if a new spreadsheet model passes at least fundamental tests for accuracy.

The trick: As you're building new models, stop from time to time and save the current state of the model in a temporary file—say, TEST1.WK2. Then load that test version, and enter the digit *1* in every single data-entry cell on the sheet. Recalculate the 'sheet, print it out, then *get away from the computer* for a minute, so you're not tempted to start banging on the keys.

Look through the rows and columns of the worksheet. Since you've entered the simplest of values in every value-cell, your eye can tell you whether the logic in the formulas that drive that 'sheet seems to be working. If you have 17 rows in a column you've footed with an @SUM formula, is the total in that footing cell 17? If you have a similar series of footed columns across the worksheet, do they *all* add up to 17? If not, you probably made an error in one or more formulas' cell-range arguments.

Look at computed cells (cells that are based on formulas' calculations) to see if the values returned make sense. Again, since you entered all those *1s*, you don't have to be an Einstein to do the test math in your head.

When you've made that first pass over the worksheet away from the PC, come back to the computer and go over it again, comparing it to the model shown on-screen. You may want to use a felt-tip highlighter to mark on the printout every cell that is supposed to have a computed value. Because those cells are likely to have values other than 1 if they're correctly calculated—that is, if the formulas in those cells actually do what you think they're doing— making a second pass through the printout to examine and challenge those highlighted cells can spot even more errors.

I don't know another spreadsheet-vetting trick as easy as this one. Nor one as likely to catch mistakes you'd otherwise overlook until much later in the game. In fact, stopping fairly often to make these test passes as you work on the model is one of the secrets of using quick-squint auditing effectively. You're trying to catch logical errors early in the game, before they become so deeply embedded in the model (and often, so entwined with *other* errors) that they're both hard to find and hard to fix.

Sounds like a lot of work? Not at all; actually, running and checking a few quick-squint printouts as you construct a model is less work than you'll invest in almost any other area of building that spreadsheet.

But it may be the most *important* work of all.

☙

Exploiting Workspaces

When Microsoft introduced *Excel*, it brought to the spreadsheet market a number of useful innovations. One of my favorites is *Excel*'s concept of "workspaces." Yet I've found very few *Excel* users who make much use of the feature . . . and virtually none who've taken the idea to anywhere near its limits.

The idea behind workspaces is simple. We often need to work with several related (but not necessarily linked) worksheets at once. With PC spreadsheet programs that could load only one worksheet at a time into memory, we were largely out of luck. We could use *1-2-3*'s File Combine command, for example, to go out and read subsheets into memory as part of a large virtual worksheet, but there were obvious problems when it came time to save those big 'sheets' results. And we could use linking commands to pick up values from specified cells of other 'sheets that weren't in memory. But we couldn't make any changes in those linked worksheets until we saved the current 'sheet, then loaded each one that needed changes, tracked down on each 'sheet the cell with the value that needed to be changed, and saved the file once again.

Excel gave us a new way to work. More than one worksheet could be loaded into memory simultaneously, subject only to the memory-management limitations of the version of *Windows* in use and the amount of memory installed in the PC. (With the advent of *Windows* 3.0, even those limitations largely vanished, thanks to *Win* 3.x's ability to use what is usually called "virtual memory" to swap data to disk when the capacity of the real memory installed in the PC is exceeded.)

That turned out to be much more than just convenient. We found all sorts of new tricks were possible when several worksheets could be loaded into memory at once. But we still needed a way to manage and group those several related worksheets. That's where workspaces come into play.

Workspaces: File Groups

Say you have five *Excel* worksheets loaded into memory in your PC. If you then choose from the File menu on the *Excel* command bar the `Save Workspace` command, *Excel* will construct a list of those open documents. The next time you use the `Exit` command (also under `File Save`) to quit *Excel*, the program will recall that you grouped those files in a single workspace, and will ask if you'd like to save any changes you've made in them before exiting. If you respond `Yes`, *Excel* will go through the list and methodically resave each file that has been changed since it was last saved.

The first time you select the `Save Workspace` command, *Excel* proposes the name `RESUME.XLW` as the workspace filename. If you accept that name, the files will be saved—and the next time you start up *Excel*, the program will automatically reassemble that workspace for you, reopening each of those files in exactly the same position on screen. (The windows for each file are remembered in what amounts to three dimensions, so not only do you get windows of the same size and proportion, in the same place on-screen; but those windows are also stacked in precisely the order you had them in when you last issued the `Save Workspace` command.)

That capability, using the `RESUME.XLW` filename, to reopen exactly the same set of files, with their windows in the same positions on-screen, can be a wonderful convenience. Those who always work with the same set of files, and only those files, can in effect turn their PC into a dedicated computer for those files.

But most of us do a lot more with our PCs than work with only one set of files, in just one way. So we can take the workspace idea even further.

Saving Work Scenarios

Let's say you usually work with the same set of files, but in one session you work mostly with `FILEA.XLS`, then next session work mainly with `FILEB.XLS`, then next time work principally with `FILEC.XLS`. You could save three different workspaces, each with a different file front-most in the stack, perhaps in the largest window. Then you could load whichever workspace was most appropriate for that session.

Or if file position on-screen isn't so important to you—it's pretty easy, after all, to roll through the stack of windows in *Windows,* and to resize and reposition them at will—you might want to make up different work *scenarios.* Thus you'd be able to load intact, and save intact, sets of worksheets for each of the kinds of jobs you handle with your spreadsheet program.

For example, one scenario might load your *Excel* worksheet that reproduces exactly the company's expense-account form, another worksheet that tracks expense accounts filed vs. expense reimbursement received, another that tracks expense advances received, and yet another that totals annual expenses. You could then link or simply copy data as needed among those worksheets. You might call that workspace file EXPENSES.XLW.

Another example: Say you're responsible for getting the managers of your company's half-dozen regional offices to submit their proposed budgets for the next fiscal year. You've sent each a floppy disk with an *Excel* worksheet file as a template for them to use in preparing their budget forecasts, thus assuring consistency in reporting categories and form. You've also kept a separate blank template for yourself, to use as a roll-up, or summary worksheet, of those individual files' figures. You'll link that cover 'sheet to the regional 'sheets as each arrives, so the roll-up is automatically recalculated and always up to date.

Linking those worksheets is easy. And since the links to the roll-up are straightforward, those supporting worksheets won't have to be loaded into memory along with the roll-up. (That is, they use what *Excel* calls "simple external references.") But you've found that your boss likes to come look over your shoulder as you're building that file, and is always asking questions about what kind of numbers Detroit turned in, or what San Jose wants for next year. So you really do want them all in memory, and available at a couple of keystrokes, along with the roll-up 'sheet.

The answer is simple: Create a workspace file called BUDGETS.XLW. Load that file just as you would any other *Excel* file, and the program will display the regional offices' worksheets one after another. If you saved the workspace file with the ROLL-UP.XLS window at the front of the stack, *Excel* will position it there once again. Now you're ready to field those questions in a flash.

As these examples show, individual worksheet files can belong to many different workspaces, so that, say, listing a worksheet in workspace file MAYSALES.XLW doesn't keep it from also being part of the workspaces FEBSALES.XLW, COMSNS91.XLW, or IRSTRACK.XLW.

One last warning about using those .XLW workspace files: They're only *lists* of your individual worksheets' .XLS filenames, not duplicates of those files. So you can't delete the original worksheet files just because you've listed them in an .XLW workspace. You'll lose all your work!

❧

Spreadsheet Compilers:
Canned Worksheets

Businesses are increasingly using worksheets as fill-in templates. I know of many companies, for example, where standardized worksheet models are distributed to managers for turning in budget estimates for the next year. I know a few that use worksheet templates for reporting travel expenses. And I know of hundreds of special-purpose worksheet templates used by companies of every size to gather, report, and assess information.

Every employee who uses one of those worksheet templates has to have a copy of the program used to create it, of course—or at least, another program absolutely file-compatible with it. Every employee who uses those templates has to know how to use that program. And every employee who uses those templates thus has the potential to unintentionally wreck the logic of a template by making changes in it.

Those changes can seem innocent enough. Most of us, for example, when confronted by a worksheet without enough space to enter the data needed, would simply open up that 'sheet by adding more rows or columns—or both. That could easily destroy the validity of the formulas that perform calculations on the data we enter. But unless the calculated values at the bottom looked really screwy—unlikely in all but the simplest models—we'd never know we'd caused a problem.

Or we might move a group of cells from one part of the worksheet to another, expecting, quite plausibly, the worksheet to open up to accommodate those cells. After all, that's how word-processing software works, doesn't it? Except that with spreadsheet programs you have to open a space for the moved cell-range *first* . . . or it overwrites the formulas and values that reside in those cells.

Requiring that each employee using a template have a copy of, say, *1-2-3*, and expecting him or her to know how to use it with some proficiency, may be a boon to the bottom line of Lotus Corp. and to those who sell training materials and stage training classes for new *1-2-3* users. And people who build templates for others can, in theory, save themselves from disasters by using cell protection liberally. But it doesn't make much economic sense for those companies that use templates to be funding Christmas bonuses at Lotus and the training companies. And relying on cell protection is a paradox: Someone who knows *1-2-3* well enough to use it to fill in a template may also know it well enough to know how to turn cell protection *off*.

The Power of Compilation

In not much more time than it takes to build and test an original worksheet model, you can reduce that model to a self-running, fill-in-the-blanks template that can operate independently from the program (such as *1-2-3*) used to construct it. You can protect absolutely as much of the worksheet as you wish from changes, so that neither a rank beginner nor the office's resident *1-2-3* wizard can foul up the model. And you can add on-screen notation, your own application-specific help-screens—even put a whole new menuing system up atop the screen, complete with slick drop-down menus, and consisting only of choices that apply to *that* template.

Maybe best of all, you can get faster recalculation of that template than if you had loaded the file under any version of "real" *1-2-3*.

Magic? Nope, just a spreadsheet compiler at work.

The term at first sounds a little odd, but in fact it's perfectly descriptive. Consider the analogy to a database compiler, such as Nantucket's *Clipper*. You sit down and build a database application with the *dBASE* language, then run it through *Clipper*, which compiles all those *dBASE*-language statements into an executable file. That file runs a good deal faster than native *dBASE* running under true *dBASE* (or under anything else), because it's down on the machine-language level. And once compiled, no one can change that database application.

So the term "compiler" for these software packages is perfectly appropriate, even if my analogy is a little inexact. You still need *1-2-3* to build the original model, for example—though I'd argue that's actually an advantage, since *1-2-3* can be a very nice "development environment" once you see it that way.

But once you've constructed the *1-2-3* model, tested it, and built and saved any macros you want users to be able to run, you then run it through the compiler, and you've got an executable but unalterable file. That executable file can include all the data values users need, so they can use the model as a very large, fast, and smart calculator; or it can contain some of the data, with users prompted to insert the additional values needed for recalculation; or it can consist exclusively of structure and formulas, with all data coming from the user. The choice is yours; compilers take it from there.

Baling Your Work

I've worked with several spreadsheet compilers. Of all of them, *Baler*—and especially the newest version, *Baler XE*—is my choice by a mile. It has superior development tools, more flexibility and power, provides more options for re-organizing the display and menus . . . and delivers the fastest compilation times *and* execution times for completed templates of any compiler I've ever used.

On its most basic level, *Baler* creates a simple executable file from your *1-2-3* worksheet that looks exactly like that worksheet did when you loaded it under *1-2-3*. But if you take a few minutes with *Baler's* CUSTOMIZ program, you can completely change the look of the worksheet on-screen, from adding a customized sign-on screen, to building a new drop-down menuing system, to using color and lines, boxes and solid-area fills on-screen in ways that can completely conceal the worksheet's *1-2-3* origins.

(In fact, two smart in-house corporate developers I work with use *Baler* to create what they then pass off as entirely new programs, without ever men-tioning *1-2-3* or spreadsheets. They're not trying to commit fraud, and they aren't trying to take credit for others' work. They've found that mention of "*1-2-3*" still strikes fear in some mid- to low-level employees at their company . . . whereas these programs they bill as purely company-developed software are much more readily accepted. They use the *1-2-3*-plus-*Baler* route as they would any other computer-language development environment: to produce finished programs for specific jobs.)

A major issue for those who may be considering using *Baler* or another spreadsheet compiler is the integrity of the finished work. How bulletproof is the compiled template against accidental (or intentional) changes? If any half-way-savvy *1-2-3* user can figure out how to turn off cell protection in a plain .WKS or .WK1 worksheet and change the formulas, are these templates really that secure?

Yes. A "baled" worksheet's "secured cells" simply can't be modified. The cell protection is more sophisticated, and actually easier to use for the devel-oper, than *1-2-3's*. Cells can be protected absolutely, even from changes by another *Baler* user, thanks to a developer-level password system. Unless, of course, you choose to use one of *Baler's* sneaky secret weapons, the OVER-RIDE option, which lets users change specified formulas so they can do logical as well as value-based "what-if'ing." But even if you've chosen to let them fiddle with some formulas through OVERRIDE, the original formulas aren't overwritten by those changes, and thus are never lost.

Running worksheets through a spreadsheet compiler doesn't make much sense unless you're going to "publish" them by distributing them to others. But if you are, even the incredibly quick process of running them through *Baler's* compile-as-is BALE command is worth the effort. And if down deep you really want to become a software developer, you'll *love* the accessible power of *Baler's* CUSTOMIZ-level commands.

❧

II

PRINTER MADNESS

Buying
Enough Printer

The last few years have brought amazing progress in personal computer print-ers. The daisy-wheel, once a marvel of technology ("How *does* it spin so fast?") and king of the hill for good-looking output, is dead. And while newer dot-matrix printers are faster, cheaper, and offer much better print quality than many of us ever expected, PC-scale dot-matrix machines generally have been relegated to low-cost, low- to medium-quality work, especially where mul-tiple-part forms, such as overnight-courier waybills or pharmacists' labels for pill bottles, must be produced.

Thank God.

The machine-gun *tat-ta-ta-tat-tat* sound of the daisy-wheel (and worse, the sound of a whole fleet of them) was a major contributor to a decline in the quality of office environments. And the grating *neeeeah, neeeeah, neeeeah* of the dot-matrix printer was a close second. Getting that noise out of the work-place was at least as important, most workers will tell you, as the greater speed and vastly better print quality delivered by the successor to both machines: the desktop laser printer.

Desktop lasers haven't completely captured the better-printer market. Tiny ink-jet units make good traveling companions (see *Why Carry a Printer?*) or compact adjuncts for "executive PCs," those rarely-if-ever-used electronic totems some senior managers like to stick in a corner of the office, to show they're hip to this PC stuff, too. And color printers using thermal-wax and sublimated-dye technologies tease us with intimations of high-resolution color for overheads and graphics, while we wait for the real thing: color laser printers.

But those are strictly sideshows. Today, the laser printer is the peripheral of choice, and it gets all the attention.

Redefining the Low End

Most recently, what's getting most of the press, and a great deal of buyer interest, is the new generation of under-$1,000 laser printers. Created by Hewlett-Packard's spectacular IIP, the low-end laser market teases and tempts with high-quality output, compact size, the nearly silent operation of almost all laser printers . . . and those seductive prices. A few months after HP rolled out the IIP, IBM joined the fray with its similarly small, quiet, and cheap Laser Printer E; then the QMS 410 one-upped both, with better print quality and more features.

H-P, IBM, and QMS aren't alone in the game; other compact, low-cost printers are available from the usual crowd of printer vendors. But those three manufacturers deserve the credit for creating the "cheap lasers" market.

Especially for local area network use, the price of these printers is very attractive. If you subscribe to the "if many users, then many printers" philosophy espoused elsewhere in this section, the idea of widely scattering $1,000 laser printers around the office, hooking them up directly to those PCs whose users have particularly output-intensive needs, sounds perfect. No more hikes down the hall to pick up pages from a distant shared printer; no more complaining about the wrong paper stock some malevolent soul left in the printer—discovered, of course, only after you've run off that 53-page proposal that has to be ready for the FedEx runner in ten minutes.

The idea is right; it's the printer that's wrong.

Saving Pennies, Losing Face

For many PC jobs, it's important to have a printer readily available. Sure, the "paperless office" is coming—someday. Sure, the local area network promises less paper-shuffling in most offices—if not yet in mine or in any other office I've seen.

But it's just as important to buy *enough* printer as it is to have enough *printers.*

The paradox is as inevitable as it is dismaying. The producers of these low-cost printers, which deliver such high-quality output, have to cut something, somewhere. Those cuts fall primarily in the output speed of the units—the number of pages printed per minute—and in the "design life," that combination of the monthly recommended duty cycle and the estimated total life of the laser engine inside the box. And yet we just agreed that what we're trying to do is put dedicated, single-user laser printers at the elbows of . . . those very PC users who crank out a *lot* of paper.

In other words, at the desks of the very people for whom the number of pages produced per minute, and the monthly duty cycle, are likely to be big issues.

Office Printer Strategies

Beyond slow printing and limited duty cycles, there's another flaw in the notion of moving these low-end printers into offices *en masse*: There are much better alternatives, at only slightly higher prices.

In the Hewlett-Packard product line, for example, there's the top-of-the-line LaserJet III, which prints twice as fast as the IIP (eight pages per minute versus the IIP's four), has a longer design life (300,000 versus 200,000 pages), and offers substantial advantages, such as more and better built-in typefaces, any of which can be rotated and scaled to smaller and larger sizes, costs only about 50 percent more than the IIP. H-P also built new technology into the LaserJet III, allowing it to change dot size and float dots around to produce sharper, better-looking letters and numbers. (But don't be fooled by this last bit of technical razzle-dazzle: If you use a magnifying glass, you may be able to see the difference that resolution-enhancement circuitry makes—but how many of your coworkers, customers, or other correspondents examine your work with a magnifying glass?)

Not to be naive, the 50 percent higher price for the LaserJet III—again, just one example of printer price/performance spreads—isn't trivial. For the price of 20 LaserJet IIIs, you could buy 30-odd LaserJet IIPs. But the more expensive machine delivers a lot more value in the office than that price difference suggests. Remember too that the issue of printer longevity comes in second here: While yes, the $1,500 printer will probably last longer than the $1,000 machine, the real issue is that the better printer delivers faster throughput and better-looking results *from the day it's installed.*

Buying Reliability

With greater day-to-day reliability as well. Reliability is hard to measure in the computer business, despite such official-sounding and highly quantified measures as Mean Time Between Failures (MTBF), Mean Time Between Jams (MTBJ), and Mean Time To Repair (MTTR). And the amazing reliability of PCs themselves has for many of us created an unrealistic expectation for computer-related equipment: It will never break.

But computers—and, much more often, printers—*do* break, and when they do, the cost to repair them is often the least of the problem. In many offices, disruption of the work flow, the cost in expensive staff time of finding alternative methods of performing their work, and the fearsome lost-opportunity costs lurking in possible missed sales make breakdown-prevention a bargain at almost any cost.

The good news: Printers that are operated at a relatively small fraction of their monthly recommended duty cycle tend to be far more reliable in day-to-day use than printers operated near their recommended monthly limit.

This is tough to quantify, and my numbers are hardly scientific. But my experience and that of many others who have worked over time with large numbers of business PCs is that laser printers operated at 30–40 percent of their recommended monthly duty cycle are *four to five times more reliable* in day-to-day service than those driven at 90–100 percent of their recommended duty cycle. That's a far greater return on the additional investment in those more-durable machines than could usually be expected, and in many cases, reason enough to opt for the more expensive printer.

One last note on prices: Printer manufacturers are well aware of these pricing issues, and of how we as buyers respond to price points. Much as Sears, Roebuck has for many years nudged prospective purchasers up-line with Good-Better-Best labeling and pricing—aiming to keep as many people as possible out of the lowest price range, by making it relatively inexpensive to make that jump up to the Better grade—printer makers, too, try to make the leap from lowest-price to midprice units smaller than we'd expect.

Thus, the performance gained by making a low- to midline jump is usually far greater than the ratio between the lowest and the midlevel prices predicts.

If this sounds as if I think there's no good use for $1,000 laser printers, or as if I'm trying to warn you that they fall apart soon after you open the box, that's dead wrong.

The new generation of low-end lasers has many appropriate uses. While they may not make much sense in paper-intensive applications on networks, they make great sense as *convenience* printers. Low-end laser printers can be a superb fit in out-of-the-way spots, away from faster, shared printers, where the need for convenient output is nonetheless important.

They can also be a perfect fit in the home office—or simply in the home, period.

When Enough Really *Is* Enough

When we hear the term "home office," many of us think immediately of small-time one-person shops, tucked away in someone's basement or unused bedroom. Sure, such tiny entrepreneurial businesses can benefit greatly from the leverage provided by PCs, laser printers, fax machines, compact copiers, and other tools that were once the exclusive province of big business. But today the great majority of "home office" setups aren't used by solo entrepreneurs but by 9-to-5-ers who stretch the workday (and get out of the office a little earlier at night) by bringing work home, sneaking in a couple of hours of PC time after dinner or once the kids are put down for the night.

(A contemporary philosopher observed that there is no such thing as "home work" in this context, but only OVERwork. I agree: Much as Dwight Eisenhower's cardiologist snorted that a round of golf was a perfectly good way to ruin a nice walk, there's no better way to spoil an evening than to bring home some budget-forecast figures on a disk. And yet I do it, too. And far too often.)

For that home office, where size, quiet, and price may count equally—and where output quality is also important—these small, low-cost laser printers can be a godsend. Duty cycles, resolution enhancements, and rotatable fonts become nearly irrelevant when you're printing just a couple of hundred pages a month and simply want to get *through,* so you can read Graham his favorite story about the little red lighthouse.

Buying
Enough Printers

If it's important to buy *enough* printer, as the last chapter argues, for those PC users who work in shared-printer settings, it's also important to buy enough *printers*, period.

I've helped plan a lot of corporate local area networks. Though I don't do the nuts-and-bolts work, like pulling cable and installing network cards in PCs—clients rely on contractors, and sometimes their own inside PC-support staff, for that—I often find we've invested many more hours in *planning* a network than it took to actually get it installed, up and running. A great deal of that planning time is spent not on such computer-engineering issues as which kind of cable to install, or which networking protocol to use, but rather on *human* engineering: making the network easy to use.

In LAN planning meetings, I sometimes find myself in a corner, so to speak, arguing for what some of my colleagues complain is a distinctly *un*-networking idea: installing lots of printers. Sharing such expensive peripherals as printers is one of the premises upon which networks are built, after all; and it is that economy of means—sharing a few tools among many users—that is the economic justification behind the installation of a great many networks.

So why do I want to undermine those sound economics?

One Step Forward, Two Steps Back

Almost every time I've worked on planning a network, I've returned to the offices once the network's been up and running for a month or two to do a very useful, if informal and decidedly unscientific, survey of how the new network users like the system. What do they like best? What surprised them about working on a network? Do they fully trust it? And what do they like *least* about it?

Over the course of dozens and dozens of these surveys, the loudest complaint has almost always been from PC users who used to just turn around and pick up their print job from a printer behind them or at their elbow—but who now have to go trudging down the hall to the printer they share with others to pick up that job.

Which, of course, they often now find is printed on the wrong paper (someone switched letterhead for draft paper), or is in the wrong typeface (someone "borrowed" the printer's font cartridge to use in another printer), or the printer was out of paper (but the network didn't alert the user), or the job still hasn't printed 20 minutes later (the network printing queue was full, and the new job went to the bottom of its first-in, first-out stack).

There are other complaints, to be sure, from slower access time to too many new things to learn, to unease about just how secure files saved on the server can be. But nothing is so loud nor so enduring as the howls from people who feel put-upon by no longer having easy access to a printer.

"I spend an hour a day walking back and forth to someone else's printer!" a secretary once almost screamed at me. "*THAT'S progress?*"

She was exactly right, of course.

How can it possibly be so economical, so smart, so technologically advanced, to spend tens to hundreds of thousands of dollars setting up a networking system that many users will come to dislike so much that they try to avoid it, or even subvert it?

And so I often argue, a lonely voice in these meetings, for putting far more printers on the networks we're planning than my colleagues think necessary. (Of course, those colleagues rarely print much themselves; their secretaries do their printing for them. Or worse, they hardly ever use a PC themselves, anyway. . . .)

If you're involved in setting up a local area network for your company, consider the human part of the equation as well as the technical aspects. If people have print-intensive jobs, put a printer near them. Maybe give them their own directly attached printer. What we're after here is *improved productivity,* not a Scrooge-like, bean-counter's parceling out of as few printers as people who don't use the system much in the first place believe they can get away with.

The Ghosts of Peripherals Past

The idea of sharing those "expensive peripherals" has rapidly become outmoded, at least in those terms. If we were talking about $5,000–$10,000 printers, maybe that would make sense. But while many were preaching so sanctimoniously about those "expensive peripherals," things changed: Printer prices fell through the floor. Today a $1,500 H-P LaserJet III is the most common new LAN printer; and $1,500 is cheap enough by anyone's standard for a tough, reliable, shared printer.

Yet the "expensive peripherals" cliché is alive and kicking.

Once, attaching a networked printer meant hooking it up to a network user's PC, then watching performance on that PC degrade into an infuriating torpor, as managing the flow of work to the printer took more and more of the machine's power. To say nothing of all those people trooping through to pick up their print jobs, load or change paper, and grumble for awhile about the &!*@&&%$!ing network.

That was really great for *that* person's productivity, eh? The one with the shared printer attached to his PC?

Or we bought aging PC-XTs to use as print servers, stood them in hallways next to the network printers they controled, and wondered why the great new technology of networking relied so much on a machine built in 1983? (To say nothing of the network manager's worries about someone using that print-server PC as a point of unauthorized, and essentially untraceable, illegal access to the network. . . .)

Today, the difficulties and much of the expense of attaching multiple printers to a network are over. Instead of keeping the used-PC-XT market alive, today we can simply buy printer-connection boxes from Hewlett-Packard, Intel PCEO, and other vendors. At about $500 each, these black boxes let users connect a printer anywhere on the network, *directly to the network,* without an attached PC. Add $1,500 for the printer and you've got a $2,000 answer to a million-dollar problem with employee productivity and satisfaction.

If you help plan a local area network, stand up for productivity, not parsimony. Even if you have to take on my occasional, curmudgeonly role as a lone, irritating voice crying out for more printers, it's worth it. Your coworkers will thank you.

Remember: It's at least as important by buy *enough* printers as it is to buy the *right* printers.

❧

Laser-Printer Myths

A curious thing has happened as laser printers have taken over the largest part of the business PC-printer market: Laser-printer myths have taken over many PC users' minds, replacing their innate good judgment with the oddest kind of old wives' tales.

Strange, isn't it, that such a high-tech product could engender such low-tech thinking . . . ?

Let's knock down some of the silliest myths.

No. 1: You Can't Recycle Toner Cartridges

When the first LaserJets arrived, we marveled at how economical they were. Thanks to the disposable drum system of the Canon laser engine used in those early LaserJets (and, in succeeding versions, in most other laser printers sold since then), printed pages cost just three cents each. What a bargain! How clever of Canon to package all those messy supplies in that one, neatly disposable toner cartridge!

It didn't take long, though, before our sense of economy was offended by the use-it-and-toss-it approach of the single-use disposable laser-printer cartridge. That cartridge looked pretty complicated, which meant it had cost a lot to make—and to buy. And the drum and the mechanical parts looked perfectly OK, even after the little window on the side of the cartridge had gone from green to red, Canon's signal to replace the drum.

Conspiracy-theorists decided Canon was getting rich by urging us to toss out drums long before their useful life was over. Corporate purchasing agents hated to replace *anything* before it was thoroughly, visibly, and irredeemably trashed. And the environmentally conscious wondered if we weren't contributing needlessly to America's growing mountain of nonbiodegradable trash by throwing out these cartridges.

But most of us just wanted to reuse them to save a buck.

Early efforts to reload and reuse Canon toner cartridges were pretty sloppy. Garage-shop toner-recycling entrepreneurs drilled holes in used cartridges, poured in some more toner powder, slapped a piece of Scotch tape over the hole, and returned the cartridge to its owner, who often then found that mechanical abrasion during reinstallation of the drum peeled that tape back, or shortly thereafter, as the printer's fusing element heated up, the tape simply curled back on its own. And then the insides of the printer filled up with toner powder.

Have you ever had to clean up toner powder? It's the most maddeningly fine-grained and tenacious substance known to mankind. Like black talcum powder, it sifts and blows into every crevice. Once on a surface, it's hard to remove; as you clean, it smears. Get it on your clothes, or a carpet, and you'll *never* get it out.

Toner-recycling began to look like a very bad idea, indeed. It didn't help when rumors spread that printer makers would cancel the warranty on your printer if they found you'd been using recycled cartridges, or, more ominously, when word spread that there was a grit in the recycled toner that would destroy printers. Both stories were false, but they scared a lot of businesses away from recycled cartridges.

That didn't last; the economic imperative to recycle was too great. As more companies bought more and more LaserJets, and looked more closely at the obvious economies of recycling cartridges, suppliers began to find better ways of refilling them. Toner powder was more carefully measured, to avoid spills from excess toner. Seals were improved. In the best shops, cartridges were taken apart, cleaned, then reassembled before being refilled.

Throughout, care had to be taken not to mark the delicate drum surface. While Canon had originally specified its toner cartridges for just 3,000 copies, many users had found they could get more like 4,000 pages out of a cartridge before the output became dim and gray. Canon's second laser-printer cartridge design, the LBP-SX unit, was spec'd for 4,000 pages—and usually delivered more like 5,000. *If* the drum surface wasn't scratched.

With care, the drums were fine and the cartridges hardly ever wore out. They simply ran out of toner. It has became clear that with careful refilling, both Canon toner-cartridge designs can deliver 10,000–12,000 pages of high-quality output before the drum surface is exhausted. Which means that with superior refilling techniques, recycling cartridges is a very practical idea.

I've used refilled Canon toner cartridges for a long time, and so have many of my corporate clients. Over the years, we've found several principles important for continued success.

- **Use top-notch refillers.** There are no economies in using cheap, quick-and-dirty "drill-and-fill" laser-cartridge refilling shops. You want an outfit that will refuse to refill a damaged or worn-out cartridge; that disassembles and cleans cartridges before refilling; that uses top-grade toner, measuring it accurately and sealing the refill opening tightly; that tracks the number of times a cartridge has been refilled; and that delivers refilled cartridges in sturdy packaging, with new fixing-roller felt cleaners. The prices charged by the best and worst refillers are within a few dollars; don't cut corners here.

- **Limit the number of refills.** Though they last a lot longer than Canon says, cartridges don't last forever. Never refill a cartridge more than four times—for a maximum of five cycles, including the original "factory load"—and for best results, limit cartridges to three refillings.

- **Protect drum surfaces.** A slight mark on the drum surface will mean a "dead zone" across every page printed thereafter with that cartridge, no matter the care taken by the cartridge refiller. Drum surfaces are physically sensitive, and light-sensitive, too. Handle them carefully.

- **Store recycled cartridges in a cool place.** Both drum surfaces and toner are very sensitive to heat. Keep 'em cool, or you'll have problems.

- **Refill only your OWN cartridges.** Don't accept randomly refilled cartridges from a recycling shop. Even the best shops buy empty cartridges from firms that don't intend to refill them; you have no idea how those cartridges were handled. Save and recycle only your own cartridges; affix a distinctive mark—perhaps even number them—before sending them to the refilling station. And demand that you get your own cartridges, and *only* your own cartridges, back.

Follow those rules and you'll cut your cost per page for running laser printers by at least half, without the slightest loss of quality.

There are many good laser toner-cartridge refilling shops across the country. The best refills I've used come from LaserCharge, an Austin, Texas-based franchisor of laser-refilling shops (800-999-8134), and Laser's Edge, a large Fairfield, Iowa refiller (800-635-8088). But mentioning only those firms is in a sense unfair. Others do fine work, too.

No. 2: Laser Printers Demand Special Paper

This one reminds me of the early days of Xerox copiers, when businesses by the thousand bought case after case of "special" Xerox-brand copy paper. That paper was not fundamentally different from many other grades of copy paper available from the major paper mills; it just cost more. While Xerox machines did run better with Xerox-brand copy paper than with cheap, poorly made groundwood paper, you could buy a grade of copy paper directly comparable to Xerox's paper stock for much less from many mills—some of which produced Xerox's own paper.

Today, we're still stuck with two myths about paper and laser printers: that they won't run reliably with "ordinary" grades of paper; and that every laser printer user would benefit greatly from using special papers.

Nonsense. Any grade of fairly good office bond runs fine in laser printers. I use and recommend Boise Cascade's 20-lb. Cascade OM/Bond for ordinary work. At about $25 per case of ten 500-sheet reams, it costs just a half-cent per sheet; you'd be hard-pressed to find a piece of paper you'd be willing to use for *anything* in your office for less money, yet Cascade OM runs superbly in laser printers.

And those special, premium-quality laser papers? I use Hammermill's Laser Print for work that is going out for reproduction, because its smooth, highly polished surface produces sharper images and better solid-black areas than standard paper. But Laser Print is a pretty unattractive sheet for most uses. Its bright, white surface is harder on the eyes, and it simply *feels* odd. So we never use it for anything but those repro masters. (Hammermill also produces Laser Plus—the same paper with "wax holdout" for laser-printed pieces that are going to be pasted up into layouts. That simply means the paste-up wax is less likely to come up through the sheet and stain it; it serves no purpose unless you're producing paste-up copy—for which it's the paper of choice.)

Note that even though Laser Print is a useful special-purpose laser paper, it's still an inexpensive one, at about $5 per ream, or a penny a sheet. I've seen many much-more-expensive "laser papers." Some cost as much as $15–$20 per ream . . . yet offer no real advantages.

One last note on paper stock: Heavily textured papers, such as Beckett Cambric's linen finish, or Kimberly-Clark's Strathmore Classic Laid, don't work well with the laser-printing process—which is, after all, nothing more than a copy-machine mechanism. The final image consists of fine grains of black powder baked onto a sheet; for best appearance and durability, the process wants a smooth page, not a textured sheet.

That's unfortunate, because so many businesses (including my own!) rely on classy papers such as Strathmore Classic Laid for stationery. In our case, we've decided that the slight imperfections in the laser-printing process on Classic Laid are more than offset by the speed and convenience of laser printing, and by the look and feel of that sheet. You may reach the same conclusion . . . but it's worth taking a look. If you use a very heavily textured paper—and if you use even a lightly textured sheet for envelopes—you may find much of the laser-printed image flaking off from the normal abrasion received in the handling of your printed work.

No. 3: Heavy Paper Won't Work

Because the specs in the owner's manuals of most laser printers specify a fairly narrow range of paper weights, many laser printer users believe they can't feed heavy, cover-weight stock through their printers. Surely such heavy sheets will damage the printer?

Again: nonsense. We routinely run up to 80-lb. cover-weight sheets through our laser printers, and we've never had a problem. Many of those heavy sheets don't take well to the tight turns they have to make when fed from the printer's paper tray, and again when they do a 180-degree turn out into the paper basket. So we simply hand-feed them, one at a time, through the manual-feed slot in the printer.

Without problems.

That's not quite as convenient as sitting back and running the paper through the automatic mechanism. But it's a lot better than not being able to print those pieces at all.

We use those heavy sheets for many kinds of office signs, report covers, posters, "table tent" name-signs we put in front of speakers on the dais at conferences, for *No Smoking* signs on tables, for name tags at meetings, for invitations, and a hundred other uses. In fact, we'd be lost without the ability to produce those so quickly and easily in-house . . . on our laser printers.

I won't say there aren't some kinds of heavy papers that shouldn't be fed through laser printers, or that you *cannot* damage a printer this way. To avoid problems, we use 80-lb. stock as our upper limit. And some special-surface papers—such as those coated with colored powder, or foils—shouldn't be fed into laser printers. They can melt and even cause fires.

So this isn't a guarantee; I won't come fix your printer if you try to stuff something really heavy into it and it chokes. But for ordinary office uses of cover-weight stock, you're probably safe.

No. 4: You Can't Print on Both Sides

Hah! The people who started this one had good intentions, but it's gone much farther than they intended.

With the earliest H-P LaserJets and other printers based on the Canon LBP-CX toner cartridge, there was a possibility that pages fed twice through the printer—first to print on one side, then on the other—might transfer some unfused toner remaining from the first pass to printer parts touched during the second pass.

The problem was rare, and not serious. And today's second- and third-generation laser printers handle this kind of "manual duplexing" just fine. Indeed, Hewlett-Packard even sells the LaserJet IIID, a LaserJet III built around the same Canon LBP-SX cartridge, which automatically flips pages and immediately prints on their back sides.

If you're manually refeeding a few pages you've already printed on one side—or just one sheet—you can probably print that second side right away. But if you want to feed a whole stack of printed pages through a second time via the printer's feed-tray, for backing up with second-side printing, you'll be happier if you let them sit for a few minutes to cool off. Otherwise the curliness of the paper (caused by the heat of the printer on that first pass, which baked some of the moisture out of the paper) may lead to misfeeds.

Note that this is really a *paper* problem, not a laser printer problem, and doesn't involve any potential risk to the printer.

In my office we have a Formica countertop near one of the laser printers, upon which we stack freshly printed pages headed for a second pass through the printer. We put a heavy book on top of them, and let that cool plastic-laminate surface draw the heat out of the stack. Ten minutes to a half-hour later they go back in—and we virtually never have a misfeed.

No. 5: You Must Use Special Label Sheets

Yes and no. The problem with many cheap label sheets is that the adhesive between the sheet and its peel-off backing has a very low heat tolerance, and can ooze out and muck up the inside of your printer as it passes across that hot fuser-bar near the back of the machine. So in some cases, those special, expensive, just-for-laser-printers label sheets may be a good idea.

But there's a major problem with those lasers-only lines: the choice of label sizes, shapes, and colors is very limited. Many kinds of labels we use regularly simply aren't available in laser-tested versions. And virtually none of the bright DayGlo-colored label stocks are available in laser-printer versions.

So we usually use the regular label sheets—and have never had a problem. The key here may be to buy good-quality label sheets, from a well-known manufacturer. We use only Avery labels and, laser-tested or not, we've never had a hiccup.

No. 6: You Must Use Special Overhead Sheets

Again: yes and no. Some clear-acetate transparency material won't stand up to the temperatures of that fusing mechanism in your printer. I've seen two cases where old, cheap transparency sheets actually melted to the fuser, producing a terrible mess (and a terrible stink). Both printers needed expensive repairs; one was simply scrapped.

But you don't necessarily need those unpleasant, lighter-weight overhead-transparency acetates sold for laser printers. I like more rigid overheads—in large part because I often don't mount overheads in frames, but simply use them loose—and I'm unwilling to give up that rigidity.

Several companies produce good, relatively thick and rigid overhead-transparency material, which works fine with laser printers. Ask your paper supplier, office-supplies dealer, or audio-visual specialist for advice.

❧

Getting Those
Odd PC Characters
From LaserJets

Almost everyone who uses IBM PC software with Hewlett-Packard LaserJet (and compatible) printers has run into an occasional problem with the differences between the character set defined by IBM for the PC—and thus adopted by virtually every producer of PC-DOS/MS-DOS software—and the character set defined by H-P as the standard for the LaserJets.

"Character sets" can include not only the letters and numbers of the Roman alphabet, but also punctuation marks, accent marks, and foreign characters. Computer makers typically use the "lower" ASCII codes, from 0 to 127, for basic characters, such as upper- and lower-case letters, numbers, and punctuation marks. Some computer makers also define extended character sets, using the upper ASCII codes from 128 to 255 for additional useful characters. Examples from the IBM extended character set include line-drawing segments such as corners, vertical and horizontal lines, and intersections (| ┬ ┴ ╔ ╗ ╠ ╣), background-shading characters (▓ █ ▌ ▐), foreign-language characters (ç û ä), math symbols (Ω ∈ τ π), bullet-marks (■), currency symbols (£ ¥), fractions (¼ ½), and even some silly stuff (☺ ● ♥ ♦ ♣ ♠).

That IBM Extended Character Set is one of the few really widely accepted standards in the PC business. When IBM supported the full Extended Character Set (ECS) in its early IBM Graphics Printer, the IBM PC ECS became the *de facto* standard for PC hardware and software. Epson, which built the Graphics Printer for IBM, adopted most of that character set for its own machines, and soon almost every other printer maker angling for a slice of the PC-printer market came into line.

But Hewlett-Packard has always gone its own way, so when it introduced the first LaserJet a few years later, it ignored the IBM Extended Character Set, and instead substituted its own Roman-8 Character Set. The letters and numbers still looked the same, of course; it was in the other characters—the *extended* characters—that surprises lay waiting for unsuspecting users.

Confusing ASCII Codes

When your software inserts ASCII code 157 in a document, for example, which that software believes will produce a Yen sign (¥) on the printed page, LaserJets instead print a blank space; the LaserJet assigns ASCII 188 to the Yen sign, and doesn't recognize ASCII 157 at all. When your PC software inserts ASCII 174, it thinks you'll get a pair of left-hand chevrons («), the European-style open-quote mark, but the LaserJet prints a û instead; H-P's Roman-8 set assigns the left-hand chevron pair to ASCII 251.

Since most of us don't use those extended characters very often, that isn't much of a problem. Doing without the silly IBM ECS happy-face characters, for example, is hardly a sacrifice. But some IBM extended characters, such as the line-drawing and shading characters, are really useful, and when PC software attempts to use those characters, things often go awry.

The drawing characters are particularly important when you need to make a quick screen snapshot—say, for a software training manual, or simply for a cheat-sheet to help a colleague remember how to use an obscure feature in a program—and when you want the printout to be as close as possible to what you saw on-screen. Use the standard PRINT SCRN key and the page that comes rolling out of your LaserJet will look all wrong.

Where characters merely have different ASCII codes in the two systems, the problem can be solved by using the LaserJet printer drivers supplied with each application. By now, virtually every commercial PC program is accompanied by LaserJet printer drivers that access those changed-code characters directly, without problems. The big problem comes with characters that exist in the IBM ECS but are not found at all in the H-P Roman-8 set: You'll get the wrong character, or no character at all, when you print your document.

Hewlett-Packard eventually showed users some mercy, and beginning with the H-P LaserJet II model, started including the IBM ECS in ROM chips inside all LaserJets. *But these machines still rely on the H-P Roman 8 set as their standard;* you won't get the IBM ECS unless you specifically request that the IBM character set be substituted for the H-P set.

This is only a problem when dealing with text screens. Programs that produce printouts of graphics screens—that is, displays that arrange many tiny points on-screen into letters, numbers, graphs, and drawings—are required when you get beyond simple text-only screens. But many PC programs effectively simulate the *look* of graphic screens by using characters from that IBM ECS—typically, the very line-drawing and shading characters with which the LaserJet has so much trouble—and so the odds that you'll want to print a text screen are high.

There are three good ways to wring those IBM characters out of your LaserJet. Which you use depends on which model printer you have, and on how you value your time vs. your money.

If you're using a LaserJet II or later printer, you can either switch over to the IBM ECS from the printer's front panel, or send the printer a simple line of instructions from your PC. Either way, you'll switch the printer into using the IBM ECS until it is turned off or otherwise reset. I'll come back to these techniques in a minute.

Using the H-P "Y" Font Cartridge

If you're using the original LaserJet, LaserJet Plus, or LaserJet 500—the early models—those IBM ECS characters don't exist in your printer's memory, so you must add them by plugging in the little-known H-P "PC Courier" IBM ECS font cartridge (H-P Part No. 92286Y, also known as the "Y" cartridge). This gem, which you can buy for about $175, includes the usual LaserJet 10-pitch/ 12-point Courier typeface, in standard, bold, and italic fonts, all in portrait (vertical-format page) orientation only, plus the LaserJet's tiny 16.66-pitch/ 8.5-point Lineprinter font, in both portrait and landscape versions. Except for adding an italic and a true boldface (rather than merely thickening the strokes of standard Courier, which is how the original LaserJets produced a boldface character), this font cartridge simply repeats the characters found in the printer itself.

But with a big difference: It provides those characters in the form of the full IBM Extended Character Set. By plugging that cartridge into your LaserJet— *any* LaserJet, including the latest models—you can in effect turn them into IBM ECS printers without having to make any changes via the printer's control panel or send special setup strings from the computer. (Though ordinarily you'd need to send the printer a control-character string to choose the cartridge fonts, when the LaserJet detects that cartridge it changes automatically to make the standard-weight IBM ECS Courier 10 font the default font.)

Actually, screen shots produced by any of these methods on LaserJets won't be exact duplicates of the image you see, because none of the H-P IBM ECS options includes the inverse-video option used by the IBM ECS to create good-looking screens. But the result will be close.

If you need an absolutely accurate representation, you'll need to use one of the more complicated screen-capture programs, such as *Pizazz Plus* or

Hotshot Graphics. There's more on those programs in *Quick: Grab That Screen* in the **Analysis and Persuasion: PC Graphics** section of this book.

Switching Characters from the PC

As I said before, if you're using a LaserJet II or later printer, you can change from one character set to another either by using the controls on the LaserJet's front panel or by sending a setup string from the computer. Using the front panel is simple enough, and probably preferable if the printer is at your elbow. But many LaserJets are shared by a number of users—some, via simple printer-sharing devices; most, via more complex local area networks, on which the LaserJet appears as a "print server." If your LaserJet doesn't sit next to your desk, but in a closet or alcove 50 feet down the hall, you'll want to switch character sets from your computer.

In fact, the printer doesn't even need to be way down the hall to justify switching character sets from the computer. My LaserJet is in the same room with me, but it's a ten-foot roll of my chair away from the PC to which it is connected. It's faster and easier for me to switch character sets from the keyboard than to roll across the room, tap in the new instructions, roll back to the computer, print the IBM ECS job, then scoot back over to the printer and reset it to the H-P Roman-8 set, then roll back to my desk.

Which brings up a good-manners point for those using shared LaserJets: Remember that once you switch the printer from its native H-P character set—which most other users, and their software, expect to find in place on the printer—it's going to *stay* in IBM mode until you switch it back to the H-P standard, or turn the printer off and then back on. If you change the character set on a shared printer temporarily for a job, remember to change it back as soon as that job is printed, or your coworkers are going to get some funny-looking printed pages.

Remember, too, that the person in charge of supporting your local area network would like to know what you're up to on shared printers—*before* you start switching the printer around.

Using the LaserJet's Front Panel

To switch from the native H-P Roman-8 character set to the IBM character set on a LaserJet II or later model, follow this sequence:

1. With the printer turned on and **READY** showing in its LCD display, press the printer's ON LINE key once. (This is a simple toggle switch; since the printer was already on-line, this takes it off-line, so you can make the adjustments.)

2. Hold the MENU key in for several seconds, until **SYM SET=** appears in the LCD display.

3. Repeatedly tap the + key on the panel until the display reads **SYM SET=IBM-US**.

4. Press the ENTER/RESET MENU key on the printer control panel to get an asterisk next to the letters **IBM-US** on the control panel.

5. Press the ON LINE key once again.

6. Press the CONTINUE/RESET button on the panel *and hold it in for several seconds.* When the LCD panel reads **07 RESET**, release the CONTINUE/RESET button. Note that the LCD display changes to **READY**.

The printer is ready to use.

Sending a Setup String from the Computer

Though the character-string that will force the LaserJet II and later models into their IBM ECS mode can be embedded in documents, that's usually impractical for such simple jobs as snapping screen shots. It's much faster and easier to send a simple control sequence from the DOS prompt, then load your application, bring up the screen you want to print, and hit the PRINT SCRN key.

First, you create a one-line DOS file with the character string. Then you use the DOS `COPY` command to send that file—consisting only of instructions to select the IBM Extended Character Set as its default—to the printer.

To create the DOS file:

1. Using your word processor, type in this line:

   $^{E}s_{C}$&l00$^{E}s_{C}$(10U

   There are two tricky points here: getting that $^{E}s_{C}$ character into the line, and making sure that you differentiate between zeros and Os, and ones and lowercase Ls.

   The $^{E}s_{C}$ character is a problem because computer software publishers have never agreed on how it should be handled from the keyboard. That $^{E}s_{C}$ character is ASCII 027, so it should be easy; but since there is also an ESC key on almost every computer keyboard—which, paradoxically, does *NOT* insert the $^{E}s_{C}$ character!—you have to find out how your word-processing program handles $^{E}s_{C}$.

   With Microsoft *Word, PC Write,* and *WordStar 2000,* for example, you simply hold down the ALT key while you type the digits 027 on the numeric keypad at the right end of your keyboard. In *Professional Write,* you simply type in *P27*. In *WordPerfect,* you hit SHIFT + F8, then type OPPC, then 27. In *MultiMate,* you type ALT + A, then 027. Only *XyWrite* lets you do the logical thing: Simply hit the keyboard's ESC key to insert an $^{E}s_{C}$ code!

The second requirement when setting up LaserJet control strings is to carefully distinguish between zeros and the capital letter "O," and between the numeral one and the lowercase letter "l." H-P's Printer Control Language, the computer language used to set these parameters, is full of such traps for the unwary; clearly such similar-looking characters should never have been used for commands.

When you've figured out how your word processor handles the $^E{}_{S_C}$ sequence, enter that line; at the end of the line hit the ENTER key.

2. Although it's not essential, I suggest that you also add a form-feed or page-ejection code, ASCII 012. That code can often be entered by typing CTRL + L from the keyboard; but once again, you may need to check your word-processing software's manual to see how it handles these control characters.

   The reason for adding the form feed? To be absolutely sure you've cleared the printer of any data left from an earlier job, so your first IBM ECS page prints properly.

3. Save the new file under a name you'll remember. I use 2IBMCHAR.BAT, since this switches the printer *to the IBM Extended Character Set.* I also like to keep that file in the root directory on my hard disk, so I can always access it from the DOS command line without having to issue a **CD** (Change Directory) command.

Now, to use that new file:

At the DOS prompt, type this line:

```
C>COPY 2IBMCHAR.BAT LPT1:
```

(I'm assuming that you put the file in your disk's root directory, and that you used the same filename I chose; substitute your own path and filename if they are different. And I'm assuming your LaserJet is connected to the PC's first parallel printer port, LPT1:. Change that too, if necessary.)

That will send the file to the printer, and you can now print the IBM Extended Character Set without problems.

If you're going to switch printer modes from the computer, you'll also want to be able to switch back to the H-P Roman-8 set from the computer. The procedure is exactly the same, except that you use a file with the setup string, which changes the printer to Roman-8 as its default. Here's the character string for that file, which on my PC is called 2HP8CHAR.BAT:

$^E{}_{S_C}$&l00$^E{}_{S_C}$(8U

Use it just as you use the 2IBMCHAR.BAT file, sending it to the printer with the DOS **COPY** command.

Ejecting Printed Pages

"Page printers" such as LaserJets—so named because they construct the image of a whole page in memory, lay it down on paper, then eject that page and go on to the next one—don't print and eject completed pages until they get a code telling them the page is completed. Thus once your screen image is printed, you need to send to the printer a form-feed, or ejection, signal.

Once again, you can do that from the printer's front panel, or you can do it from the computer. If you're sitting near the printer, just tap the ON LINE key, then the FORM FEED key, then the ON LINE key once more. Your page will be printed and ejected immediately.

If you're not near the printer, you'll want to create one more little one-line .BAT file so you can send the eject instruction from the computer's keyboard. Here are the contents of that escape-code file:

$^{E}s_{c}$011

Add an ENTER at the end of the line, then save the file under a name such as FORMFEED.BAT. Put the file in your hard disk's root directory, so you can always get to it without typing a PATH statement. To send a form-feed instruction to the LaserJet after your screen shot has been sent to the printer, type the following line at the DOS prompt:

```
C>COPY FORMFEED.BAT LPT1: <ENTER>
```

You can also find tiny utility programs, often named something like FF.COM, for free on many computer bulletin-board systems, or on shareware/ freeware disks available from PC user groups, which accomplish the same thing.

Easy Laser-Printer Sharing

I'm not a big fan of small-scale printer sharing. Just because there are three or four of us who work in fairly close proximity to one another, and just because laser printers can turn out printed pages a lot faster than we can create those pages, doesn't mean laser printers necessarily *ought* to be shared. That kind of reasoning can lead to unhappy workers and a real sag in productivity. If an office worker's job is reasonably paper-output intensive, then that person ought to have a printer at his or her elbow.

Obviously, the world doesn't agree with me, because printer-sharing devices have long been one of the most popular categories of PC peripherals. There are dozens of these devices available today, from simple A-B boxes you must set by hand to direct one or another PC's output to the printer, to large, elaborate, and expensive switching devices so complicated and feature-packed that they're often called "sub-LANs," since they mimic the lowest-level connectivity features of local area networks.

If you don't share my lack of enthusiasm for printer sharing, and believe sharing would work well in your office, at least get off on the right foot on the hardware: You don't want a printer-sharing box at either end of that spectrum. You certainly don't want—and wouldn't long put up with!—the clumsy manual A-B units. And if you need a LAN, buy a LAN; avoid the sub-LANs.

Simple Hardware Answers

Since most printer sharing these days consists of providing access to a desktop laser printer for three or four people who sit relatively close to the shared printer, I'll recommend two devices that in my experience fill that need well.

The first is Extended Systems' ShareSpool 2094A, a tiny, elegant solution that fits inside the printer itself. Extended Systems distilled the printer-sharing circuitry down to a small card, which plugs into the I/O option slot on H-P LaserJet IIs and IIIs. Rather than relying on expensive, bulky, hard-to-hide serial cables for the run out to each connected PC, the 2094A uses telephone wire and connectors. It's quick, quiet, inconspicuous and, at $845 for a four-user printer-sharing answer, very cost-effective. The 2094A also includes one megabyte of RAM for buffering incoming print jobs (see *Smart Buffers, Smarter Spoolers*), so you won't, under ordinary work loads, be waiting for the printer to finish and hand your PC back to you.

The Extended Systems unit only works with those three H-P printers—other laser printers don't have the slot it requires—and it can't accept more than four connected PCs. Sometimes you'll want to connect more users to one printer, and of course you may be using another brand of laser printer, so I'll offer a second recommendation.

Elsewhere in this book I rave about LaserTools' *PrintCache* as the best print-spooling software I've used. The company also produces a companion printer-sharing box, the oddly named Local Union, which serves four or eight connected users. The two work perfectly well separately, but if you're going to install a Local Union box, I strongly recommend you put a copy of *PrintCache* on each connected PC as well. Since spooling is then done at each PC, the box doesn't need a big buffer (which is fortunate, since it has no buffering at all), but your connected PC users still won't notice any delays, thanks to the automatic spooling. The Local Union 41 connects four PCs to one printer, and costs about $500 (including a four-user-licensed copy of *PrintCache*); the eight-user version, Local Union 81, costs about $650 (also including *Print-Cache*).

Beyond the Hardware . . .

When you're planning to share a printer among several PC users, human factors become at least as important as the hardware and software issues. Each of those PC users is probably accustomed to having a printer devoted to his or her exclusive use, and if you deliver a shared-printer answer that is materially less convenient than the former separate-printer answer, you'll have unhappy PC users.

Ninety-five percent of shared-printer unhappiness, in my experience, comes from convenience issues. People used to having a printer at their elbow are used to the convenience of picking up finished print jobs, switching kinds of paper, swapping font cartridges, and doing other printer-related tasks by simply swiveling around in their chairs. Make them get up and walk down the hall to do those things and you'll make them unhappy.

That suggests that a primary criterion for happy printer sharing is *proximity:* how close each user is to the shared printer.

The most successful shared-printer arrangement I've ever installed was in a law firm, where secretaries already sat back-to-back in two-person cubicles divided by an attractive low rosewood "fence." We mounted LaserJets on custom-made Lazy Susan-style swiveling bases, and placed one of those swiveling LaserJets between each pair of secretaries, recessed into the low dividing wall between their individual workspaces. That way, either could swing the printer around for easy access to its front (for changing paper or font cartridges), to its back (for turning the printer on), or simply leave it in a mid-position, with each having easy access to the printer's output bin on top.

Because we met the convenience issue head-on, and because we only asked two people to share each printer, the change was accepted very well.

(We had another, less-obvious advantage, which probably had as much to do with that instant acceptance as did our savvy about positioning the printers. These LaserJets replaced NEC Spinwriters, which formerly sat on every secretary's desk. Spinwriters are among the noisiest and most irritating daisy-wheel printers in existence. We promoted the changeover much more as a way to deliver a better, quieter, more serene workplace than as a step-up to a newer printing technology with better-looking output.)

Ignore the human factors and you'll soon forget about the economies you forecast for the new shared printers. Unhappy people are almost by definition unproductive people, and no printer-cost savings are great enough to justify turning your workers into a grumbling, discontented lot.

☙

Soft Fonts, Hard Fonts

Today, many PC users have come to rely on soft fonts—typefaces stored digitally on a PC's hard disk, then downloaded to the printer as needed—to produce good-looking documents. It's easy to see why: Soft fonts offer an essentially unlimited number of typefaces and sizes available on disk, and those fonts are much less costly than typefaces bought in other forms.

No doubt the slow drift towards a graphical-interface world on PCs, a trend accelerated by improved versions of *Windows* and OS/2-*Presentation Manager*, will increase soft fonts' popularity. People who work in a graphical environment on-screen tend to use a greater variety of typefaces and type sizes than those who plod along in character-mode systems.

But before soft fonts became so popular, we relied on hard fonts. These came built into the laser printers that first exposed us to the possibility of typeset-look work from our PCs, or as font cartridges we could plug into those machines. Because of the high cost of the ROM chips required to hold those fonts in the printer or in the cartridge, hard fonts were expensive. Many who bought the very first LaserJet font cartridge, with its marginal Times Roman and execrable Helvetica-style typefaces, soon came to marvel at the look of their printed work . . . but remembered much less fondly the hundreds of dollars they spent for that cartridge.

Today, font cartridges have fallen dramatically in price, and often now fit many typeface and size variations into a single cartridge that sells for half or less the price of those early, very limited cartridges. And font-cartridge vendors have gotten serious about the quality of the typefaces they provide. Often the type designs are licensed from such major digital-type houses as Bitstream, and are true to the original designs.

When Hard Fonts Are an Easy Choice

Despite the popularity and apparent economy of soft fonts, there are several good reasons why you might want to use hard fonts in cartridges as well as, or perhaps instead of, soft fonts stored on disk.

- **Hard fonts stored permanently in cartridges installed in laser printers are much faster to use.** Soft fonts must be downloaded from the computer to the printer, and perhaps scaled to the correct size, before they can be used, and often must be downloaded again and again throughout the day as the PC user changes programs. Indeed, some word-processing programs with poor soft-font management require that the *same* sets of soft fonts be downloaded again at the beginning of each print job.

    If you're going to be using the same typeface and size over and over, all day long—say, 12-point Times Roman in standard, bold, and italic weights for correspondence—it's silly to be forced to wait through this cycle of downloading, time and again. With a font cartridge in the printer, those typefaces are immediately available, every time, for every document, in every application.

- **Using hard fonts saves hard disk space.** If you still have megabytes galore available on your PC's hard disk, this may not be so important. But a lot of business PC users find their hard disks are getting close to the edge: nearly full, with only a few megs of storage space left. Soft-font files are large—from 30,000 bytes for a single, standard 12-point typeface to 100,000 bytes for that same typeface in 24-point size, and as much as 200,000 bytes for a 36-point size. And remember that you'll need a separate soft-font file for every variation (standard, italic, bold, bold-italic) and every size (6-point, 12-point, 18-point, 30-point) you think you'll need.

    The subdirectory you use to store soft font files can take as much as five to ten megabytes of disk space. Especially on an older PC, with a 20- to 40-megabyte disk, that's a lot of magnetic storage to devote to "pretty print" typefaces.

- **Creating soft font files with programs such as Bitstream's *Fontware* can be very time consuming.** Some soft fonts are delivered in specific sizes on floppy disks. But many programs today use Bitstream's very good *Fontware* system to create custom-sized fonts from typeface outlines. You might choose to ask *Fontware* to create and store on your hard disk its Swiss (a Helvetica look-alike) typeface new font files in 6-, 8-, 10-, 12-, 14-, 18-, 24-, 30-, and 36-point sizes. Extend that range to include italic as well as boldface versions in each size, and you may as well go out for lunch—or for the afternoon—while your PC chugs away, creating those files. To say nothing of the huge chunk of hard-disk space they'll occupy once *Fontware* has done its job.

- **Using soft fonts requires a good deal of printer memory.** And that usually means an expensive memory upgrade from the printer's basic 512KB or 1MB of memory. Memory still isn't cheap, though prices are dropping steadily; you could buy a font cartridge with a lot of typefaces in a lot of sizes for the price of that memory.

- **In networked or shared-printer situations, shipping downloadable soft fonts to the printer can slow down the network for everyone.** A LAN can nearly choke, temporarily, on all that typeface data you're shipping over the network.

- **In shared-printer situations, installing a font cartridge or two in the printer gives *everyone* on the network immediate access to a known group of typefaces and type sizes.** Rather than letting each user download fonts, which absorbs a lot of network capacity (and of course also costs a bundle as each user *buys* those soft fonts), installing the cartridge at the printer provides extensive, certain, cost-effective typeface support for everyone on the net.

  Note that this means that even users of portable PCs, who hook into the network only when they need to, and typically don't have enough space on the relatively small hard disks in their machines to store many soft fonts, have access to those good-looking cartridge-based typeset-look fonts, too.

- **No scaled typeface looks as good as one carefully crafted for a certain size.** Typeface-outline systems—whether using the *Fontware* approach, which creates specific-type-size bit-mapped image files for you in advance, or Adobe's *PostScript* system, which turns typeface outlines into real characters on paper in the printer as the page is created—inevitably produce compromises, especially in medium and small sizes. Often smaller letters and numbers look thick, chunky, and unattractive.

  But hard fonts are precisely drawn for the 300×300 dots-per-inch (or other) resolution of your printer. A human being who knew *exactly* how that letter or number should look hand-tuned each character for that resolution, at that size. No matter the claims made for computer-based scaling systems (including Adobe's famous "hinting" system to produce better-looking small typesizes), the human eye and hand are always better in this kind of letter-by-letter, size-by-size fine-tuning.

  Good hard fonts simply *look* better, in many cases, than scaled type fonts.

Better Fonts, Better Choices

Today, exceptionally good font cartridges are available from IQ Engineering, Pacific Data Systems, Hewlett-Packard, and others. Such products as IQ Engineering's Super Cartridge series include many typeset-look fonts, in several sizes; special-purpose cartridges such as Pacific Data Systems' Headlines in a Cartridge unit add very large typefaces, up to 48-point Times Roman and Helvetica, for titles, overhead transparencies, and headlines in desktop-published documents. (See also *When Tiny Type Is Big Enough* for information on the special small type fonts intended for reducing large spreadsheets to single-page printouts.)

I don't want to be a hypocrite here. I have a wide range of soft fonts, and rely heavily on them. I especially like PostScript fonts and printers, because of the wide variety of typefaces they make available. But I also use font cartridges, and often recommend them to corporate clients.

Before long, this question of soft or hard fonts will become irrelevant, thanks to the wider typeface support being built into newer printers. The H-P LaserJet III, for example, makes external type fonts of whatever sort superfluous for many users, by including Times Roman and Univers (yet another Helvetica look-alike) typefaces in the printer, scalable to almost any size and rotatable to any angle. We can expect to see more printer makers building a greater variety of typefaces into their machines as a competitive measure.

But there are still millions of earlier laser printers in daily use in corporate America, and they'll be in use for a long time to come. Users of those printers will increasingly find, I think, that font cartridges, with their quick, easy-to-use, and precisely drawn hard fonts, are the better choice.

Special-Purpose Printers

We're pretty much accustomed to the wonders of the typical PC printer found in offices today. If it's a laser printer—they constitute about half of the installed PC printers in business use today—then we expect it to be either a Hewlett-Packard LaserJet or a LaserJet clone, or an Apple LaserWriter or a LaserWriter clone. If it's a dot-matrix machine, chances are it's a recent model from Epson, C. Itoh, Okidata, or Panasonic, perhaps with an 18- or 24-wire printhead, that provides better print quality than the old standard 9-pin head.

The laser printers take letter- and legal-size paper; the dot-matrix machines may also accept $11 \times 14\frac{7}{8}$ inch "greenbar" paper—the kind traditionally associated with computer-printed reports.

Ho-hum. So what else is new?

In fact, while our expectations for PC printers have converged around those few models and conventions, printer makers have been coming up with really interesting and unusual machines for special needs. If your vision of what's possible with a PC printer is limited to those models listed above, you may be missing some tools you'd find very helpful.

A complete review of unusual, special-purpose printers could fill this book. Instead, let me look at three little-known, out-of-the-mainstream printers that are both superbly crafted tools and superbly crafted answers to not-so-uncommon business needs. You may not know any of them exist; I'll be amazed if you're aware of all three. Their nature as special-purpose tools has limited their coverage in the computer press . . . but among those who know and use them, these are high-profile products, indeed.

I hate for this to sound like an ad for these three machines, but I find them so useful, and my clients have found them such eye-openers and problem-solvers, that I can hardly restrain my enthusiasm for them.

On the Road Again

The printers that made taking it on the road with you practical, the wonderful Kodak/Diconix machines, have gained an intensely loyal following among those for whom portability is a high priority. This is one of those rare cases of a company getting it just right the first time. When Diconix introduced its first model, the 150, in 1987, those of us who had been searching for years for a truly high-quality, truly portable machine fell on it like a loose football near the goal line.

The machine is full of clever tricks. It uses the Epson command set, which means it works properly with virtually every commercial PC software package ever published. It runs on both internal batteries and external AC power—and in a bit of design genius, it hides its batteries, usually one of the bulkiest parts of a portable device, inside the platen roller.

The ink-jet printing mechanism in the Diconix is licensed from Hewlett-Packard, and thus uses standard H-P ink-jet cartridges, which are reasonably easy to find in larger cities—and so small and leak-proof that it's easy to carry a few extras, if you're going to be away from those larger cities for awhile. And I can attest that its tough, plastic housing protects the printer's innards against the rigors of travel: my Diconix has been bounced cruelly across North America, yet has never failed to work properly.

That original Diconix 150 has since been joined by later models, one of which accepts wider sheets of paper. Kodak now owns Diconix; its name appears on the more recent machines, which cost about $350.

All in all, the Diconix has proved a marvelously well-designed tool. Later developments, such as Canon's new portable bubble-jet printers, may threaten Diconix's hold on the serious portable-printer market—but they aren't likely to topple the champ anytime soon.

Bigger Sometimes *Is* Better

As marvelous as today's laser printers are, I long for printers that never were . . . and ask why not?

One of my longstanding complaints about laser printers has been that they're only available for paper sizes up to legal-sheet size. I've often needed larger sheets, for flyers, posters, proof pages with trim-mark corners shown, short-run oversize newsletters, promotional pieces, and many more items. But excepting only the very expensive 600 dots-per-inch Varityper models— really meant for typesetting, and expensive both to buy and to maintain— large-sheet lasers have simply been unavailable.

Not long ago QMS changed that. Tucked away in Mobile, Alabama, QMS has been quietly rewriting the rules in the laser printer business for some time. They produced a PostScript upgrade for the original LaserJets that was so good that H-P never introduced their own planned LaserJet PostScript upgrade, and recommended that their customers buy the QMS unit. QMS produced an exceptionally high-quality PostScript add-on for LaserJet IIs, which uses an expansion card in the PC, tied to a card installed in the LaserJet II's expansion slot, for very fast PostScript printing—while maintaining full H-P PCL compatibility. And QMS one-upped Apple with its PS-810 Turbo, a better, faster PostScript printer than Apple's top-of-the-line LaserWriter IINTX—about which, more in a minute.

Recently, the good ol' boys and girls at QMS introduced that big-sheet machine I'd been waiting for: an 11 × 17 inch (or tabloid-page size) PostScript laser printer. This wonder, the QMS 2210, turns out about 20 8½ × 11 inch pages per minute, or 10 11 × 17 inch pages per minute. (Those figures, measured in the real world of typical usage, are a little slower than QMS's specifications: like every laser printer manufacturer, QMS is a little optimistic in its specs.)

The print quality on the 2210 is absolutely stunning. Though still managed by a QMS-designed 300 × 300 DPI controller, the 2210's output is sharper and finer than that from any other 300 × 300 DPI laser printer I've seen. Solid-black areas are especially outstanding: dead-black, velvety, and smooth.

The printer is available with either one or two feed trays. It includes H-P LaserJet emulation, Diablo daisywheel emulation, and also HPGL graphics-language emulation (more, below), so it can print architectural drawings and other plotter-output work that would otherwise take forever as it scratched its way through a pen plotter.

Like only a few other high-end laser printers, the 2210 also has a SCSI port for connecting a dedicated external hard disk for font storage. The 2210 also includes several built-in interfaces: Centronics/parallel, the PC standard; RS232C serial; and RS-422/Appletalk, for Macintoshes. It's hard to imagine a business computer in anything like wide use that can't be connected to the 2210.

All in all, the QMS 2210 is one of the most satisfactory PC tools I've used: fast, reliable, with beautiful results. At $12,950 list, it's not cheap, but if you need what the 2210 offers, you won't mind paying the price. (Because QMS's high-end printers can be hard to find, it's difficult to come up with a real-world street price. But I've seen the 2210 sold for as little as $9,995.) If there is a flaw in the 2210, it is the more complicated toner and drum replacement process, which reminds me every time of the genius of Canon's all-in-one, throw-away system. But if that's the price for printing big sheets with such quality, I'll happily pay it.

So Long, Plotters

Finally, if someone in your office uses PC CADD (Computer-Aided Design and Drafting) programs, they should know about QMS's PS-810. As indicated above, it's essentially a clone of Apple's pricey LaserWriter IINTX that is faster, of better quality, more-versatile, and lower-cost. On those grounds alone, it's a winner.

But QMS introduced in the PS-810 series their extremely accurate HPGL emulation, which also makes the PS-810 (and other QMS HPGL-emulation models) a joy to use as a replacement for slow, cranky pen plotters. Since virtually every CADD program, on almost every hardware platform, supports HPGL output (as a result of the dominance of H-P's plotter line), switching to the 810 from a plotter is incredibly simple: no new printer drivers are needed, and existing files print properly without modification.

Desktop lasers can't yet quite replace the pen plotter, whose last logical domain is the production of very large working drawings. When you need E-size drawings, you need a plotter. But increasingly, design and engineering firms and departments are discovering that letter- and legal-sized printouts have a lot of uses, too. They're easy to scan for errors before committing to that long process of plotting an E-size drawing. They're easy to file. They're easy to include in proposals and bound specifications-books for contractors and bidders. They're easy to present to clients—who won't understand the drawing in that size any more than they will when it's a wall-size blueline, but will feel comforted by being given their very own 8½ × 11 inch copy of the drawing to put in *their* files.

Enter the PS-810. You could also use the larger-format QMS 2210 described above, but the PS-810—at $3,300, about a third the typical actual selling price of the 2210—is going to be an easier first step away from the plotter . . . or rather, an easier-to-cost-justify *addition* to the plotter, than the 2210.

Using laser printers for small, fast, presentation-quality plots is not widely accepted today among technical people. But the idea is catching on fast . . . and high-quality if little-known machines like these QMS printers are leading the way.

Smart Buffers,
Smarter Spoolers

There's a lot of sloppy language thrown around in the PC world. From intentionally misspelled words to baffling acronyms to ambiguous and often tortured meanings to widely misused terms, we've built a PC culture based, it sometimes seems, on illiteracy. One of the most confusing and persistent examples of misusage among PC users and experts alike is the interchangeable use of the terms "spooler" and "buffer."

Buffers and spoolers are both designed to help with the same problem, but they work in critically different ways. And unless you understand that difference, you'll be hard-pressed to pick the right one for your needs.

The problem that led to the development of both of these productivity-boosters is simple: slow printers. No matter how fast your printer is—even the 400 characters-per-second dot-matrix machines, and the 8–10 pages-per-minute lasers—your PC is a lot faster still.

When you finish preparing a six-page document and send it to the printer, the PC starts pumping that data down the parallel or serial cable to the printer. But the printer quickly falls behind. Its small "receive buffer," the block of memory chips set up to hold incoming data, fills up fast, so to avoid overflowing and losing incoming data, it sends a "busy" signal back to the PC: *No more data for awhile!* The PC pauses, and only when the receive buffer has room again does it resume transmitting your print job. This back-and-forth, stop-and-go routine continues until the document is finished printing.

Unfortunately, your PC is tied up during the entire process, so you sit there staring at an apparently frozen screen, waiting for the printer to finish the job. And if you specified multiple printed copies of the document, be prepared for a *long* wait.

If printers could turn out finished pages as fast as those pages were received from PCs, there wouldn't be a need for that receive-buffer, and we'd regain control of our PCs almost instantly once we issued the print command. Sadly, though, printers aren't going to catch up to PCs anytime soon: the disparity in speed is far too great.

Buffering Print Streams

Buffers and spoolers are both designed to end this nuisance, by making the printer's slow effective printing speed invisible, or at least irrelevant, to the PC user—who, once having issued the "print" command, can then go on his or her way, exiting that program, loading another, beginning a new piece of work, all while the printer slowly chugs its way through the print job.

Buffers were the earliest answers to slow PC printers. Using a buffer is a brute-force answer: it substitutes brawn and cash for brains. PC buffers are small boxes crammed full of RAM chips, connected between the cable coming from your PC's printer port and the printer's input jack. Buffers effectively amplify the data-holding capacity of that tiny internal receive-buffer, adding from 256 KB to 1 MB or more of external memory. To your PC, and to the application programs you use, that huge chunk of memory looks like the world's fastest printer: a program ships a print job, and *whoosh!* it's accepted, in one big bite. (Providing, of course, the amount of RAM in your buffer is greater than the size of the document to be printed.)

The buffer then trickles the data out to the printer in the dribs and drabs it can accept. You're not bothered again; the interaction is hidden, and exists entirely between the buffer and the printer.

Buffers work well. They ought to: there's not much to them. And if they are inelegant solutions, remember the high cost of elegance in the PC world: a quick and dirty but highly reliable answer often makes more sense than an incredibly elegant but tricky and sometimes unreliable one. So adding a print buffer can be a smart way to increase your productivity. You won't be waiting around for your printer anymore.

Printer buffers abound; recommending one over another is almost impossible. I've long used and admired Practical Peripherals' buffers, which are available in both parallel and serial models, with RAM capacities up to one megabyte. I've also had great success with large-capacity buffers from Enhanced Systems. But almost any buffer offers a quick and easy alternative—if at $100–$300, an expensive one—to letting your printer control your workday.

Spoolers to the Rescue

Aside from their cost and the need to find space on or under your desk for that buffer box (which in fairness is often as small as a couple of packs of cigarettes), I have one more reservation about buffers. And this one is more serious.

Buffers waste RAM. Once you've bought the megabyte of RAM in that buffer box, it serves no other purpose. You can't use it to stretch your PC's expanded or extended memory, or do anything else useful with it. And while memory prices are falling, memory is still too expensive to use in so cavalier a fashion. I'm convinced big chunks of RAM chips belong in PCs, where memory-management software can turn them into extended or expanded memory, and use them in a number of different ways to enhance overall system performance.

Enter spoolers.

PC spoolers are hand-me-downs from the mainframe business. Rather than relying on a dedicated, external block of RAM to hold and dribble out data to the printer, spoolers instead use a slice of your PC's existing memory, and maybe a chunk of your PC's hard disk, to produce the same no-wait, no-pain perceived improvement in system performance. In other words, spoolers make use of what you have *now* to deliver the same benefits buffers provide through the brute-force answer of buying a box of RAM chips.

Here's how a spooler works. When you first install the spooler software, it asks whether you'd like it to use only your PC's RAM memory, or whether you'd like to devote some hard disk space to the spooling job as well. Then as you work, the spooler, which is always running invisibly behind your application, intercepts the print jobs you've sent to the computer's printer port. The spooler stashes the print-job datastream in the block of RAM you've assigned to it, or passes the data through that RAM to the temporary holding space you created on the hard disk. Then it dribbles the data out to your printer from either RAM or the hard disk as fast as the machine will accept it—exactly as if you were sitting there waiting for the document to print, exactly as if an external printer buffer were managing the job.

All this is utterly transparent to you. You issue the print command, and typically regain control of the PC in two or three seconds. Everything else happens in your PC's memory, as the spooler program manages the print queue.

Queue? Yes, indeed: good spoolers let you submit print job after print job, without worrying about whether preceding jobs have been completed or not. It stacks them up in that holding pen in memory or on your hard disk, then ships them, one after another, to the printer, on a first-in/first-out basis.

Some spoolers even let you see on-screen, at the touch of a couple of keys, the current list of documents waiting to be printed. You can then shuffle the deck, moving a last-minute, end-of-the-queue document up to the top of the list, or even temporarily suspending the job currently printing so you can rush a later one through. You can also delete any pending document from the queue if you've changed your mind and no longer want to print it. (Buffers provide *de facto* spooling too, simply stacking up one incoming print job after another. But usually they provide few or limited tools for actively *managing* that queue, which makes queueing of limited value.)

Assigning System Resources

Downsides to spoolers? There aren't many. My favorite spooling program, *PrintCache*, costs just $100 or so; it's available from the developer, LaserTools, and also from any Hewlett-Packard dealer or regional office. *PrintCache* can be installed in many ways, so the amount of RAM it takes varies greatly, but you can cut its RAM requirements to just under 6KB and still get fine performance.

While *PrintCache* can work with only RAM, or RAM plus a hard disk, I strongly recommend the latter choice. If you can set aside 100–200 KB or so of disk space, you'll need to devote only a very small amount of RAM to *Print-Cache*, but you'll still get superb performance. (Indeed, though there is a theoretical speed advantage to spooling directly out of RAM, I find the speed using a *PrintCache* hard-disk parking lot so incredible—and so far ahead of what any laser printer I know can handle—that I happily spool from disk.)

PrintCache doesn't offer much in the way of queue-management tools— you can cancel the current print job, but that's about it—but once again, I choose to forego more advanced queue management for the rock-solid performance and blinding speed of the program.

Most network operating systems have their own spoolers built in; spooling is essential on a shared, networked printer. But I've found *PrintCache* even more efficient than some LANs' spoolers. And while some applications (for example, Microsoft *Word*) offer their own built-in spooling routines, those internal systems very often use so much computing power that using the PC while the spooler is emptying itself becomes almost impossible: the screen image and the cursor move so jerkily that you'll soon give up any attempts to spool your print jobs through the application.

All in all, *PrintCache* is one of the most satisfactory programs I've ever used, certainly one of the best two or three utilities I've encountered. For me—and, I suspect, for you, once you've tried it—*PrintCache* falls into that category of programs I can't imagine doing without.

Spare Yourself
Serial Grief

Once upon a time, long, long ago, in another epoch of human existence—say, around 1980—the most common method of connecting printers to personal computers was via serial connections. The name for the serial connection specification, which set out how many wires were needed and which signals were to be sent on each wire, was "RS-232C," and among *cognoscenti*, that term became a kind of shorthand for serial connections.

To make an RS-232 . . . oops, *serial* . . . connection between a computer and a printer involves dealing with several related phenomena, from XON-XOFF "handshaking" to strobing to baud rates. If the DB25 plug-and-jack combination usually used for serial connections itself became more or less standard— at least until IBM introduced a new serial-connector standard with the PC-AT in 1984, and Apple redefined serial connector standards again with the introduction of the Macintosh in 1985—very little else about serial connections was standard at all. With the result that making that computer and printer actually *work* together was a matter of trial and error, time and frustration.

The introduction of the IBM PC in the Fall of 1981 marked a fundamental change. While it was certainly possible to connect serial printers to IBM PCs (with the attendant trial and error, time and frustration), it was far easier to use the parallel connection found (oddly enough) on the video-display card plugged into the PC's bus. Based on a system developed by the once-powerful printer maker Centronics, parallel connections for printers became the dominant standard.

And not a minute too soon.

If for any reason you are tempted to buy an older serial printer and connect it to your PC, think twice—or as many times as you have to, to convince yourself that it is a *verrrry* bad idea. Don't do it.

Actually, it's not only the maddening details of getting serial printer connections to work—after all, modems are also connected serially, and we seem to handle that perfectly well—but also the inefficient performance of serial connections vs. parallel connections, that should steer you away from serial madness.

Eight Versus One

Imagine baseball players warming up in the hot sun before a game.

On one side of the field we have a line of eight pitchers tossing balls to a line of eight catchers. There are 200 baseballs in a big communal basket at the pitchers' feet; each ball must be thrown across to a catcher before everyone can knock off and go back into the dugout for a break.

How long will it take them to throw those balls? Beats me. But let's say that if each pitcher throws at a constant rate of five pitches every minute, it's going to take five minutes to get all the balls from pitchers to catchers. That's eight pitchers times five pitches times five minutes, so we get the 200 balls across to the catchers' side pretty fast.

Meanwhile, on the other side of the field we have one pitcher throwing balls to one catcher. The basket at the solo pitcher's feet also has 200 baseballs, and he, too, must get all those balls across to the catcher before the two of them can head for the cool of the dugout. He can only toss them as fast as the pitchers in the group across the field, so his progress is much slower. At five pitches a minute, it's going to take him 40 minutes to get all those balls over to his catcher. They may both suffer heatstroke before he gets those balls across the field.

That's a rough analogy to how parallel and serial communications protocols work. In the PC/Centronics-style parallel cable, eight lines, or wires, carry data simultaneously. It's an efficient means of moving data from Here to There—or from the computer to the printer, in our case. It's fast because several things can happen at once, in . . . parallel.

But in a serial connection, just one bit of data is passed at a time, serially, one bit after another. So all other things being equal, it's going to take a lot longer to move the same amount of data from PC to printer. (There are other complications that slow things down even further. For example, at the beginning of each group of seven or eight individually transmitted bits that form one letter or number, a "start" bit is sent; at the end of the group, a "stop" bit is sent. Without these "framing bits," the printer could never make any sense of this undifferentiated stream of bits coming in.)

Suffice to say, serial data transfer is *s-l-o-w.*

Bring On the Lasers . . .

All this didn't mean much a decade ago, when fast letter-quality printers, such as top-of-the-line daisywheels, ran at 40 characters per second (cps), and *really* fast dot-matrix machines turned out a sizzling 150 cps. If it took ten bits to represent each character, and the printer could handle 150 cps, we only needed to ship 1,500 bits per second (bps) to the printer to keep it running at full speed. Since the standard for serial-printer transmission speeds was (and remains) 9,600 bps, the connection, or data pathway, was far faster than we needed.

But then came laser printers, which assembled printed pages not a character at a time, line by line, but a whole page at a time—and could print a page every eight to ten seconds. I'm talking about the earliest LaserJets, of course, which set the standard for PC page printers.

Serial connections could support that rate, barely, if we stayed with plain text. But one of the glories of these amazing new laser printers was their 300×300 dots-per-inch resolution for graphics. And shipping enough bits over to the printer to handle the 7,560,000 addressable points in the 8×10.5 inch usable image area of those pages was simply beyond serial connections.

Serial connections were dead. Technical complications aside, serial transmission according to the RS-232 standard had simply become too slow to meet our needs.

Smart Cabling

If after reading all this you're *still* thinking about setting up a serial printer, there is one trick that can probably cut your setup time (read: frustration time) by a large percentage: buy a Smart Cable.

Produced by IQ Technologies, the little-known Smart Cable has an electronic-switching module at one end and a variety of connectors at the other. The multiplicity of connectors lets you get around problems caused by different and incompatible connectors of the wrong gender. Trying to plug a female DB25 connector into a male DB9 connector isn't going to be very easy, just as plugging a male DB9 into another male DB9 isn't going to work. The hydra-headed end of the Smart Cable solves that problem.

The electronics module at the other end of the Smart Cable solves most which-wire-should-carry-which-signal problems. By flicking a small switch on the electronics module until a certain combination of red, yellow, and green LEDs lights up, you can electronically search for signals and reassign them within the sealed cable—without knowing anything about what you're doing. Just match the picture in the Smart Cable manual of the right combination of LEDs and you're set.

The Smart Cable is just that—smart—and makes setting up serial connections much easier. The price you pay for that convenience is, however, steep: about $50, or three times what standard, nonintelligent serial cables cost. Still, for many PC users—and especially for those who must frequently switch several different serial devices (such as modems, plotters, printers, and digitizing tablets) back and forth on the two serial ports PCs can handle—the Smart Cable can be a very smart buy, indeed.

❧

TIME OUT I

If It's Right Here
In Black and White
On Greenbar Paper,
It *Must* Be Right!

Of all the traps PCs can lead us into, none is so pernicious as the tendency to automatically accept as gospel anything that comes out of a computer.

It's odd that it would work that way, because if anything, our growing experience with computers ought to make us more *skeptical* of the inherent accuracy of computer-generated information. It isn't (usually) that the computer is going to add something up wrong; it's that at every human link in the chain, there's so much chance for error.

Part of the problem, of course, is that PC output often looks either like big-computer database reports, or, in the case of work run off on a laser printer, like something fresh from the print shop. Either way, a computer printout these days carries an innate credibility that is absolutely groundless in real-world experience. Both kinds of "veracity by association" are phony; both can be costly.

We see and hear stories all the time about people getting monthly utility bills for $345,556.78, or IRS refund checks in the millions of dollars when they earned $25,000 that year. If the big systems that turned out those huge bills and checks can produce such grossly mistaken results, why would we think our PCs are immune to similar errors?

Often there's a question about the origin of an error in PC work. In a celebrated case a few years ago, for example, a Florida construction company sued Lotus over an alleged deficiency in the spreadsheet portion of Lotus's multifunction program, *Symphony*. Someone at the company had made a change in a spreadsheet they were preparing for a bid, forgot to adjust an @SUM XX..XX formula used to add up a column, and wound up leaving the topmost item in that column out of the total. The error was discovered too late, and the company lost money. Their lawsuit, which never came to trial, claimed it was Lotus's fault—a design error in *Symphony*—that allowed the error to happen.

Was it Lotus's fault? Or was it the fault of the person using the *Symphony* spreadsheet, who forgot to check the ranges in the column-footing formulas?

Do you *care?*

(For the record, I thought then and still think that it wasn't Lotus's fault at all. The user simply wasn't sufficiently familiar with how *Symphony* worked. Powerful tools can get us into powerful trouble if we're not careful with them.)

The point is simple, I hope: finger-pointing after the fact isn't very helpful . . . and if we're to use these amazing machines effectively in business, we also need to keep their results in context. No answer from a computer ought to be accepted at face value in making an important business decision.

Healthy skepticism is part of being a PC power user. Because the more you know about PCs, the more you know just how wrong those pretty reports on greenbar paper can be.

❧

Don't Tell Me What
The Computer Says;
Tell Me What *You* Say

A senior executive in a Fortune 500 company was talking to me a couple of years ago about how he thought PCs fit into large companies. I listened attentively and admired his perspective, because his focus wasn't on the technology or on specific applications, but on the human issues he'd observed at work: how people use PCs on the job, and how PCs change their perspective and behavior.

And then he said a very interesting thing.

"The one thing I really hate about computers in general," he said, "is how they encourage people to come in and tell me what 'the computer says.'

"I don't give a damn what the computer says! We bought those computers for people to use to become better managers. I don't want to know what the computer says; I want to know *what he says.*"

In a couple of sentences, he had cut to the heart of how computers, and especially PCs, are used and misused in large companies. These are decision-support systems, not decision-*making* systems. They can make us far more powerful, more effective, by helping us tap into more sources of information, consider more options, quantify the heretofore unquantifiable. But computers don't make decisions; they just process information.

And I agree with him: it infuriates me, too, when I ask someone what they think, and get back a lame little tap dance along the lines of "Well, I put all the information into the PC, and what the computer says is. . . ."

Don't tell me what the computer says; tell me what YOU say. If someone made a plaque with that line, I'd hang it on the wall behind my desk. And a thousand thousand other managers would, too.

❧

I Don't Want to Look Stupid in Front of My

☐ Secretary ☐ MBA Assistant
☐ Ten-Year-Old ☐ All of the Above

What's the dumbest reason you know not to use a PC? How about "Because I don't want to look stupid . . ."?

Yet we see that often enough to know that it's a common, if usually unspoken, reaction, especially among older businesspeople. It's funny to turn that same phrase to other business skills. For example, "I don't want to learn how to close a sale because I don't want to look stupid." Or "I don't want to learn how to do a performance review with my direct-reports because I don't want to look stupid." Or "I don't want to learn how to read a financial statement because I don't want to look stupid."

Or my favorite, "I don't want to learn how to use a telephone because I don't want to look stupid."

I certainly don't think you can't be successful in business today without using a PC. But in almost every white-collar job in business, skill in using a PC can be a real help in doing your job better. And thus some facility with PCs can be a real career boost.

We're all afraid of looking stupid. I give about 40 speeches a year, and have been doing that for many years. Yet every single time I get ready to walk out in front of an audience, I get that old, scary feeling: *What if I make a fool of myself?* That's as deeply embedded in our psyches as our DNA chains are embedded in our cells, I suspect; I don't know anyone who doesn't get the sweats at the prospect of looking dumb to someone else.

But we don't let that keep us from learning to drive a car, or make a cold call, or pitch a proposal to top management. So why should we let it get in the way of learning to use what is, after all, just another business machine? Would you avoid using a copier because you didn't want to look stupid by asking someone how? Or a fax machine?

I know you don't have this problem. If you did, you probably wouldn't be reading this book. But you almost certainly have colleagues who would find a PC an important business tool, if only they could get over their fear—that fear of looking stupid during the process of learning how to use the machine. Their fear may be well masked, and thus may appear as something very different . . . but fear it almost certainly is.

Which means that once you understand what's standing in their way, you have a real opportunity to help. After all, a PC is just another business machine. . . .

Do It Yourself?

I know: You have someone to do that *for* you.

That's the credo of the Modern Manager: Do as little as possible yourself, delegate as much as possible to others. And never, ever perform a support function, even when it makes more sense to do it yourself. Keep that up and you'll stay on the fast track until you reach the very top. Otherwise, you'll bring into question your abilities, and your sense of yourself as a *manager of people,* not a mere doer of things.

Phooey.

Sure, good managers delegate, and sure they use aides and assistants and secretaries well. But sometimes it *does* make sense to do something yourself—even if it looks like one of those menial tasks you routinely deal off to others.

I have in mind, of course, working with a personal computer. And knocking out the occasional memo or draft proposal or outline of a speech—word-processing tasks, all—are good places to begin.

You wouldn't be reading this book if you weren't interested in PCs, and almost certainly using one now. So I'm not trying to sweep in the "never touch 'em, myself" crowd here. Whether from fear of things technical or fear of looking like a fool, or fear of losing their Joe Cool status, these people have forsaken the leverage a PC could bring to their work and their careers. (Great: that makes it easier for you to roar past them.) Instead, I'm going after those among you who are devoted single-task users of PCs—or maybe even two-task users—and who look down your nose at other things people do with PCs.

If you're a frequent spreadsheet user, for example, and maybe a fairly active electronic mail user as well, you've accumulated a solid base of knowledge and experience working with PCs. You're way past the stage where you felt you were always dealing with the computer itself, trying to figure out how to make it do this or that. You're working now with *information* and *ideas,* concentrating on the business at hand, not on getting the underlying technology to work. And you have a pretty good sense of what works and what doesn't, generally, with PCs: when it's worth handling something on the computer vs. scribbling on the back of an envelope or dealing the job off to someone else. That's an enormous advantage: you've assimilated the tool.

That means you're in an ideal position now to *leverage* your PC knowledge and experience by adding some other useful work to your time at the computer. Why sneer at the idea of becoming even *more* productive?

Reaching Out

Maybe you should try using a simple outlining program to lay out the structure of proposals or contracts or sales pitches for your field salespeople—even if those documents are eventually going to be written by others. Maybe you should try a personal-calendar program, such as *Calendar Creator Plus,* or a daily to-do list keeper, such as *Top Priority.* Maybe you should get a simple word processor, such as *Q&A,* or *Professional Write,* and try your hand at your own first drafts of important sales plans or budget capital-spending plans, or at organizing those occasional speeches you make to professional groups.

Maybe . . . but I hear you already: *You have people to do that for you. It's not a good use of your time. You're a Big Picture kind of guy, not a keyboard-pounder.*

Again, phooey.

Once you've tasted how powerful a PC can be, why put artificial blocks in the way of getting even more out of the tool? I'm not suggesting writing your own routine correspondence on a PC, or endlessly polishing and formatting "pretty-print" documents, or designing the new company logo on your PC, or laying out the next issue of the company's employee newsletter with a desktop-publishing program.

Because you *do* have people to do those things for you. And those probably *are* poor uses of your time.

I just want you to try getting your feet wet in some other areas on the computer. *Not because there's any special glory in using a PC*—PCs are simply business tools—but because I suspect you'll be amazed at how much you like what you try, at how quickly it becomes part of your normal routine and makes you more productive.

And in my experience, for most businesspeople, scientific and technical professionals, that first additional step is to try using a word-processing program.

Sure, you have people to do that for you. But do you like it that way? Is that always the best way to get things done? Are you always satisfied with the results? Do things always turn out the way you expected them to?

I didn't think so. Keep reading.

III

SMART DOCUMENTS

When GUIs Make Sense

Following at least five years of hype and overclaim, the graphical user interface (or GUI) finally arrived for real in the DOS world in mid-1990. The advent of *Windows* 3.0 meant that PC users could finally see what all the cheering had been about over in the Macintosh world: GUIs really were a swell idea, after all.

Earlier versions of *Windows* had been so sluggish and bug-ridden as to be nearly unusable. If you doubt that, talk with any of the ordinary PC users—as opposed to the people who love to play with their PCs—at any of the several companies that attempted to standardize on *Windows* 2.0, 2.03, *Windows/286,* or *Windows/386.* But be prepared to hear some strong language.

The alternatives for GUI true believers had been the Macintosh itself, of course; the feeble *Windows* competitor, *GEM;* the clumsy IBM/Microsoft joint development, *OS/2 Presentation Manager;* and early beta versions of the feuding Unix twins, *Motif* and *OpenLook.* Of those, the Mac was the best choice, and also the best illustration of how much graphical interfaces can contribute to an individual's productivity at the computer. But the theological wars that raged over the idea of bringing Macintoshes into some companies kept them away from many people who would have benefited from using a GUI-based computer. Apple's own mismanagement in the late Eighties and the resulting loss of momentum for the Macintosh as a business computer didn't help, either.

Whatever the options, it's clear that GUIs didn't make many inroads into the business-computing mainstream before the appearance of *Windows* 3.0. But A.W.3.—after *Windows* 3.0—applications with true graphical interface appeared, running under *Windows,* and the computing community generally began to appreciate the merits of the GUI.

The business community, characteristically, has been a lot slower to move towards standardization on GUIs as general-purpose office-automation systems. In part that may be due to lingering confusion over whether the enduring standard will be *Windows* or *OS/2 Presentation Manager;* but likelier, it simply represents the conservatism and inertia historically so much a part of businesses' management of their information systems.

Cheerleading the GUI Revolution

I've been a big fan of GUIs, and certainly am willing to be labeled by the anti-GUI forces as one of the "GUI cheerleaders." (The term wasn't coined by me. In the Q&A following a speech I gave to a group of corporate MIS managers a while back, an MIS officer at a midwestern bank rose to his feet and began his query by calling me "one of the infamous GUI cheerleaders." It irritated him when I not only repeated the line in my answer, but took obvious pleasure in the intended insult, and kept referring to it throughout the rest of the question-and-answer period.)

Because I *am* a GUI Cheerleader, and if I've gotten some notoriety for it, so much the better. I think GUIs make important contributions to PC productivity. Those benefits are evident not only in the early stages of becoming a PC user—a shorter learning curve for the machine itself and its system software, for example, plus the carryover of knowledge about how applications work from one program to another—but also over the long term, in day-to-day work.

And despite what some say, those benefits aren't limited to graphics programs, desktop publishing packages, or graphing and charting programs, but apply to almost every kind of PC work. The high-quality on-screen preview offered by a GUI saves time for users, often a *lot* of time, by reducing time-wasting rounds of printing files again and again to get a decent-looking printout. The ease of manipulating such tools as 3-D spreadsheet models under a graphical interface is another example. Compare navigating and linking among related worksheets in *PC Excel,* under *Windows,* with the same steps in a character-oriented program such as *1-2-3* 3.0, and you'll immediately appreciate the benefits of a GUI for everyday work.

And yet, and yet . . . I hardly think character-oriented systems are going to go away overnight. Nor do I think that in every company, every PC user should be pushed into a GUI world right away.

Word-processing programs seem to me the best illustration of this "not everyone, not right away" principle. Among the early GUI word-processing packages, for example, was Microsoft's *Word for Windows.* It's a sensational product, bringing many desktop-publishing-like characteristics and features to ordinary office word processing. The computer magazines fell all over themselves about *Word for Windows,* and it was widely touted as the kind of program we'd all be using soon. WordPerfect Corp. was perceived as being in trouble, since its mass-market GUI product, a *Windows* version of the best-selling *WordPerfect* package, didn't appear until a year later, giving Microsoft and *Word for Windows* a huge advantage in a notoriously time-sensitive business.

But a funny thing happened during that year: *WordPerfect* held onto its market-leading status, and despite good sales for *Word for Windows,* the world hardly converted to GUI word processing overnight.

Avoiding the Bleeding Edge

Cynics might say that's because Corporate America is too timid in its assessment of and commitment to new technology. I say it's because the people who make new-technology buying decisions know what they're doing.

First, the character-based version of *WordPerfect* is a widely accepted, widely installed standard. Most of the people who use word-processing software intensively in corporations aren't PC buffs, hanging on the edge of every technological advance. They just want to get their work done: to do a good job, and go home at five o'clock. Disrupting their work lives by pushing them into a new and unfamiliar product, full of new work habits and new features to be learned, would be a massive disruption for them and for the company. And it would inevitably produce a productivity sag until those people learned, then began to internalize, those new habits and features. There are huge and very real if intangible costs associated with that kind of changeover.

Second, while the advantages added by bringing a graphical user interface to word processing are undeniably worthwhile for some users, they have little to offer the person doing production typing. And a great part of the use of word-processing technology in American business is just that: turning out production typing. Today's distributed-work office landscape might not look much like the old "typing pool," but the principles remain the same. If those people doing grind-it-out production typing aren't going to benefit from the advantages of a GUI—and arguably may even become a little less productive with one, since the computation overhead for a PC of running a graphical display inevitably slows down truly fast typists—then why make the change?

And third, the PCs in use by many of the people doing high-volume production word processing either won't run *Windows* and a GUI word-processing package at all, or will do so only very slowly. Upgrading by adding a new processor, more memory, a better display, and a mouse is one possibility; simply tossing the old (paid-for and fully depreciated) PC and installing a new, more powerful one is another. But what about the third alternative: leaving the old PC, the old program, and the old habits in place?

Lest my banker-antagonist and others think I'm shrinking from my support for GUIs, let me make a very clear no-retreat statement: I think GUIs can make a big difference in productivity, and most of us will be using them in a few years.

But I also think the business of business is doing business, not trying to drive technological change for the sake of change. And I've seen too many instances over the first decade of the personal computer era where a gung-ho technology advocate turned things upside-down at a company by implementing new technologies across the board, rather than adopting them selectively and incrementally. Deciding that because a large number of PC users in a company would benefit from using *Windows* (or any other graphical-user-interface-environment), *everyone* in the company should make the transition, is an expensive, disruptive, and short-sighted view.

Indeed, I'd argue—and often have—that that kind of decision is actually profoundly *anti*-technology. If the proper role of new technology is to help us work better, smarter, and faster, but adopting a new technology forces some to work less well, less intelligently, or less quickly, then that's technology gone berserk: new technology violating its own premise and promise.

The transition to new technologies is never easy, and I don't predict a smooth glide into a GUI future. We'll make the move in fits and starts, lurching forward, then consolidating our gains; then lurching forward once more. Those applications with the most self-evident gains under GUIs, such as PC graphics packages, will steadily knock off older, character-oriented market leaders. Applications such as word processing, where the gains are real but of immediate value only to selected users of that kind of application, will advance much more slowly, and will probably be the last areas to adopt the GUI as the standard interface.

Five years from now, a character-oriented word-processor—*WordPerfect*, for example, or Microsoft *Word*—will still be a viable product for a lot of PC users. Even though a lot of those whose use of a PC isn't focused primarily on word processing will have switched to GUIs.

The question, it seems to me, is not how fast we can move everyone to a brave new GUI world, but how willing we're going to be to recognize that reality of a diverse workplace, and how smart we'll be about matching tools to office workers' individual needs.

❧

Type-Over Templates

If you always like to use the very highest-tech answers, you'll hate this chapter. You'd better skip to the next one fast, or your blood pressure is going to start rising fast.

While today's best word-processing packages offer many ways of speeding up your work, from style sheets to glossaries full of boilerplate text to built-in macros, one of the simplest and most useful timesavers is available to users of even the most basic program. Just pick two or three letters, reports, contracts, or other documents you've created that are generally representative of how you like your work to look when printed. Choose documents of different sizes, lengths, degrees of formality and finished "looks" on the printed page, then save an extra copy of each as a template.

You might pick a short one-page letter, with wide margins all around and just a couple of paragraphs of text; a long, narrow-margin letter that gets about as much text on one page as will look good; and a still-longer multiple-page letter, with slightly more generous margins, plus page-numbering headers. Each has exactly the type faces, margins, line and paragraph spacing, paragraph indentations and so on that you like in your correspondence. Save the first file as SHORTLTR.TPL, the second as ONEPGLTR.TPL, and the last as LONGLTR.TPL.

Then use a utility program or a DOS command (see below) to make each file read-only, so you don't alter those permanent templates by saving the letters you write with them under the same names.

Using Your Templates

Now, to write a new letter without having to pay any attention to formatting issues, just call up within your word processor the template that comes closest to the kind of letter you're about to type, and write the new one atop the old one. That is, either literally type the new text over the old (a bad idea, usually, because you'll invariably wipe out some line breaks and other formatting information), or just push the old text ahead of the cursor as you type. Then delete the old date, inside address, and text, and print the letter.

Yeah, I know: it's pretty basic.

But it can be a wonderful productivity booster. I've taught this trick to hundreds of secretaries. Sometimes that was because they were new to PCs and wanted a crutch, to get started; sometimes it was because the company wanted to establish certain styles for PC-generated reports and correspondence, and wanted to use templates to maintain those styles and formats.

In every case, the PC users loved it. Especially when someone's just come to a PC from a typewriter, or from one of those creaky old dedicated word processors, this can be a big help in climbing up the learning curve and getting productive *fast*. But this isn't just a trick for newcomers; I've taught it to dozens of executives, who though savvy indeed with *1-2-3* or *dBASE* or *Paradox,* don't often use the word-processing programs on their PCs' hard disks. But when they do, they want to get something out fast.

Protecting Templates

If you do decide to use this template trick, but don't have a utility program (such as the *Norton Utilities,* or Central Point Software's *PC Tools*) that can set the read-only attribute for a file, here's how to do it manually with a DOS command. First, save each file you want to protect as outlined above, with a .TPL filename extension (or any other standardized filename extension that will remind you that these are reusable templates).

Next, use the DOS ATTRIBute command to set the read-only bit for the files to "on." To do this, use the syntax shown here, substituting the correct path to the subdirectory where your .TPL files are stored:

```
C>ATTRIB +r c:\wp\docs\*.tpl
```

The example assumes that your files are stored in the DOCS subdirectory of the WP directory on drive C, and that you have used the filename extension .TPL for each template. The asterisk is a DOS shorthand that means "all files, regardless of their filename" to the left of the period in the filename. The +r turns on the read-only protection.

Now when you load those template files, your word processor will respond to a command to save your new letters—the ones written with a template's help—with a request for a new filename, and will refuse to save the real letters under the template filename. Hence, that file has now become "read-only," and you can't accidentally alter it.

You hate this? It's a retrograde step that takes people backwards? Well, I warned you that if you always go for the slickest, most elegant, most techie answers, you'd hate this one. So I understand.

But don't tell that to all those people around you in your office who use this trick every day to speed up their work. They're going to think you're a little confused about just why you have that PC on your desk.

Not you and me: Now we know that you're a propellor-head at heart.

Two-Handed Productivity

If you're a mouse-hater, or simply haven't yet seen any reason to put one on your PC, I want to suggest that you consider adding one for the application many PC users would say would benefit *least* from using a mouse as an on-screen pointer: word processing. But only if your word-processing program makes good use of a mouse. In the PC world, for now at least, that limits the list to *Microsoft Word*, plus *Windows* and *OS/2 Presentation Manager* word-processing programs.

Every good word processor provides plenty of keyboard alternatives to using a mouse—including *Word* and the *Windows* and *OS/2-PM* programs. So you can certainly use them satisfactorily without a mouse. Indeed, many good typists argue that the time involved in moving their hand away from the keyboard to a mouse, then returning, can sharply reduce their effective typing speed.

I agree: using a mouse as you write is actually an impediment to real productivity with word-processing programs.

But writing—by which I mean your first-pass inputting of the text—isn't all there is to turning out documents with a word-processing program. The key to the greater word-processing productivity possible with a mouse attached to your PC is to use it during *editing*.

And the trick is to keep one hand on the mouse, another flicking across the keyboard.

Reserve the mouse movements, with your hand staying on the mouse, for *selecting* text: individual characters, a word or two, part of a sentence, a paragraph. Then use your other hand to enter the necessary keyboard characters, when only a few keystrokes are needed. For longer passages, of course, bring your "mouse hand" back to the keyboard, and type as you normally would.

A program that makes good use of a mouse—*Word* does, and virtually every GUI-interface word-processing program does, as well—uses that mouse primarily for jumping around through your text, plus selecting the text you want to move, change, or delete. For most of us, editing changes in the text typically consist of adding missing letters or removing unneeded ones, adding an *and* here or a comma there, removing a redundant word. Your left hand can handle that work very quickly, once you get used to this pattern.

Until you've tried it, you'll be skeptical of the difference this style of working can make in the speed and ease of editing a document. But try it for a few minutes, and you'll never edit text any other way.

(While I use the word "mouse" here for clarity, I much prefer trackballs to mice and believe you will, too, once you've tried one; see *So You're a Mouse Hater: Try A Trackball* in the **Analysis and Persuasion: PC Graphics** section of this book.)

This two-handed game sounds odd—it *looks* odd, too, frankly—but it works superbly.

❧

Good Design versus
Ransom Notes

This one's quick and easy: don't use too many different typefaces and sizes in your documents.

Remember those funny-looking ransom notes that kidnapping victims' families used to get in 1940s movies? The ones that were obviously pasted together from a wild variety of letters and numbers, cut out of the big-type grocery ads in the local daily newspaper . . . supposedly, so there was no incriminating handwriting to tie the note to the kidnappers?

That's the kind of "ransom note" look you want to avoid. But unfortunately, it's one that too many PC users who've just bought some soft fonts, or maybe a font cartridge, turn out. And worse, for some, the look that their documents never *lose.*

We've kept for some time in my office a Desktop Publishing Wall of Shame, on which we post the most egregious examples we've gotten in the mail lately from practitioners of this Ransom Note School of Design. A few entries are readers' letters, but far more of these painful-to-look-at pages come from press releases, promotional materials, computer and software manuals, and other easy targets for the Alcatraz Typographers.

One look at that wall makes clear that overuse of typeface, type-style, and type-size variations is by far the single biggest bugaboo of the neophyte type user. *If only,* we've often dreamt, *people were limited to Helvetica and Times Roman. . . .*

But even *that* wouldn't be enough. Because you can produce really *terrible-*looking documents with only one typeface—say, the ubiquitous Helvetica—if you twist it into enough unfortunate varieties. By mixing many sizes, and adding some italic type, some boldface type, and maybe even some boldface *and* italic type, then using such excesses as outlining, drop shadows, underlining, and gray fill-patterns, you too can look like an idiot to your correspondents, coworkers, clients and boss.

Most documents require few type variations. Using 12-point Times Roman for the body of your letters, for example, with the occasional word in 12-point Times Roman Italic, is fine. If you want to get really elaborate, maybe you should make the company name, in the formal inside address at the top of the letter, Times Roman Bold. *And then stop.*

You don't need more fonts, which would be confusing and unattractive; and you don't need a more exotic font, such as Broadway or Script or Cooper Black; those will distract the reader from what you're trying to say. You don't need boldfaced words scattered throughout your letters, as a second form of emphasis. This only leads to an interesting question in the reader's mind: Which is supposed to be *more* emphasized . . . the parts that are in italics or the parts that are boldfaced?

And please, please, please avoid the two cardinal sins of typeset-look work: underlining and setting words in ALL CAPITAL LETTERS. An underline in text is simply a code to a typesetter that a certain word or phrase should be set in italics. Underlining on the printed page—especially in the typeset-look but modest-resolution typefaces many of us use on laser printers today—looks awful. And material in all capital letters is much harder to read than words using the usual combinations of capital and lower-case letters. The VERY occasional word in all capital letters for emphasis is acceptable. But avoid all-capital-letter text if you want your work to appear clean, bright, and readable.

We all see lots of examples of bad type usage around us—from packaging to magazine pages to those ugly desktop-published flyers on the community bulletin board down at the supermarket. And sometimes, unfortunately, those ugly pages even come with an *imprimatur,* such as the horrible-looking ransom-note-school spreadsheet printout featured in one of the PC magazines a while back . . . as a supposed paradigm of good design.

But resist. Keep it simple.

And don't send people ransom notes.

Drawing the Line:
Word Processing Or
Desktop Publishing?

As mainstream PC word-processing programs have grown larger and more capable—cynics might say even more bloated with 'featuritis'!—one of their publishers' loudest claims is that for many jobs, these latest high-end WP wonders can take the place of desktop-publishing packages. With features such as multiple-column pages, vertical and horizontal rules, great flexibility in using typeset-look type, the ability to put scanned photos and artwork into documents, the ability to lay a screened pattern over text, and other new features, the major word- processing packages are the Swiss Army knives of software.

Which is exactly the problem.

With enough time and patience, you could probably build a house with just a Swiss Army knife . . . but *would* you?

Multiple-function tools inevitably sacrifice power for versatility. Swiss Army knives add saws, magnifying glasses, rulers, teaspoons, toothpicks, and more to the basic jackknife, but those additions hardly match the usefulness or quality of even mediocre-quality saws, magnifying glasses, rulers, teaspoons, and so on.

Software pioneer Bill Gates coined a great phrase some time ago, one that's useful here: Some products, Gates said, have depth; some have breadth. In his own company's case, for example, Microsoft *Word* offers remarkable word-processing power, and Microsoft *Excel* is a spectacular spreadsheet program. Yet both those functions (and more) are found in the company's $99 Microsoft

Works package. But no one is going to confuse the much more limited word-processing and spreadsheet functionality of *Works* with the state-of-the-art, power-user depth of its two elder siblings. The former are for serious users of those computer functions; the latter, for those who need to do a little of this, and a little of that. By Gates' definition, *Word* and *Excel* have depth; *Works* has breadth.

Power Users, Power Tools

That definition fits exactly the claimed desktop-publishing prowess of programs such as *WordPerfect,* Microsoft *Word, MultiMate, XyWrite,* and other high-end WP packages. With great effort and a lot of fiddling around, you can induce these packages to turn out finished pages that may not be quite as good as those produced with a true desktop-publishing program such as Aldus *PageMaker,* but produce remarkably desktop-publishing-like results, certainly acceptable for some purposes.

But those same pages—actually, more precise and better-looking versions of them—could have been produced more quickly and easily with a real desktop-publishing package.

There is an appealing economy of means to using high-end word-processing software for desktop-publishing jobs: You don't have to buy and learn a new program and store it on your computer's increasingly crowded hard disk. And for some work—simple flyers about the upcoming softball game between Accounting and Telemarketing, or a relatively straightforward employee newsletter, or a client proposal that looks better than the old, plain typed ones ever did—the better word-processing packages' DTP-like features acquit themselves decently.

But remember the Swiss Army knife, and Bill Gates's definitions. If you need to do a little desktop publishing from time to time, then using your word processor may be just the answer. But if you're at all serious about desktop publishing—in other words, if you need *depth,* not just breadth—then you're fooling yourself by trying to do the job with a word processor.

Style Sheets:
Making Life Easier

Perhaps the least-used feature of sophisticated word-processing programs is their ability to use style sheets to format your documents. Style-sheet formatting was introduced years ago in the first version of *Microsoft Word*, but can now be found, in various forms and under other names, in most of the major word-processing programs.

I can understand why relatively few *Word* users use style sheets, especially if they started using the program in its early days. Until fairly recently, using style sheets in *Word* was a pain in the neck. To make things worse, the process was badly documented in the manuals that accompanied *Word*. Reading the first few pages of the chapter describing *Word's* style-sheet feature made you want to take a couple of Excedrin and close your eyes for a while. But starting with *Word's* Version 3.0 a few years ago, the style sheet feature became much easier to use, and much better documented. Today, it's a snap.

Perhaps too many of today's *Word* users have long memories and little patience for reading the manuals that came with their later-versions' disks.

Among users of other word-processing programs, I find the general aversion to style sheets baffling. Style sheets can make your work go so much faster, and produce such attractive and consistent results, that they ought to be central to every PC word-processing user's bag of tricks.

Formatting by Styles

Here's how style sheets work. You identify every part of your document that has a unique style, or look. In a typical business letter, that might include the date line at the top of the page; the formal, inside address; the salutation; the body of the text; indented paragraphs within the text; the formal close; and maybe a "secretary sig" in the lower left-hand corner.

Let's take a closer look at those styles.

- You might like the date to appear 12 lines down from the top of the page, and indented 4.3 inches from the left margin.

- You like the inside address of your letters to begin two lines below the date line, flush with the left margin, followed by a line and a half of vertical spacing.

- You like the "Dear So-and-so" salutation to print flush with the left margin, followed by two-thirds of a line's space.

- You like the standard paragraphs of the letter to follow the document's margins, with the first line of each paragraph indented .3 inch (in lieu of tabbing), with a half-line between paragraphs.

- You occasionally like to use indented paragraphs, with the text indented .7 inch from the left margin and .5 inch from the right margin, with a .2 inch first-line indent. Indented paragraphs should also be preceded by an extra half-line's spacing, and followed by an extra two-thirds of a line's spacing.

- You like the formal close to consist of the word "Cordially" followed by a comma, then three blank lines, then your name; and you want the left edges of the word "Cordially" and your name to line up vertically, each 3.7 inches from the left margin.

- You like the "secretary's sig" line—the little "JD:SL" line that indicates this letter from John Defoe was prepared by Sally Lewis—to print at the left margin, in capital letters, three lines down from the line with your name.

- Oh, yes: The letter should be printed in 12-point Times Roman, with 2 points of space between each line of type within a paragraph; and those indented paragraphs should be printed in 12-point Times Italic.

To use a style sheet to produce such attractive, consistent documents, just create a list of the styles, and add to each the specifications for that style. Your word-processing program largely automates that job; some even offer a "styles by example" feature, which lets you create a sample of the way you want the style to look, select that text, then ask the program to take a style-sheet snapshot of the selected text. Those individual styles are collected into a master style sheet.

Then, as you're writing your letters, you simply apply each style, or "tag," to the appropriate part of the letter, typically by using a two-letter code. For example, in Word you might have assigned the code *IA* to your inside-address style; to use that style you'd simply type the inside address text, select it, then type ALT + IA. The text will be instantly reformatted into the appropriate form.

Diversity and Consistency

It's easy to create and save on your PC's hard disk many different style sheets: one for the double-spaced text of a draft, for example; another with very large, black type for a "reading copy" of a speech; another with small type and justified lines for contracts; and so on. Switching to the right one for a new document takes just a few keystrokes. And a hidden advantage for some to using style sheets is that if your word-processing output is sometimes incorporated into larger documents created with a desktop publishing program, such as *Ventura* or *PageMaker,* those programs can often read your style-tags, and will format the text properly without any further intervention.

As you can imagine, many companies develop standardized style sheets for several kinds of corporate documents, from correspondence to proposals to press releases, then distribute copies of those style sheets to everyone who uses a PC, to assure that corporate documents have a clean, consistent, attractive look.

But you don't have to work at a huge corporation—nor at one that has adopted this distributed style sheets idea—to make good use of the concept. It's sitting there in your word-processing program, just waiting for you to put it to use to save time and produce better work.

❧

Design Templates

I like to think the reports we prepare for my consulting firm's clients are attractive and professional-looking. There's a lot more to them than good looks, of course—it's the quality of the *ideas,* not the quality of the typography, that counts most—but an attractive, well-organized and well-designed report has an authority, an *open-me-first* feeling, and an implicit credibility, that you don't find in sloppy or dull-looking work.

To establish a standard for our reports, we devoted some time to coming up with a few good-looking, consistent, reusable formats. We knew that just one or two designs wouldn't cover the range of our work, but we also knew that having a hundred different choices would be a disaster. So we focused on the kinds of reports, proposals, analyses, and recommendations we produce most often, then devised some more-or-less-standard ways of handling them.

We knew that standardizing would make it a lot faster and easier to turn out good-looking work, since conceptualizing a piece of printed work in one of those forms leads directly to writing, illustrating, and preparing "infographics" that are *appropriate,* rather than wandering off on costly and time-consuming false starts.

We also knew there would be an advantage in developing a kind of savvy, in-the-know corporate identity: As clients see more and more of our work, and notice the attractive, consistent design, the perception of the firm as a group that has its act together grows.

Finally, we knew that a failure to show that we ourselves knew, understood, and used well the publishing tools computers put at our disposal would reflect poorly on us. If we didn't know them well enough to use them intelligently ourselves, how could we possibly hope to advise others on how those tools should be designed and sold, or chosen and used?

What we *didn't* know before we decided to get more serious about a rich, attractive, and consistent design scheme for our outgoing work was that it would become a kind of internal quality-assurance program as well. When one glance at a finished piece of work shows it doesn't stack up very well against other recent, similar work—the analysis is slight, or the writing is clumsy, or the ideas muddled, or too many ideas rely on too many words and not enough on simple "infographics"—it's hard to get that report out the front door. Peer pressure and self-respect are amazing motivational forces among professionals; quite aside from their innate competitiveness, people don't want to be associated with a body of work, or even with a few individual items, that fall below the standards that prevail around them.

I bring this up not to brag about our graphic standards, but to provoke and perhaps irritate you a little about *yours*. If your company scatter-shoots odd, uneven, inconsistent, and often not very good-looking work around your markets, what does that tell prospects and customers about your company?

Better Design on the Macro Level

I won't claim to be able to quantify the benefits of bringing good design to your printed output. But any businessperson who appreciates the perils of opportunity costs—the high price of *what might have been*, of opportunities lost not least because they were never understood—will immediately understand that quantifying precisely the return from good design is quite unnecessary: the high opportunity costs of *bad* design are all too evident.

On a global level, fixing corporate design standards can be a huge task, involving the use of graphic-design and corporate-identity firms that redesign everything from logos to doorknobs, come up with design specs for the painting of delivery trucks and the signs on rest room doors, and often engage senior staffs in solemn metaphysical discussions about What This Company Is Really All About.

Developing better corporate design practices and standards on that scale starts at maybe $100,000 and quickly goes up into the stratosphere—a bargain, often, but beyond the scope of what you're going to do when you put this book down in a minute.

What I want to encourage you to do is to spend a few minutes doing what we did: thinking, talking, and arguing about the few kinds of pieces you send out most often: proposals, contracts, reports, price lists, whatever. When you come across printed materials that you think capture the kind of look you want, hold onto them for reference. And then get a little professional design help on making your own computer-printed pieces look better *within the limitations of the computer-based tools you already own.*

A Few Good Templates

In managing this macro-scale better-design process, focus on developing templates: a few stock designs that include the repeating elements, or building blocks, from which you construct finished documents. Those may include cover-page designs; body-copy standards for typefaces, type sizes, and spacing; headings and subheadings; positioning of text on the page; the scaling and positioning of graphics; preferred types of graphs; the format for captions on graphics; binding standards; paper color, texture, and weight; and much more.

Watch, too, for ways to extend the look and feeling of these core templates into related materials, such as overhead transparencies. For example, if you develop a few simple standards for overheads—you'll get a lot of good ideas for that in this section—stand-up presentations of your company's work can start echoing your accompanying printed materials. (That's exactly what large advertisers are doing, of course, when they repeat the visual themes, ad copy, and slogans from their television commercials in their print ads, and the jingles and audio trickery from TV spots in their radio commercials.)

It's often surprising how much small, simple but not-so-obvious decisions can affect the quality, sense of design, and *read-me-first*-ness of proposals, reports, and other commonplace business documents. Simply turning the paper sideways—for example, printing on standard 8½ × 11 inch sheets turned horizontally—in what computer people call "landscape format," can open up the pages of text, making the document at once more substantial and easier to read, and can greatly enhance its attention-getting clout.

Using multiple-column pages can help, too. But generally you'll get even more impact by using just one column that is perhaps 60 percent as wide as the page, then placing that column markedly off-center, cheated well to the right, for example, if the document is to be bound along its left edge.

Remember that while you want striking documents, you want them to be impressive because they're clean, attractive, and easy to read. Avoid tendencies towards "ransom-note" design and other excesses that work to your disadvantage by drawing attention—very often, *unfavorable* attention in this conservative business world!—to the design, not the content, of the document.

Enough examples. I don't want to encourage you to develop these templates yourself, but to suggest that a design professional's ideas can fit within existing resources, deadlines, and budgets, and that the process doesn't need to be elaborate or expensive.

The PC tools at our disposal today are capable of producing astonishingly good-looking output. Most often, the greatest impediment to getting to that result is our own failure to demand it, our failure to ask for something better than we're used to seeing, our failure to use computer tools if not to their fullest, at least to the point where they give us great leverage.

That kind of use of technology lies at the heart of what PCs are really about: increasing productivity in its largest and best sense.

Two-Bit Mail-Merging

True Confessions Time: Sometimes when I need to turn out a handful of quick mail-merged letters (read: fake personalized letters), I just do them manually, rather than dealing with my word-processing program's mail-merge "features."

That's heresy, of course, to PC zealots, who believe as an article of faith that if there is a feature in a program that will accomplish what you want, you should always use that feature, whether it makes any sense for the job at hand or not. Tough, guys: When I have to do some piddly little job, I just want to get it *done.*

I can't think of a better example than mail-merged letters. Virtually every word-processing program sold today has some form of mail-merge facility. Many are very powerful, with all sorts of conditional expressions that let users construct form letters that do things like including stored boilerplate paragraph 37G *IF* *CITY=CHICAGO* *AND* *IF* *ACCTBAL=>0* *AND* *CUSTNAME=SMITH* *OR* *CUSTNAME=JONES* but *NOTIF* *CUSTNAME=WALKER* *ELSE* *SKIP* *ENDIF*.

You get the idea.

In my experience working with thousands of PC users at hundreds of large corporations, no area of any major category of PC software is so baffling and frustrating to real-world PC users as mail-merging in word-processing software. I'm not surprised. It *can* be puzzling—precisely because of the power and flexibility of that extensive range of database-like conditional statements software publishers have added.

Yet mastering mail-merging isn't hard. I use the mail-merge feature in my favorite word processor, Microsoft *Word,* frequently and without much trouble, even though *Word's* mail-merge facility is probably the most powerful, versatile, and thus (necessarily) complicated of any presently available.

But I also have enough sense to know when NOT to use automatic mail-merging. One case is the large-scale mail-merge operation, based on an existing database of names and addresses, that I describe in the next chapter, *Serious Mail-Merging: Use a Real DBMS*. But even more often, my mail-merge needs are at the other end of the spectrum: I simply want to send fake personalized letters to four or five people or companies.

When I do that, I invariably just write the first letter, complete with the first name, address, and any other personalized information. I save it, proof it, then print it. Then I save a second copy of that first letter in the series, under another name—usually, as TEMPLATE.DOC. I call up that TEMPLATE.DOC file, and insert an asterisk in front of every "variable," or personalized item, in it. I save the file again, under that same TEMPLATE.DOC filename.

Then I simply replace the personalized information in the letter, one addressee at a time. After each entry I use the word-processing program's search feature to chase down that next asterisk, so I can insert the next personalized bit. As I finish each letter, I print it, then clear that file from memory, call up old TEMPLATE.DOC again, and enter the new set of personalized information.

Inserting the asterisks is a small touch, but an important one. Otherwise, it's just too easy to overlook one item that gives away the whole game—using the name of the previous letter's addressee somewhere in the body of the letter, for example. (Have I ever done that? You bet; and I usually catch my mistake about ten minutes after the mail has gone out.)

There has to be a threshold of pain here, a crossover point at which it's more trouble to go on using this disgustingly manual, template-based, one-at-a-time system instead of using the power of your PC to do a true mail-merge. For me, that's somewhere around five letters. Beyond that, it's worth using mail-merge.

If you routinely send personalized form letters to even short lists of the *same* groups of people, clearly it's worth using real mail-merge then, too. If you like to pound on your local city council members regularly, or frequently distribute new corporate-policy memos to the same group of managers, true mail-merging makes sense even for groups of four or five.

Otherwise, why make life difficult?

I'd much rather have an extra 15 minutes at the ballgame this afternoon, or another 20 minutes on the racquetball court, or maybe just a few minutes to look out the window and relax, than chase after that noble feeling of having Really Used A Complicated Feature Of My Software, By God.

I leave that to the PC Zealots.

Serious Mail-Merging:
Use a Real DBMS

The complexity of the mail-merge features built into the best of today's word processors is matched only by the complexity of *using* those features. But their apparent sophistication in applying those mail-merging commands within a letter—offering extremely complex conditional statements, for example, that appear to turn word-processing programs into something like sophisticated database report-writers—can lure innocent users into asking more of these programs than they can deliver.

That's most evident in mail-merging features' marginal capability to select information from the data lists they make it so easy to construct. If you want to use a word processor's mail-merge routine to send "personalized" letters to each of the seven city council members in your city, then go ahead and build that data list of the council members with the word-processing program. You'll be happy with the results . . . especially if you find you like the power of mail-merging so much that you become a frequent, if one-way, correspondent of those public officials!

But if you're going to be sending letters to a hundred or a thousand people, that word-processing data-list approach is quickly going to become inadequate. Most important, no matter how certain you are when you begin that you don't really need the power of a real database program to manage your list, I can almost promise you that if you're in the business of writing letters to a hundred- or thousand-name list, you'll soon find things you want to do but cannot do within those very limited sort-and-select commands of your word processor's conditional mail-merge functions.

Then you'll wind up reentering all that data in a database program. And you won't be nearly so impressed with the data-management capabilities of your word-processing program anymore.

Rather than making that detour through your word processor en route to the true database file you need, why not enter that data just once, the first time, in a simple database program? I'm a fan of flat-file database programs, such as Symantec's *Q&A* and Software Publishing's *Professional File,* for this kind of work—you don't need the greater power of relational programs, such as *dBASE* or *R:base,* so why put up with their greater complexity?—but nearly any database program will work find for such simple tasks. Some word-processing programs can read *dBASE* files directly, but virtually every database program can write ("export") a file in the "CSV" (comma-separated variables) format, which is what you'll want to feed into your word processor's mail-merge process.

For those without any great attachment to their present word-processing software, I should add that *Q&A* combines a superb word processor *and* a superb flat-file database program in one box, which makes it particularly easy to use for mail-merging. (These are two separate programs, called from a single menu, so this doesn't violate my principle of using a database program for managing data, and a word-processing program for managing mail-merging.) There's no need to change if you're happy with your WP program . . . but if you aren't, and plan to do much serious mail-merge work, you really ought to take a look at *Q&A.* It's state-of-the-art *easy,* yet plenty powerful for any mail-merge project you can imagine.

Some might argue that if your word processor's feeble list-management capabilities can nonetheless be stretched to handle your mail-merge needs, going through the extra step of exporting a file of the selected data from a database program every time you want to get out a mail-merge run is just adding unnecessary work.

I disagree. Word-processing programs' mail-merging features may be powerful when it comes to manipulating data within an individual mail-merged letter, but they're lousy for selecting that information from a word-processing document's data list. It's well worth the extra time and trouble to set up that database, then turn to it first to select the people or companies you want to write.

Otherwise you're heading for an expensive and frustrating fall . . . and the possibility of having to repeat all that data-entry work from scratch.

Using Dummy Pages

Warning: Producing good-looking printed documents is highly habit-forming. Once you get used to turning out great-looking work, it's hard to go back to that old "typewriter look." Or to let little things pass as easily as you might once have.

An example: When you're creating a multipage document that has graphs or other PC-generated graphics dropped in along with the text, you want those graphics to look perfectly integrated into the document. If the graphs are small and have been dropped into the text using your word processor, the text probably wraps right around them, and they look just fine. But sometimes small, drop-in graphs are hard to read and interpret, and you want to use full-page graphics.

Sounds easy enough—and it is—but then when those separately printed graphics pages are dropped into the report, they don't have the same page-numbering, headers, and footers you used on the text-only parts.

An easy fix: Insert two forced page-break commands at the bottom of each page that precedes an all-graphics page you'll later insert. Your program will then print a page with the repeating header and footer you've used throughout the report printed on the otherwise-blank page. Then use that blank piece of paper—a dummy page—to print your graphics.

Obvious? Sure . . . once you've thought of it. I include this tip because clients have told me literally dozens of times, when they saw reports of mine that used this trick, that they wondered how I got my word-processing program to print those graphs so perfectly.

It didn't, of course: I just ran those pages through the printer twice. And then they give me a sheepish look and say "Of *course*! Why didn't *we* think of that . . . ?!?"

Tab, Don't Space!

One tell-tale sign of a novice user of word-processing software is the use of the spacebar to move across the page to insert a new line—say, the "Cordially" in the formal close at the bottom of a letter.

It isn't just that it takes longer to space all the way across the page to the insertion point. Nor is it only that you then have to carefully eyeball whether any succeeding lines that are supposed to line up with the spaced-over one are accurately placed, such as the "John Doe" and "Vice-President" lines that follow that "Cordially," after a few blank lines.

The big problems come when you use the more-attractive proportional-spaced typefaces most of us prefer over typewriter-look Courier or Letter Gothic. And when you make revisions. And when you try to right-align columns of numbers at their decimal places (explicit or assumed). And when you send an electronic copy of that file to someone else for review or revision. And when someone pours that text file into a desktop-publishing program. And . . .

It's no accident that today's word-processing programs give us a rich set of choices for installing tab stops in documents. Beyond the usual "left" tab setting, used for traditional indented lines, such as at the beginning of a paragraph, or for vertical columns of data in multiline tables, word-processing packages also offer right tabs, center tabs, and decimal tabs.

Center and decimal settings are obvious. Right tabs are like decimal tabs, but work without decimal points; they simply move the line over so that it *ends* at a certain point, just as left tabs assure that a line *begins* at a certain point.

It's always easy to succumb to the "quick and dirty" instinct: doing something the simplest, lowest-tech, most self-evident way. That's especially true for the casual user of PCs, someone who doesn't do this very often, and who just wants to get a letter or report or proposal out quickly, hang the protocols and procedures.

In the case of tabs in word-processing documents, though, they're well worth the slight extra trouble to set up and use. You'll save time, get better-looking documents, and charm any coworkers to whom you send electronic copies of those documents.

Running The
WP Format Maze

In the beginning, so to speak, there was ASCII—the American Standard Code for Information Interchange, an almost universally accepted standard for representing the characters in computer-generated documents. The widespread adoption of that standard meant documents, once created and stored, could easily be shared with other PC users, and used with other software programs, with some certainty that they'd read as they did when they were first created. But the range of formatting instructions in ASCII coding is narrow indeed: spaces, tabs, and carriage returns. So while they might *read* right, those documents might *look* very wrong.

As we moved away from the early, primitive text editors—really suited only for programmers entering lines of code—towards true word processors, with extensive formatting (such as page margins, type sizes, line spacing, and much more), we needed a new, more complex industry standard for encoding, saving, printing, and exchanging formatted documents. Otherwise, each word-processing software maker would wind up devising its own system for indicating something like italic type, and as likely as not, no two systems would be compatible.

Unfortunately, that standard never emerged—or rather, *many* of those standards emerged, the useful ones so late that the war was already long since lost. And so we have today's word-processing Tower of Babel: every program encodes formatting instructions its own idiosyncratic way, and many programs compound that confusion with oddball, proprietary file formats for storing documents.

The result is that I can't open a colleague's *MultiMate* file under *Word-Perfect*, or a *WordPerfect* file under Microsoft *Word*, or a Microsoft *Word* file under *Displaywrite*, or a *Displaywrite* file under *XyWrite*, or virtually any other program's file under any other word processor, and expect to get something on my screen and on paper that looks anything like the document that that colleague created.

Sharing and Revising Files

We could use the conversion features built into most up-to-date word-processing programs to reduce files to plain ASCII text files before shipping them back and forth. That would get the text itself from Point A to Point B in good shape, but the formatting information would be lost. At Point B, someone would have to reformat the file, flying blind, without any idea how it was *supposed* to look. And if the people at Point B revised the file and sent it back to Point A, it would have to be completely reformatted once *again.*

ASCII text is perfectly acceptable for such things as short electronic-mail messages, but it is essentially useless for any more demanding document interchange.

If we only exchanged files on paper, the lack of standardization wouldn't matter so much. But the trend towards circulating drafts and final messages in electronic form is growing rapidly, accelerated in many corporations by the ubiquitous local area network. And increasingly, text created in one program is later used by another, as when word-processed material is poured into complex page layouts via a desktop-publishing program.

All that document-swapping, combined with the PC industry's profound aversion to meaningful standards, means we need a convenient and reliable form of document interchange that converts the formatting information of the original file, rather than losing or garbling it.

That need has been turned into a commercial opportunity by several producers of word-processing file-format conversion programs. These programs can be lifesavers for those who have to exchange formatted text files with others.

The two leading conversion programs are *Software Bridge* and *Word for Word Professional*. I use and prefer *Software Bridge*, though both programs work well, and at under $100 apiece, either would be a good choice.

Automatic Conversion

Software Bridge accepts a file in any of 24 word-processing formats—including *MultiMate*, Microsoft *Word, Displaywrite, DIF, Navy DIF, DCA/RFT, Samna Word, Smart, Sprint, DEC WP, Total Word, Volkswriter, PFS:Write, Wang PC,*

WordStar, WordStar 2000, and more—and converts the original file to any other file format on that list. The program allows batch operation, converting groups of files you've defined by filename extensions, or by directory or subdirectory, or even whole disks full of files, without further user intervention. The original files are unaffected. *Software Bridge* simply creates a new, converted copy of the file and writes it to the disk.

As useful as these little-known gems can be, their conversions are not perfect. They get confused occasionally with boldfacing and italic-type codes, hanging indents for paragraphs, unusual (especially fractional) line spacing, headers and footers, and especially footnotes and endnotes. You'll still need to spend some time cleaning up the formatting in some converted files. Most problems occur with such arcana as footnotes and endnotes, though, so regular business documents should give you few problems.

If you routinely send or receive word-processing files from users of WP programs other than your own, you'll find that *Software Bridge* or *Word for Word* can save time, money, and frustration out of all proportion to their modest cost.

❧

Envelopes And
Laser Printers

Boy, doesn't it kill you to go back to a typewriter after you've gotten used to using a PC? Me, too. I can hardly write on one anymore: I keep trying to go back up a couple of lines to fix a spelling mistake, then swap this word for that one, then . . .

But typewriters survive still in my office—and, I suspect, in yours.

We use typewriters for some envelopes and virtually all office forms we have to deal with. Because as much as we hate using typewriters—and "correcting" typewriters don't take away much of the pain—we dislike even more trying to do that work on personal computers.

But envelopes are an exception, if only sometimes. We've looked at virtually every envelope-addressing program for IBM-style computers that's come out over the past few years. We've used the prewritten macros for envelope-creation provided with most of the leading word processors, and we've written our own. But still we turn to the typewriter a few times a day, roll an envelope in, and return for a minute to the Dark Ages.

Because all those envelope-printing utilities and envelope-creating macros have irritating little problems that, after awhile, have chased us away from using PCs for quick, one-off envelopes. Most of those utilities and macros were appealing and promising at first; few were very appealing after a few days; none survived here more than a week. They're still slow, inconvenient, and even worse than using a typewriter.

We do, however, use PCs and laser printers for producing most of the envelopes we use . . . and thereby hangs a tale.

One day about two years ago I was grumbling about the inconvenience of using a PC to print addresses on envelopes. I was sitting with a group of friends at a client company, at the end of a couple of days of hard work. Our team had been immersed in a fairly brutal review of networking decisions, and we were beat. I had to run to the airport in a few minutes, and this was our quiet wind-down over the last cups of tepid coffee and the crumbs from that morning's stale donuts.

A secretary we'd recruited as part of the group—a great decision: she kept holding our feet to the fire to make sure our decisions were workable in the real world of that company's daily routine—listened quietly to my complaints about how we could put a man on the moon, but couldn't find an easy way to get envelopes out of a PC and laser printer. The she dropped her bomb.

"I tried that too," she said. "And I didn't like any of the things the PC support office suggested to make it easier. So I just print envelopes in advance. Now we only use a typewriter for maybe one envelope in ten."

In advance?

"It's not hard to print envelopes on my LaserJet; it's just a nuisance to print them *one at a time.* So I set up an envelope template in *WordPerfect,* and one afternoon I printed about 20 envelopes for each person or company my boss writes to. I figured that would take care of most of the problem, so I'd only have to do the occasional one-time envelopes on the typewriter. I keep a box of a few hundred of these preaddressed envelopes I've printed in the bottom drawer of my desk. When I finish a letter and print it, I just reach into that box for an envelope. Ninety percent of the time the one I need is there, and pulling an envelope out of a drawer is a lot faster than printing them on the PC *or* typing them on the typewriter."

And that's how this computer expert came to use a computer to produce envelopes.

When I got back from that trip and talked about this weird notion with my secretary, she said she figured that about 90 percent of our mail went to the same few dozen people and companies, too. So she ran off 20 envelopes for each of those addressees, stuck them in a couple of envelope boxes and . . . we usually find the one we need right there. Faster than typing it, and faster by far than turning the PC and laser printer on their ears to print one lousy envelope.

When someone notices that the supply of envelopes for one of those addressees is getting low, we run another batch of them. When someone notices that we've had to manually prepare envelopes for an addressee a couple of times on the typewriter, we knock out 20 or so preprinted envelopes, and they go into that loosely alphabetized file of ready-to-go envelopes.

The system works *superbly*.

It's the best answer I've ever found—an absolutely *no*-tech answer, you'll note—to trying to get decent-looking envelopes out of a computer. And as much as I'd like to tell you I dreamed it up myself, there's this secretary in Phoenix who'd know I was lying. And who also has a couple of hundred colleagues who'd know I was lying, because nearly all the secretaries in her company now do exactly the same thing.

Where, as you may have guessed, she's now tagged as something of a computer expert. With good cause.

Computerized Form-Fill

"Anything to keep me away from the typewriter!"

I suspect that was the motivating influence behind the development of the first PC-based form-fill software. Once you've freed yourself from the tyranny of white-out bottles, strike-over tapes, and the rest of the frustrations involved in working with typewriters, turning back to one—especially for such mundane tasks as filling in preprinted forms—seems unbearably *retro*. Isn't there a more elegant solution?

Well yes, there is . . . but sometimes elegant solutions can get you into a lot of trouble. And PC-based form-fill software is one of my favorite examples of the perils of elegance.

The ads for the form-fill packages look inviting. There's always a big photo, usually of a neatly completed Federal Express waybill rolling out of a PC printer. Every space is filled in correctly; each little box has a nicely centered "x" in it. The form looks great; and if your job evaluations depend on how neatly you fill in FedEx forms, you should run, not walk, to the nearest software store and buy one of these packages.

On the other hand, if you're working in the Real World, consider just how important filling in overnight courier waybills is to you. And are you really that obsessive about neatness . . . ?

Computerized form-fill is a wonderful idea—for shipping clerks, who do dozens or hundreds of them a day. It's so fast and easy to fill in stock forms such as waybills on a computer that your company absolutely ought to provide a dedicated PC and printer for people who do that work.

(In fact, PC-based waybill-completion is such a nifty idea that a few years ago Airborne Express started pulling customers away from its competitors by offering to put a PC, printer, and Airborne-developed software into large companies'

shipping departments—for free. They figured that if they made it irresistibly easy to send things by Airborne—and thus correspondingly hard to use another service—customers would opt to use Airborne for all or essentially all of their outgoing shipments. It worked: clerks found it so easy to type all their outgoing packages' addresses into that PC—which then turned out nice, neat waybills for each package, plus a manifest for the Airborne driver who picked them up at the end of the day, and also an errorless electronic daily summary sheet for the company—that FedEx and others soon found themselves nearly frozen out of the few companies that took Airborne up on the offer. It was a great idea, and a nice example of an external strategic system based on technology simply not available before inexpensive PCs came along.)

But unless you fill in a *lot* of forms—and always the *same* form—you don't want to get involved with form-fill software, because you'll go crazy endlessly threading and unthreading your dot-matrix printer's forms tractor with one stack of forms after another. (You'll probably waste a lot of forms, too, unless your printer is one of the very few that offer a special "demand printing" tractor that rolls the completed form up for you to tear off, then rolls the next one back down into the printer, ready to go. Otherwise you'll be ejecting—wasting—an extra blank form every time you fill one in and roll it up to tear it off.)

Oh, yes: that has to be a *dedicated* printer, too, of course—you won't want to be changing back and forth between preprinted forms and the letterhead and other paper you use for ordinary work.

Well, it sounded good for a while, didn't it?

I'm entirely serious about form-fill software being a great idea for those who work with insurance claim forms or purchasing orders or waybills all day long. I've even set up arrays of five or six cheap dot-matrix printers, connected to a single PC through a printer-switching box and each loaded with a different form, so a department could keep a whole array of forms "on line," by simply devoting a printer to each kind of form. The PC-user just turns the switch to the correct position before printing, and the computer's output is directed to the printer permanently loaded with the correct form.

But that doesn't sound much like your office, does it? Nor much like what you're paid to do. . . .

❧

IV

KEEPING UP:
PIMs, Calendars,
To-Do Lists

What's Wrong with PIMs?

Boy, I like the idea of PIMs—Personal Information Managers. If no new category of PC software introduced in recent years has been preceded by so much overblown hype and breathless copy in the computer magazines—*mea culpa,* dear reader: my hands are a bit smudgy here—I think we also have to say that no new category of PC software introduced in recent years has held such bright promise.

A promise the highest-flying PIM packages fall short of fulfilling.

I remember well the first time I saw the half-finished *Agenda.* Lotus founder Mitch Kapor was showing a couple of us his much-rumored Work In Progress, which Lotus would publish a year or so later. Mitch is one of the most brilliant product designers in the software business; I always look forward to his little product-preview salons. As we sat on the edge of a bed in a Las Vegas hotel room in a brief respite from the COMDEX madness outside and squinted at the screen of his Compaq portable, I was dazzled. Mitch whipped through all the categories and views and associations and the rest of it. *Amazing!* He could even flip through his personal list of favorite sushi parlors.

This was just how people worked, of course—gathering random bits of information, which soon came to cover their desktops and fill their pockets, purses, wallets, bedroom dresser-tops, and, too often, wastebaskets. Lurking somewhere in all those bits of information was some kind of pattern. Everything was tied together in a maze of invisible, interlocking, cross-pollinating relationships, but mere mortals never seemed able to make those connections, see those relationships, find just the right bits, remember things in time.

But here, in a tawdry hotel in a tawdry city, was a peek at the future: We'd put in all the bits, and the computer would help us with the associations and relationships—the hard stuff. Thereafter, of course, every factoid in our personal universes would be immediately available at the touch of a key.

Even the phone number of that wonderful sushi joint in Toronto. . . .

Unfortunately, when *Agenda* hit the market, we learned that while it was a brilliant design concept, the product had holes in it large enough to accommodate those sushi bars themselves. All that data had to be *input* by someone, and while it sounded fine to theorize that an assistant could do that work, the way in which items were entered shaped, in large part, how they could later be used. So things worked really well only if the person who was going to use the information typed it in him- or herself. And getting information *out* was no easy job either: Creating those "views" of related information took a fair amount of planning and keyboard time. Worst was the job of getting information out in printed form. *Agenda's* printing controls were few and feeble.

Why worry about printouts from such a wonderfully *computerized* tool—one that seemed to promise freedom, finally, from at least some of that blizzard of paper that clutters our lives? Well, unless you had printouts, you had to have the computer *with* you to look something up. So when you made a quick trip to Toronto, you either printed out the Toronto-related information, or hauled the portable computer along . . . or wound up settling for a burger and fries.

With the result that *Agenda* was added to few PC users' personal agendas.

In that Las Vegas preview of what was still incomplete both as a product design and as final code, I'd been fooled. My enthusiasm for a paradigm was not supported by the product that subsequently appeared.

Other programs have come along, however, that illustrate that the concept behind *Agenda* and the whole class of PIMs wasn't far off—only those early stabs at turning that concept into products.

If you tried a PIM and gave up—and a lot of you did; PIMs constitute a large part of the "shelfware" overhead carried by American business, programs retired to a high shelf by purchasers eager to forget how much time and money they spent on something they never really used—then look again. There *are* PIMs that deliver real value.

Elsewhere in this section you'll find pointers on evaluating your real information-management needs, and on picking PIMs with working styles that suit your own.

Remember: It wasn't the *idea* that was wrong. . . .

A PIM Strategy

As much as I love the idea of personal information managers, none of the PIMs released so far really lives up to the hype surrounding this new category of software.

As I looked at each new PIM that appeared, I came to a depressing conclusion: no product on the market (or in the pipeline to market) met my needs very well. And the compromises in trying to bend each of those programs to my purposes were so great that, in the end, I simply gave up. I wound up with a two-foot tall stack of PIM packages, each of which purported to be, reminiscent of those late-night television commercials, all the software I'd ever need. . . .

It wasn't that the products were bad, just that they were incomplete. Now if only I could take *this* feature from Program A, and graft it onto *that* feature of Program B. . . . Which, of course, I finally realized I *could* do—by adopting more than one PIM.

That decision came out of my analysis of just what I expected from a PIM. I decided that I had two very different kind of personal-information-management needs, and that was why no one PIM was right for me. One need was for storing and retrieving highly structured information—the kind we usually keep in standard database programs, by filling in specific fields. The other was much more *ad hoc*: that constant need for quick, on-the-fly notes about the million little things that pop up every day. No personal-information manager I could find worked both ways, and probably none should; it would be an oddly schizophrenic package.

So in the end I devised what a friend called my "PIM Strategy": I'd use two different products, each for the kind of information-recording it did best. My choices were—and remain, happily, to this day—Broderbund's *MemoryMate*, and Symantec's *GrandView*.

Over time I've become convinced that my needs aren't at all unusual. Most of us have a body of structured personal information we'd like to keep handy at the touch of a key. And we also accumulate lots of tiny bits of information—those little yellow Post-It notes, and the business cards, receipts, newspaper clippings, and hastily scribbled notes that fill our jacket pockets. Trying to set up a database focused on the former, with sufficient flexibility to accommodate the latter equally well, would be madness. And yet I wasn't willing to take the opposite route, casting aside the quite natural and often very useful structure of the former, in an effort to accommodate the eccentricities of the latter.

The *MemoryMate/GrandView* combination eliminates that kind of decision. It also makes the most of the *structuredness* of the former group of data, and the *free-formness* of the latter. It's been a good answer.

A quick look at how I use each program will help illustrate the differences in the kinds of personal information each manages best.

Structure, Structure, Structure

Some complain that *GrandView* is really just an outliner, not a true PIM. That's partly true, but it's irrelevant.

If you were one of those marked for life by a junior high school English teacher who demanded that you outline everything you were about to write, in a Roman numerals-capital letters-etc. outline, you may never like *any* program that looks like an outliner. On the other hand, if you were the rare, nerdy type who actually *liked* outlining—or if, like me, outlining was an after-the-fact exercise: you faked it by writing the book report first, then went back and produced a feeble outline from your final text—then there's some hope that you can approach *GrandView* with an open mind.

It's easy to see how *GrandView* earned its not-really-a-PIM reputation. First, it comes from the publishers of *ThinkTank,* an unabashed outlining program that was one of the early hits in the PC software business. And second, *GrandView* LOOKS like an outliner. The difference lies in what *Grand-View* can do with that outline, and how you can, in effect, query, extract from, reorder, and otherwise manipulate it.

Much of the material we want quick access to is inherently structured. There are relationships in the material, and often those relationships are the keys to understanding and using the information. For example, many *Grand-View* fans use the program to keep their daily appointment lists, or to-do lists. That's because entries in an appointment book have no meaning without an attached time, which is a chronological link, and an attached day and date, which becomes a categorical link. By building a *GrandView* outline in which each major heading is a day and date, then listing each day's appointments in chronological order beneath that day's heading, you can maintain the relationships among appointments, and between those appointments and the days on which they're scheduled.

Sticking to the Agenda

Another kind of personal information many of us need access to consists of agendas for meetings, with subsequent annotation of actions to be taken on items in the agendas by those who attended the meetings. Ever since *Grand-View* appeared I've used it for this kind of personal information management.

I hate going into meetings without agendas. I don't call meetings myself without distributing an agenda in advance, so participants can come prepared; I generally refuse to attend others' meetings unless they have similarly alerted me in advance to the substance, structure, and purpose of the meeting.

Normally it's a huge nuisance to construct and maintain the many active meeting agendas required at any given moment by most of us; and it's even worse to have to add to those agendas afterwards the details, or annotation, of just what happened on each item on the list. And if you want to also track who agreed or was assigned to do what, how and by when . . . well, you may as well devote all your time to agenda-keeping. Or add an extra assistant to do the work, though those notes will be infinitely less valuable if someone else undertakes the work for you.

Instead, I keep all my more-or-less current meeting agendas in *GrandView*. Each resides under a primary-level heading identifying the meeting. I can quickly pound out an agenda, revise it, move things around, create appropriate subtopics and subsubtopics. Then, thanks to *GrandView's* slick formatting and typeface-selection tools, I can turn out a stack of typeset-look printed agendas, to distribute to attendees.

At the meeting, I scribble my notes in the margin of my printed copy of the agenda. Afterwards, I simply add those notes to the electronic master copy of the agenda in my *GrandView* file. Those notes include commitments by participants to accomplish certain things by certain times. *GrandView* makes it easy for me to later call up a "view" of who's supposed to be doing what on that job, or a "view" of deadlines to see who's on time and who's late.

When an agenda is fully completed, I print out that final, fully expanded part of the *GrandView* agendas file, stick the paper in a file folder as an archival record, and may erase that section from the electronic file.

With this system, I can at any moment turn to my PC, look at each related meeting and meeting-topic on a project, and find out who's responsible for handling each part of the work. It's a fast, powerful, easy-to-use tool that delivers a very effective level of project-management *simultaneously across many projects,* and across many participants, with relatively little time and effort on my part.

Note that because over time this file has grown very large—as much as I'd like to say we promptly complete the handling of everything that comes up in every meeting, so I can quickly retire past meeting's agendas, that isn't true, and you'd know as much if I said that—this big file has enormous historical value. I have available almost instantly, on-line, an enormous range of records of projects, and people's performance on those projects.

Isn't that what PIMs are supposed to be all about?

More Meaningful Performance Reviews

Though I use *GrandView* in many other ways, just one more example will illustrate the versatility and power of the program.

When you manage a group of people, regular performance reviews become essential. But too many managers fake it in performance reviews, by recalling, *sans* dates, times, and specifics, incidents of employee successes and failures. Or they go to the other extreme, filling personnel files with endless handwritten scribbles, or ominous-sounding (and ludicrous) Memos For The File. Either way, the quarterly or semiannual or annual performance review often has too few specifics, too much bluster, and far too little real content to be very useful to either party.

Instead, I like to keep another *GrandView* outline file with the name of each person who reports to me listed as a primary-level heading. Then under those headings I insert second-level heads for each year. Under those years, I list important events in each employee's work, and points I may want to cover during his or her next performance review.

At review time, I print out a copy of the past year's section of that file for each person, and have it at hand as we speak. Instead of groping for things—offering vague thank-you's for presumed good works that happened last August . . . or was it November . . . or was that someone else altogether?—I have the details at my fingertips.

I have those details because I make it a point, usually every couple of days and never less often than weekly, to enter in that *GrandView* REVIEWS file anything I found remarkable about these direct-reports' work during that time. Each entry is a subentry under the current year's heading, under that employee's heading, and takes the form of *91/03/05: John did a whale of a job on the Perkins engagement; letter from Perkins complimenting him said he'd saved them $100K a year.*

From time to time I scroll through that file and eliminate what, in hindsight, seem like distinctly minor events in the past few months' performance by that employee. I don't want a day-by-day diary of everything everyone does, just a concise listing of the highlights—and lowlights—of their work.

Those are good examples of the kind of innately structured information we need to manage, and for which a structured PIM such as *GrandView* is so well suited. But that's not enough.

Preserving Randomness

Just as some of the information I want at my fingertips is inherently structured, and that structure is important, much of what passes across my desk is highly *unstructured*—and imposing any kind of structure on it would be self-defeating. There had to be some way of dealing with that information in an effective PIM strategy, too, or the computer wouldn't be making a contribution sufficient to justify using a PC instead of a shoebox for my notes.

For unstructured work I turn to Broderbund's *MemoryMate*. It's a clever pop-up utility that, at a keystroke, springs into action with a fresh notepad page for my random jottings. When I close each note, it's saved, along with the few thousand other *MemoryMate* notes I have on file. If all those notes simply then disappeared into one giant metaphorical shoebox—and to find any one of them, I had to in effect shake them all out into a pile on my desk and look through them, one by one—*MemoryMate* wouldn't be very useful.

Instead, though, I can call up *MemoryMate,* give it a FIND command to search for some fragment of what I want to retrieve, and the program searches with astonishing speed through the whole accumulation of random fragments of information I've entrusted to it, and shows me just the one I need—and often, much more importantly—*all* of the ones I need.

After completing a search begun by my FIND command, *MemoryMate* alerts me to the number of records it has found that match my criteria. I can scroll through them with the + key at the right side of the keyboard . . . or, if the number of notes found is daunting because I've been too loose and sloppy in my FIND criteria, I can add a NARROW command, to search again among just those records originally retrieved.

Naturally, *MemoryMate* also lets me cut and paste between records, and print any selected records.

All that is highly useful, but *MemoryMate* has yet another feature I've begun to use with great pleasure. The program includes a "hypertext" feature that lets me turn any word or phrase in a note into a hypertext "button," linked to any other word or phrase in any (or many) other *MemoryMate* notes. Thus, when I scroll through a note and see that I've created a button—of someone's name, perhaps, or of a product name, or a location—I just put the cursor on that word or phrase, hit the Hyper key, and I'm instantly taken to the other record. You can create an unlimited number of these hypertext record-links, so you can ping-pong through your accumulated information as much as you wish. You can even back out of your hyper-linked daisy-chain, up to ten steps back.

I confess that I don't use that fancy stuff much yet. *MemoryMate* earns its keep on my computer through the everyday recording of quick notes from phone conversations, or great ideas that pop up in the middle of working on something else, or little reminders.

I use only about half of *MemoryMate's* capacity . . . and yet I find it an incredible bargain.

Perhaps you don't need *two* personal information managers. Perhaps you don't need even one. But if the idea of stashing away little bits of information, then retrieving them in the blink of an eye, appeals to you, consider these two programs as a highly complementary pair.

They're enough to give the whole category of PIM software a good name.

◅

The World's Best To-Do List Keeper

I'm a fanatical believer in to-do lists. I find that five minutes spent at the beginning of the day with a to-do list makes me far more productive, and far more comfortable, throughout the working day. The old saw that it's not nearly so hard to do what's right as it is to know what's right to do fits perfectly here. Being truly productive doesn't mean flailing around, trying to do a thousand things, but rather, doing the *most important* things. Keeping a to-do list is, for me, the best way to make sure I spend my time doing the right things.

Even more important, keeping a to-do list helps make sure that I spend time every day thinking about what constitute the "right" things for me. In other words, setting priorities, and reviewing and internalizing them, not just jumping after every opportunity or task that comes along during the day.

Over the years I've tried lots of ways of building and using to-do lists. I've been through those organizer books and folders, kept a daily desk-diary, and tried any number of ways of tracking to-do's on the computer. But until recently, I'd never found a system that did much better than a daily to-do list scribbled on the back of an envelope each morning.

That manual system wasn't really very effective, of course. There was no way to roll over things I'd missed to each day's new list, unless I remembered them and wrote them down again. Skip something two or three days running—no matter how good the excuse—and you simply get tired of writing it down again and again . . . so you're likely to drop it one morning. And then forget it altogether.

I did that, often.

There was also no organized way of looking forward, of reminding myself of upcoming deadlines. That ability to spot things coming up that take some preparation, and thus need to be underway long before the date they're actually due, is critical in business. The only way I got that was by scanning my daybook each morning, and adding to that day's to-do list the future items I noticed that needed advance work—or at least, some advance thinking—that day. When I neglected to add those listings, I often found I hadn't left myself enough time to prepare for events.

But I stumbled along with my freshly scribbled envelope every day—literally an envelope, because the shape made it easy to spot and it tended not to get lost on my desk—tucked into the right place in my daybook. It was sloppy and inefficient, but I hadn't found anything better.

The computer programs that purported to aid the keeping and use of to-do lists were unbelievably clumsy. Some, like Lotus's *Agenda,* were like using a cannon to shoot a mouse: the programs themselves, their price, learning curve, disk-space requirements, and, most critically, the effort involved in using them, were so out of proportion to the task that I soon gave up on them. (To-do-list-keeping is important and valuable, but when the job of keeping that list gets too unwieldy, it becomes easy to rationalize skipping it for a day. And the next day. And then for a week. . . .) Other programs I tried were too bare-bones. They didn't work as well as my envelope-and-daybook system.

Then, about a year ago, I stumbled across *Top Priority,* from PowerUp!, a low-cost software catalog-sales outfit. I was researching a story on easy-to-use products from unexpected sources—little-known and *unknown* products that nonetheless served business needs well. There are many catalog operations such as PowerUp!, and as a rule, they get little respect from most business-oriented PC users. We tend to see these catalogs as sources of Christmas-card list-keepers, recipe-filers, and banner-printers for the kids—which is true, as far as it goes. But PowerUp! had been adding business programs it has bought outright, or codeveloped, at distinctly *un*-business prices. *Top Priority* and a few others looked interesting, so I sent in an order.

What a surprise! *Top Priority* did everything I wanted, and did it quickly and easily. For just $79. I found another two or three gems in the PowerUp! realm as well (more about them later in this book) but *Top Priority* was the biggest find. It powerfully affirmed my long-held feeling that we too often look for larger solutions than many of our relatively simple business problems require. The ease and simplicity of *Top Priority* make it a perfect example.

The program is also a stellar example of why we should be wary about associating simple interfaces and low prices with low-value programs. I'd argue that a fast, powerful, easy-to-use to-do list keeper, with extensive tracking and look-forward features, is at least as valuable to a lot of businesspeople as the

$300–$500 so-called "mainstream applications" they rely on every day. The key: this isn't in any sense a low-end product; it's just mass-market priced, thanks in large part to PowerUp!'s focus on direct catalog sales. (The company has now started to branch out into some retail distribution, as well. I've found *Top Priority* and a few other PowerUp! originals on the shelves at Egghead Software stores, and in other software-retailing chains.)

Schedules and Priorities

Let's look at what makes *Top Priority*, and more broadly, the entire category of PIM-style to-do list keepers, so powerful in business.

In *Top Priority*, you first enter individual items—appointments, tasks, little personal reminders—in a master list, with due-date and other details attached, as appropriate. You can then view that information many ways, and also get a wide range of useful printouts.

In the input box you type the name of the task or other event, assign an A, B, or C priority to it, and indicate the due (or actual) date and time. You can also add an advance-warning flag, by indicating the number of days in advance of that date you want this item to show up on your daily lists as a kind of coming attraction. You can ask *Top Priority* to nag you if the task is not completed and checked off; if so, it keeps showing up on succeeding days' lists, with a naggy little "number of days late" note appended.

You can also enter regular, repeating events across a span of time—such as your regular Thursday-afternoon squash game at the club—by simply inserting a Y in the Repeat field. That will take you to a submenu with the usual choices: starting date, ending date, frequency, etc.

Finally, you can also assign a category to the entry. *Top Priority* is, after all, a legitimate personal information manager, and in the best PIM tradition the program will let you construct special "views" by category. Thus you could assign to a ROLLOUT category all events on your schedule tied to the new-product rollout you're managing next month; then when you select that category for displays or printouts, *Top Priority* would screen out all other events, showing you only those related to your work on the rollout.

After you've entered your events, which takes just a few seconds each, you can view the information several ways. There are two views I find particularly valuable.

In the first view, my day's work is laid out in three boxes, as Appointments, Tasks, and Warnings. The first two are obvious; the latter is a list of the upcoming items on which I've asked for advance reminders, with the number of days remaining until the due-date shown to the right, in countdown fashion.

Entries in the Appointments box are sorted in chronological order, by appointment times. In each box, items are grouped and rank-ordered by the priority levels I've assigned: *A's* come first, *B's* next, and so on. Each window is scrollable; a tiny arrow at the lower left-hand corner of the Warning box indicates there are more entries in that category.

As I complete work on each item, I simply move the horizontal cursor-bar to the item, then hit the F7 key to mark it as done. Thereafter a small check mark—actually, a square-root sign, the IBM PC character set's closest thing to a check mark—appears next to that item in every view and printed report.

In the second view, I see a broader master list of all my scheduled items. Here they're grouped first by priorities, then within those priority classes by dates, and in the case of appointments, within each date by time.

One nice touch in *Top Priority* is that you can at any time pop up the current month's calendar in the lower right-hand corner of the screen. To move to the display of items for another date, just move the cursor in that calendar to the day you want to see and hit Enter.

Printed Schedules

In addition to showing that information on-screen, *Top Priority* also delivers a wide range of printouts.

During the working day I usually rely on *Top Priority's* QuickPrint feature for a plain-vanilla checklist of what's to be done today, and what has been accomplished so far.

The QuickPrint daily schedule isn't elaborately formatted, but it has the information I need. *Top Priority* also provides plenty of space to write in, away from the computer, those additional items that pop up. I take this worksheet with me when I'm away from my desk during the day, so I can add those spur-of-the-moment items; later, the important ones go into the computer.

Finally, *Top Priority* turns out a very nice graphical-style check box weekly schedule.

The program is smart enough to look forward through the next six days, when printing this report, so that no matter when you print it, you get a full week-ahead view. (Many PIMs, by contrast, print only Monday-to-Friday or Sunday-to-Saturday weeks, which isn't much help when, on a Friday morning, you want to see that day's schedule *plus* the next working day's entries.) By simply checking off the boxes for work you've completed, you can turn this weekly report into a running tally of your week's commitments.

Not bad for a $79 program, eh? Actually, I could as easily have said *Not bad for a $279 program, eh?,* given the typical pricing structure and price/performance ratios in the PC software business.

Whether you adopt *Top Priority* or not, I hope I've persuaded you that daily to-do lists can be a boon, and needn't be a burden to set up and maintain. Maybe you don't need to keep your to-do lists on your PC—but when a program makes it this easy, why not?

Calendar Publishing

One of the newer and odder terms to come into use in the PC business of late has been "calendar publishing."

The idea is simple: apart from keeping your own personal calendar, strictly for your own use, it's often very handy to be able to distribute attractive, succinct, highly customized calendars to a group. Perhaps you need to hand out a company-wide annual vacation-days calendar; perhaps it's a monthly vacation schedule. For whatever purpose, it's convenient to be able to turn out these custom calendars quickly.

I've worked with several programs that let PC users assemble and print custom calendars. CE Software's *Calendar Maker,* an early *Windows* program (also available for the Macintosh, in a generally superior version), was my favorite for a long time. But it got a little long in the tooth, and CE didn't seem very interested in upgrading the package.

So when I was looking through the PowerUp! software catalog not long ago (see the preceding chapter, *The World's Best To-Do-List Keeper*) and saw a new version of a program called *Calendar Creator* listed, I gave it a try.

This wasn't my first encounter with *Calendar Creator.* The program has been around for years, but when I'd tried it before I was put off by its awful, nearly illegible typefaces and overall amateurish feeling. The PowerUp! people must have persuaded *Calendar Creator's* own creator to finally take the program seriously, because this new version, now dubbed *Calendar Creator Plus,* is one slick package, indeed.

If you haven't felt the need to distribute custom-printed calendars to your colleagues before, let me give you a few examples of how I use them. I think you may find the idea useful.

Managing Project Calendars

One good example of a customized calendar is the project, or project-group, calendar. I sometimes head, or advise, small project teams. Timelines are always important in business, but when you're part of a small team racing to bring a new strategic system on-line, or to develop a new product, they're especially critical. Within large companies, the speed with which a new strategic system can be implemented often determines how widely it will be used, and how large a contribution to corporate profits it eventually makes. And in almost every field, getting new retail products to market more quickly can dramatically increase the return on those products.

Yet small teams, especially those filled with really creative thinkers, are also often lax about completing work on time. Part of it, sometimes, is simply the old problem of underestimating how difficult the task is, and how long it will take to complete. But a larger part of the problem is that often these small groups—no matter how important they *say* the schedule may be—don't treat it with the iron-bound seriousness of larger groups and their formal timelines, deadlines, critical paths, and work-in-progress check-offs.

So for these small groups, as a way of underscoring the importance of meeting deadlines, I now often distribute project calendars that show the scope of the project and its planned duration. I can't say passing out a calendar is the whole answer; but keeping those dates in front of us as we work—and sometimes posting a large printout of the calendar in a hallway or in the conference room we use—helps. And *Calendar Creator Plus* makes that easy.

I especially like a feature of *Calendar Creator Plus* that prints out three- or six-month calendars, horizontally across three landscape (horizontal) pages. The title of the project appears centered over the middle sheet, along with the time period spanned—say, "February–July, 1991"—and each month appears as a single long, horizontal stripe across the sheets. Displaying the days of the month horizontally makes it easy to use another feature, which creates task or event boxes that spread across the appropriate period the duration of each subtask we define within the project.

Small, standard calendars for each month appear across the top of the pages, and *Calendar Creator Plus* can add to the box for each day shown in the main calendar the day-of-year number, which makes it easy to calculate the number of days devoted to a single activity. Put those three pages together, tape or paste them and mount them on a wall, and you have a very effective planning tool. And an even better *reminding* tool. . . .

Custom Calendars

Special calendars are also very useful for overviews of itineraries on complicated trips. For example, I've turned a number of computer-industry people on to the idea of using these custom calendars as overviews of their press tours undertaken to introduce new products around the country.

Such calendars are especially helpful during the planning phases of long trips, when you're trying to make up schedules, calling those you intend to visit, dealing with airlines, hotels and rental car companies. Having a visual map of the time period in front of you as you work on those arrangements makes it easy to see time-space relationships in ways that avoid scheduling conflicting events or overworking people.

Another example? In my office, a *Calendar Creator Plus* calendar is always available in a notebook on my desk, showing my schedule, so the people who book my travel for speeches and consulting engagements can tell at a glance whether I'm available for another event. A much more detailed schedule is kept in another book on my desk, of course, but hardly anyone ever looks at that schedule book. Their first, and usually their last stop, is the 24-month *Calendar Creator Plus* printout marked "Jim's Schedule."

Frankly, I don't think this is the kind of work the PowerUp! people really intended us to do with *Calendar Creator Plus.* The program is full of slick features to keep and print out daily appointment lists on Filofax-style paper; to allow users to keep their own schedules separate from, say, company vacation schedules, then combine the two as overlays at print time; and to print reminders of upcoming events.

I never use those features, but so what? I use a small subset of what the program can do—and that subset is priceless for me. If the package cost hundreds of dollars, I'd be irritated that I was paying for so many features I never used . . . but *Calendar Creator Plus* costs just seventy-nine bucks, so price isn't an issue.

Perhaps calendar publishing has no immediate application in your work. Keep the idea in mind, anyway. Before long it's going to hit you that this is the perfect answer to a communications problem you're trying to solve.

❧

TIME OUT II

It's Never Just a Matter Of 'Finding Enough Time'

Let's bury this one once and for all: In business, it's never a matter of "finding enough time" to do what we really want to do. The executive who takes that view is almost always already spending more time than he or she wants—and probably, more time than he or she *should*—on company business. The answer isn't going to be found in some kind of elastic calendar; there is no formula for adding an extra Thursday to your week.

The answer, as the B-school gurus and the $500-a-day-seminar clowns love to tell us, lies not in working harder, but in working smarter. But that's a glib and hugely unsatisfying answer. What does it *mean* to work "smarter"? To do less? To deal more work off to subordinates? To handle each piece of paper just once? To have someone screen your phone calls?

You'll find gurus who've spun careers from each of those slender threads. It's hard to quibble with any of those premises. In fact, of course, working smarter is a matter of all of those things, and many more.

For example, working smarter also means using the right tools. I'm often dismayed when, while visiting a company on a consulting trip, I get ushered in to meet the resident Mr. Big, and notice on the credenza behind his desk a PC so obviously unused I can almost see cobwebs running across the keyboard. When time and social convention permit, I often ask how he uses the PC. I can tell from the tone of his voice in the first few words whether he really uses it or not—no matter what his words say.

"Oh, you know, some spreadsheets, some *1-2-3* stuff..." means just the opposite: He rarely if ever touches it. You could run a directory listing on the hard disks in many of these machines and not find a file-creation date after the day the PC was installed in his office.

The fact is that too many of us, not only corporate CEOs, wind up with tools that don't match our needs. And that's rarely more evident than with these ghost PCs, sitting forlornly behind peoples' desks . . . never used, destined never to *be* used.

The idea of a hulking '486 power-user desktop PC sitting on an executive's credenza or side table is silly to begin with. Unless he's that very rare top-level manager who really does use a PC a lot, and has demonstrated a need for one of these muscle machines, a laptop or notebook PC makes a lot more sense. He can open it up when it's needed, close it up when it's not; move it off the desk and out of the way when it's not in use; take it along for a weekend's work in the Hamptons.

But there's never a laptop or notebook machine around, only that muscle PC someone put in his office as a symbol of rank. That's silly. And it undercuts the whole idea of setting priorities and choosing the right tools.

Finding enough time means not doing the *wrong* things even more than it does doing the right things. Indeed, this is a self-correcting process: avoiding the things you shouldn't be doing turns you towards the things you should be addressing. And avoiding the distractions of tools that only waste your time redirects your attention towards those that can make real contributions to your productivity and effectiveness.

If you've got a PC around, but make little use of it, maybe you've got the wrong tool. Maybe you got sand bagged into doing the wrong thing, saw the mistake, and swerved back to avoiding doing wrong things—in this case, using the wrong kind of PC, for the wrong jobs.

Maybe it's time to take another look.

❧

The Fritter Factor

Some years ago, my friend Stephen Manes came up with a wonderful term for one of the really insidious aspects of using a personal computer: "the fritter factor." Manes, a screenwriter and author of children's books, has a dry, wry wit, and tends to keep computers in perspective better than many people I know.

When he coined the phrase "fritter factor," Steve was talking about the many ways personal computers seem to conspire against us, sucking us into long, drawn-out exercises that later amaze us by their duration—and often, by their utter futility. We get caught up in solving what appears to be some small problem—usually something quite unanticipated—and then look up to realize we've thrown away a whole morning on something of little consequence. Even if what we want to think is a sober analysis persuades us this little side-trip really was important—perhaps we could not have continued our work without it—we look back and wonder: How did I every get caught up in *that?* For *soooo looooong?*

A common fritter-factor episode begins with the unexpected computer-system failure—often, a failure that arises from some small mistake of our own. In loading a new program onto the PC's hard disk, for example, we permit the program's installation routine to modify our AUTOEXEC.BAT file—only to find the PC will then no longer boot properly. Or we change a component, such as a video-display board, only to discover that the new one won't work with our monitor—or at least, not unless we first reset some DIP switches, install new video drivers for our software, and complete some other fritter-factor techno-drivel. Or we change parameters in system-level software, adding to the PATH statement in the AUTOEXEC file, for example, only to find one of those infuriating, baffling DOS prompts, such as "Out of environment space," popping up onscreen . . . and then the computer locks up.

Welcome to the world of The Fritter Factor. Prepare to go through an hour or two or four of obsessive behavior, thrashing around at the computer, changing this and tweaking that, trying to get things back to normal. While your secretary takes your calls, messages go unanswered, meetings and appointments get overlooked, correspondence piles up, the day goes down the drain, and you work yourself into a lather of frustration, confusion and anger.

Sound familiar . . . ?

I'd love to tell you that I have the perfect solution for that unpleasant moment. That there's a nifty little trick you can use to avoid wasting the time and blowing your stack. That a lot of us who rely on PCs have gotten past that problem, and it never happens to us any more. But that would be a lie.

And if you've spent any time at all using a PC, you'd *know* it's a lie.

Unfortunately, The Fritter Factor endures, highly resistant to organizational, structural, and economic efforts to end this infuriating waste of time. In companies with well-developed PC-support operations, for example, it's easy to call someone from "the PC shop" to come around and install those upgrades, or make those changes in your PC's configuration, or just bail you out after you've fiddled with the machine yourself and gotten in over your head.

But if your PC is still going to be down while someone else tracks down the problem and fixes it—and you needed your PC in the first place to work on whatever it was you were doing when the problem arose—then you're still going to be sitting around waiting until the machine is up and running once again, aren't you . . . ?

Gotcha.

An answer that helps a little for me, but is admittedly impractical for most PC users, is to use two machines: one as the "production" machine, on which changes and tweaks are only rarely introduced and upon which *nothing* experimental is ever tried; and a second, identical "testbed" machine, which serves as a guinea pig for new products and new ways of setting up the computer. Even assuming they had the desktop real estate and the wish to have two ugly computers, instead of one ugly computer, lurking over their shoulders, few business users of PCs could get purchase approval for a second machine.

And frankly, even that second machine doesn't always save me from frittering away time, and may actually make the problem worse, since I feel so free to try new tricks with it . . . often leading to hours and even days of fritter-factor time.

In the end, it may be better to laugh at The Fritter Factor—and perhaps, to accept it as an occupational hazard—rather than try to fight it.

As long as we recognize that the only alternative to these bouts of frittering away time at our PCs is to never change anything, and thus to accept PCs only in some fixed form as a kind of office appliance—digital toasters, if you will—then it becomes possible to see frittering around with them as an activity that is at least purposeful, if not much fun, and at least potentially productive, if only barely so.

But it's hard to remember that little mantra when you've just spent three and a half hours trying to stick a new expanded-memory card in your PC—and, oh yes, change to a newer, faster modem card while you were inside the box, and, uuh, remap high memory to use existing extended memory a little better, and change the DOS prompt to show the current path, and, ummm, now the machine won't boot at all. . . .

A Manager's
PC Software Toolkit

In most large corporations these days, personal computers are preconfigured by an in-house PC-support shop before being sent out to end users. A system's basic hardware is checked out; a company-standard set of approved-and-supported software packages is loaded onto the machine; and hardware options, such as modems, are installed.

In some cases, companies even have two or three different standard PC setups. There may be a secretary- or assistant-machine standard; a more technically oriented user machine standard; and often an "executive"-machine standard—which turns out to really be the lowest-level configuration of all, even if it's hidden inside what appears to be the most powerful system the PC shop supports.

Unfortunately, these stock configurations, while appealing as a PC-management tool, often don't apply very well to an individual user's needs. Actually, that's not true across the board. The secretary's setup, which typically focuses on word processing and the company's internal e-mail system, plus *1-2-3* if the person for whom the machine is destined needs it, is usually pretty good. That reflects our relatively good understanding of the computing needs of those whose work focuses on getting out correspondence and reports, and perhaps tracking budgets and expense accounts.

And at the high end, that powerful but crippled PC sent off to the high-ranking muckety-mucks probably won't be far off their needs, especially if, as is so often the case, the machine is destined to sit accumulating dust, more an aging yuppie's totem than a real business tool. PC managers understand very well the needs of the executive who doesn't plan to use a PC much, anyway.

It's in the middle range that these stock configurations fall down. First, because how, and how much, midlevel managers use PCs varies greatly. And second, because no one's given much thought to what really constitutes a proper "manager's software toolkit."

From my experience, that kit ought to include the following, listed in the approximate order of their importance:

- **calendar-keeper** An easy-to-use program to manage the manager's daily calendar, which should also be accessible to his or her secretary or assistant. This program should be closely linked to the to-do-list keeper.

- **to-do-list keeper** An easy-to-use program to keep lists of things to do, with automatic rollover of incomplete tasks to the next day, automatic logging by date of tasks when they're finished, and that close link to the calendar-keeper.

- **autodialer** An easy-to-use program that uses a large name/address/telephone-number database stored (preferably) on a server on the LAN to which the PC is connected, or (if necessary) on the PC itself.

- **communications** An easy-to-use program for accessing both the company's internal e-mail system and also external on-line services (Dow-Jones News Retrieval, etc.) through a dedicated modem at that PC or a communications server on the LAN.

- **database** An easy-to-use flat-file database program for use with single-file databases resident either on that PC or on a connected LAN server, with transparent links, via SQL queries, to relational database programs resident on one or more servers attached to the local area network, and to mainframe databases accessible through LAN bridges.

- **word processor** An easy-to-use word processor nonetheless capable of turning out professional-looking results. It doesn't need to be able to handle 400-page manuscripts (400-page word-processing documents are insanity, anyway). But it does need to be able to handle 30-, 50-, maybe 100-page proposals and reports—at least, to be able to load those documents once they've been produced by someone else, so the manager can read, review, edit, and comment on them. And oh, yes: it should be able to read files created by the other word processors in general use in the company.

- **spreadsheet** An easy-to-use spreadsheet program—well, at least not too hard to use, since, sadly, we seem to have accepted the idea that power spreadsheets are never going to be very easy to use.

- **graphics** An easy-to-use program for creating relatively simple presentation graphics, such as all-text and text-plus-graph overhead transparencies.

- **backup** An easy-to-use, completely automatic backup program that kicks in once a week, at a preset day and time, and dumps the entire contents of the PC's hard disk to a large-capacity tape cartridge, 8mm tape cassette, or DAT cassette. All the manager (or more likely, his assistant), should have to do is remember to swap those backup tapes so there's always a grandfather-father-son set of rotating backups available. (If the PC is connected to a LAN, these functions should be performed on the LAN's server or servers automatically without any user intervention.)

You'll note, first, the constant among all those programs: *ease of use.* It isn't that managers aren't smart enough to become PC wizards; many of the sharpest PC users I know are department and division managers. But ease of use also implies a short learning curve, which goes to the heart of the issue: managers have better things to do than play with their PCs.

(A recent story in *PC WEEK* about the use of flat-file database programs in large corporations quoted a program manager from Control Data Corp. on the value his company attaches to easy-to-use software for managers: "Learning should be consistently intuitive. We don't have time to train on the software. *If it isn't usable out of the box, we don't use it.*" Amen. And thank you, sir.)

I wish I knew a set of programs that provides all those functions, with that kind of out-of-the-box usability and seamless connectivity. I don't. But we do have a good start on that kind of software toolkit.

Symantec's *Q&A*, for example. It combines a superb, easy to set up, easy to *use* flat-file database manager with a really excellent and incredibly simple word processor. It also has a "wrap-around" feature that allows calling one other user-specified program from its menu—for example, *1-2-3*. When the PC user is finished with that other program, he's returned gracefully to *Q&A*.

Symantec has a second program that reflects that kind of intelligence: *GrandView.* A cross between an outliner/note taker and a personal information manager, it can not only pop up a to-do list, or daily calendar, at the stroke of a key; it also has its own wrap-around function: it can swap to *Harvard Graphics* to turn *GrandView* outlines into gorgeous word-charts for presentations.

Add *Hot Line II* as a pop-up phone-list manager and autodialer; a capable but simple communications program such as *HyperAccess* or *ProComm*; almost any back-up program; and those copies of *1-2-3* and *Harvard Graphics*, and you're well on your way to constructing a superb manager's software toolkit.

Nice touches such as access through Structured Query Language statements to external relational databases will have to wait. But not much longer.

The big issue here isn't so much whether we can buy the right software today, or when it's coming. The issue is to get away from assuming that the kind of word processing a manager needs is the same kind of word processing a secretary needs. Or that the kind of graphics program a manager needs is the same kind of graphics package a designer needs.

Those assumptions lead to dead ends by saddling managers with a software toolkit ill-suited to their roles, their interests, and the best use of their time.

V

DATABASE SAVVY

Poor Relations No More

Database management programs used on PCs fall into two general categories: relational and nonrelational, or flat-file. (Another way to put that, as we'll soon see, is "multifile" and "single-file.") Database theorists might reject that division as simplistic, arguing, for example, that no PC database program is truly relational, because none meets all 12 of the tests for relationality in databases, as proposed by E. J. Codd, the former IBM scientist who conceived the relational model 20 years ago. But among PC users, the concept of a world divided between relational and nonrelational programs is strongly entrenched.

Unfortunately, the idea is that nonrelational single-file databases are little more than children's toys, not up to the demands of serious users. Frankly, that's a crock.

My thesis is that for many business applications—and overwhelmingly, for those business database applications PC users create for their own use, or for small-scale shared use in their work groups or departments—flat-file products are usually the better answer.

To make sense of this argument, and to help you choose the right kind of program for your uses, it's necessary to go through a little bit of arcana. Bear with me; I'll make this as painless as possible.

Some Quick Definitions

"Nonrelational," "flat-file," and "single-file" are all synonyms for the same kind of database program. Examples of commercial programs in this category are *Q&A*, *Professional File*, *RapidFile*, and the long-time shareware hit from Jim Button, *PC File*. These programs store all of the information you create on a single subject in a single file.

You can update that file by adding to it, deleting items, or changing them; you can "query" the database by posing often-complicated questions at your PC; and you can get a wide range of printed reports from the database. Those reports include not only such traditional, computer-report-style printouts as a customer list, a list of delinquent accounts, a tally of your current inventory of parts, or an analysis of the profitability of certain product lines, but also a number of things that don't look at all like what we usually mean by the term "reports," such as payroll checks, invoices, packing slips, and monthly statements.

In other words, flat-file database programs work exactly as we expect database programs to work: storing information, then selecting, sorting, manipulating, and displaying or printing that information however we need it.

"Relational" or "multifile" database programs include titles such as *dBASE IV, R:base, Paradox, Revelation, DataEase*, and many more. These programs allow you to construct databases consisting of several files, each clustered around a single kind of data, then knit those files together through "relations" to respond to on-screen queries and print reports.

And that's the big difference between the two. When you're building large systems for businesses—say, a complicated management system for an auto parts distributor—it's often necessary to split data into several files, then set up common elements among them in ways that let you extract data from more than one file in the course of answering a question put to the database, or printing a report.

At the parts distributor, for example, let's say Gus Howard from Nick's Garage walks up to the counter and orders an auto headlamp. The PC used by the counter clerk is connected to a local area network, to which every other PC used in the business is also connected. The database program and all the related database files are resident on a hard disk in a "file server" PC shared by everyone connected to the network.

In the course of making the sale, many parts of the database system are used. A CUSTOMER file feeds in name, address, and customer-number information for the printed sales invoice and for the computer's records on the transaction. An ACCOUNTS RECEIVABLE file adds current credit-status information; an INVENTORY file confirms the in-stock status of the part and provides the exact part number, description, and pricing. All that information is shown on-screen for the clerk (a database query), and printed out in the form of an invoice (a database report). A debit is posted to the customer's account; that part is deducted from business's inventory. If the new in-stock level on that headlamp falls below a preset desirable stock level, an order may be sent automatically to a supplier listed in the VENDOR file.

The idea of a common link, or a common element, between two files is simple: one common information element has to appear in both files in order to construct a *relation*, but of course all the other information need not be duplicated. A customer-number field might appear in both the CUSTOMER file and the ACCOUNTS RECEIVABLE file, for example; a part number might be shared by the INVENTORY and VENDOR files. As long as file A shares at least one common data element with file B, a relation exists, and the database program can bridge the two files, extracting unduplicated data from both for the query or report. Files B and C must also share a common data element to draw the information in File C into the transaction—but File C need not include the *same* element common to A and B. This kind of daisy-chaining, which can go on and on, lies at the heart of the power of relational systems.

Flat-File Data Validation

However. As powerful as that idea of relationality may be, it's hardly necessary for most database work. Ashton-Tate's *dBASE,* for example, was the first widely distributed relational database product for PCs (originally under the brand-name *Vulcan*), and until the late 1980s had a commanding market share. Yet Ashton-Tate's own surveys of its customers showed that the overwhelming majority of applications built with *dBASE* used only one file. In other words, users were putting up with the expense and the enormous inconvenience of developing applications in *dBASE*—and *dBASE* is a HUGELY inconvenient program to use, to put it mildly!—when they could have achieved the same end with a good flat-file product.

In defense of those earnest *dBASE* developers, they may also have chosen *dBASE* for another reason—but a reason that is also now obsolete. In developing a database system, it's useful to be able to apply conditions, or data-validation tests, to each data-entry field, to ensure the accuracy of that field. That kind of control over individual fields in a database was once offered only by the relational database products. (That had nothing to do with any internal limitations in flat-file technology, nor with any inherent advantages of relational technology, but arose only because buyers had been trained to expect those features in relational products, but not to look for them in flat-file programs.)

This ability to apply tests and limitations to individual data elements in a database file can be powerful, indeed. For example:

- **You might want to make a field a "required" field.** It's often helpful to require that a field be filled in before the database will accept the record. You'd probably want, for example, to make sure a person's last name is provided in every record; by making that a required field, you could avoid a flawed record caused by someone forgetting to enter a person's last name.

- **You might want to have specified formats for fields.** For example, Social Security-number fields should always follow the pattern 000-00-0000. You could specify that for the Social-Security number field (a) only digits, not alphabetic characters, would be accepted; (b) exactly nine digits, no more and no fewer, were required; and then (c) you could ask the program to automatically format the field by entering the dashes, so those putting information into the database would need to type only the nine digits.

- **You might want to limit field entries in other ways.** Two-character state-name abbreviations might be limited, through a little look-up table used to test entries, to only those of legitimate states and territories. That way you wouldn't find an ambiguous, useless entry, such as TT, instead of TX (Texas) or TN (Tennessee), in the database. You might also specify that they must be typed in capital letters—or simply have the database program convert all state-name entries to all capital letters.

- **You might want to use range-limiting.** For example, you might want to limit the acceptable entries in a numerical field to figures between 100 and 9,999.

A few years ago, that kind of control was available only in relational database programs. Today, it's a common feature of the better flat-file programs as well.

Easy Queries and Report Specs

The advantages of flat-file programs don't end with creating the database. For everyday use, the commands used to search for records, or to query the database, are usually much simpler in flat-file programs than in relational programs. Here, for example, is how you ask Software Publishing Co.'s *Professional File,* a widely used flat-file program, to find every record in the data base that includes, in the field named BUSINESS CATEGORY, anything having to do with telephones, telegraph services, telecommunications services. Just type `tele..` in the blank space on-screen following that field name. Those few letters from the beginning of the root word, followed by two periods (as a "wild-card" search request) will find every entry in the database with *tele*-anything in the field.

Want to find everyone in your database who lives in the 78755 Zip code? Just enter `=78755` in the ZIP field on-screen. Want to find everyone in the database who lives in Texas? Just enter `TX` in the STATE field, or `78???` in the ZIP field. Want to find every customer whose first purchase was in the second quarter of 1991? Just type `=04/01/91->06/30/91` in the FIRST TRANSAC field.

That ease of specifying what you want from the database carries over to printing reports from flat-file database programs, too. You usually use the same search/select commands, adding any sorting preferences you may have, along with simple print-formatting commands.

I don't want to exaggerate the relative ease of querying and getting printed reports from flat-file programs. In recent years, some PC-based relational programs have taken big strides in simplifying querying and reporting. Borland's *Paradox*, especially, has easy-to-use report-formatting commands. But in every case the good flat-file products are still faster and less complicated to use.

Not Trapped or Isolated

The final nail in the coffin of relational database programs as everyday tools for managers and executives is flat-file programs' relatively newfound ability to read and sometimes write files in *dBASE* or another high-end relational-database format.

One of the arguments often used to push PC users into developing their databases with a relational program is that if a flat-file program they choose starts to run out of gas—in other words, if someday they discover they really do need the power of a relational product to do something new with their existing database files—they'll have to start all over again, entering all that data from scratch.

No more. The better flat-file programs can all *export* data in a form readily readable by *dBASE* or another mainstream relational database program—and often, can even rewrite the file directly into those formats! So you can start with an easy-to-use program, then if and when you need to grow into a more flexible program, take your data, and your entire database structure, along with you.

Incidentally, these flat-file programs can also import data from *dBASE* and other leading relational packages—again, often directly from the relational product's file, without any intervention by the PC user. So choosing a flat-file program no longer locks you out of exchanging data with other PC users who may have relational programs, or from using data that may be resident on a large-scale shared relational database system.

When you were reading a few lines ago about how relational database products can knit together data from many related files, I hope you got the sense that that kind of work simply isn't what you usually do at your PC. Certainly, relational products are essential for system developers, who write large database systems. But equally certainly, the databases most managers, professionals, and executives assemble and use don't require anything like that kind of power and flexibility.

In the PC world, power and flexibility always come at some cost, usually a high cost: costs in purchase price, ease of use, speed of use, and the level of computer power required for satisfactory performance. Why pay for something you don't need?

Don't let the PC Rambos bamboozle you into thinking you need to learn *dBASE,* or *Advanced Revelation,* or *Paradox,* simply to put together a prospects database, or to keep track of registrants for a seminar, or to build a mailing list. It just ain't so.

Database 101:
Getting Started

Building well-designed databases that are a pleasure to use is easy . . . when you've done it 10 or 20 times before. Unfortunately, nothing teaches us so well how to do something as trial and error—but investing the time and money to assemble a database of a few hundred or a few thousand records, then discovering where you went wrong, is a painful and expensive way to learn.

I want this chapter and the several that immediately follow to give you a kind of jump-start on building databases, by showing you a few dozen tricks of the trade. If you've built and regularly use PC databases, you'll probably find a lot here that's familiar . . . but you'll find new ideas, as well. If this is *all* new to you—if, like most PC users, you've found the idea of constructing your own databases forbidding, and haven't had the slightest notion how to get started using them—you'll find this a useful minitutorial on building and using your first database.

To avoid complication, I'll assume that you're using a standard flat-file database program, such as *Professional File* or *Q&A,* rather than a relational database package such as *Paradox, R:base,* or *dBASE.* That way we won't be distracted by trying to plan the splitting of data into several separate databases linked by common fields, or "relations." Relational databases are wonderful tools, but they're hardly the only nor always the best way of assembling a database (see *Poor Relations No More,* in this section). Research by the relational database software publishers shows that the great majority of relational database software users turn their applications into flat-file programs anyway, by designing databases that use only one file.

I'm also assuming that you're using a program that lets users "paint," or design, screens with fields for data placed anywhere on the screen (called a *form view*), rather than using a simple grid (or *table view*), such as is used by spreadsheet databases in their most primitive form. (As it happens, a table is a very useful way to view data when querying an existing database. But it's less effective as an input mechanism, and often hard to understand when you're getting started. So we'll stay with the form-view approach.)

We should also settle a little database lingo. In database work, the information concerning one specific person or company or part or account is called a *record*. Within those records, each individual piece of data, such as a ZIP code or a telephone number, is called a *field*. Fields are assembled into records, which are gathered into the database *file*.

Those are all the definitions you'll need to know to start building effective databases. But they're important; confuse a field and a record, or a record and a file, and soon you'll be lost.

Database design involves going through several successive stages of planning. Those include Assessment (how you'll use the database once it's constructed), Input Design (building input screens that are logical, attractive, and easy to use), Testing (making sure things really work the way you thought they would), Data Entry (in which you feed into the database file's empty shell the information you'll be working with), and Reporting and Querying (using the database for everyday work).

The next few chapters examine how you can best handle those stages.

❧

Database 101: Why?

The first step in planning a new database is deciding what you're up to: why do you want to build this database? What are you going to *do* with it?

Those seem like obvious questions, but are far too often overlooked until maybe halfway through the design process—or worse, halfway through the data-entry process. One of my favorite lines is *You've got to know where you're going; otherwise you're certain to wind up somewhere else.* I can't think of an area where this applies more than in putting together a database. Well-designed PC databases can simultaneously serve many purposes and many masters. But you've got to have a good idea of why you're doing this and, especially, how you'll use the results, before you begin.

Here's a list of questions you may want to ask yourself (and perhaps also your colleagues) as you begin to plan a database. If you're new to the game, don't be frightened by the length of this list, or by some of the implications of the questions—on database security, for example. Not every question applies in every case, and for your first efforts, many of these questions may be irrelevant.

FOCUS Do you want a list of customers, or of prospects—or perhaps a list of both, so you can turn those prospects *into* customers? Is this primarily a list of individual contacts, where company affiliations are secondary, or of companies, with individual names added only where available, as contacts at those companies?

DETAIL If it's a list of customers, do you need some credit history in the database? A thumbnail sketch of their history as customers, perhaps including last order data, last order amount, and maybe their typical order amount? If it's a list of prospects, do you need to track how you learned about them? Did they respond to ads, or walk in the door, or did you buy a prospect list? If some are referrals, do you need to be able to track by whom they were referred—perhaps for a thank-you letter or a small gift or commission?

DATA INPUT Who's going to initially input all the data in the database? You? An aide or assistant? A temporary hired for just that purpose? How much experience will be needed to extract the data for the database from existing records? Where are those records, and in what form? How much training will be required to teach someone to input data the first time around?

DISTRIBUTION Who's going to *use* the database? Is this going to be a shared database for you and many of your colleagues . . . or something you simply keep on your PC, for fast look-ups? If it's going to be shared, are you going to keep the database on a server on a local area network, or are you simply going to distribute floppies for users to copy to their PCs' hard disks? How is distribution of those disks and subsequent updates going to be handled?

MAINTENANCE Who's going to maintain the database? At what intervals should new data be added? Should that process be institutionalized—say, by adding updates and revisions every Friday, or on the last working day of every month—or can you do it as you go along? Does it matter if the information in the database is slightly out of date?

INTEGRITY Who's going to have the authority to update the data? Can one user of a shared database override another's updating, or should all updating be done by one person, to assure the consistency and integrity of the database?

OUTPUT What's going to be the most common way of using the database? Will most of its value come from quick, *ad hoc* look-ups, when you or someone else simply needs to know something stored in the database? Will printed reports, such as credit-watch lists, call-back lists, inventory lists, and other routine, formatted database-style reports be the primary printed output? Or do you plan to produce invoices, statements, collection documents, form letters, mailing labels, envelopes, and more from the data? If so, will you be using your database's report-printing features for that work, or will you export data to word processors or spreadsheets? What kind of export file formats do those programs require?

ACCESS Are there going to be limits on how the database can be used . . . or on who can use it? Will there be hierarchies of access privileges? Who should set those levels? Should some information in the database—say, employees' salaries—be protected from viewing by unauthorized persons?

SECURITY What about security? Are passwords needed for access to the database? Who will assign, change, and update those passwords? If a disaffected or larcenous employee walks off with a copy of the database, will it hurt the company? And what if the database is simply lost, say to fire, or because a burglar steals the computer on which the database is stored? Should you keep an extra copy of the database file off the premises, in a bank safe deposit box, perhaps, or simply at your lawyers' or accountants' offices? If so, how often should that off-site backup copy be replaced with an updated one?

DATABASE PUBLISHING Does the database have commercial potential of its own? Is the information in it potentially valuable to others, so that you might sell all or part of it in some form, such as preprinted mailing labels, or a printed directory, or a disk file combined with a look-up program? If so, how could or should you protect the information, and thus your company, from misuse of the database by others?

Talk through those questions and you'll have a good idea why you're assembling this database. You'll also come to a lot of implicit conclusions about the level of detail you need, about the importance of current data, about how easy it should be to use the database.

And then you're ready to start designing the database.

Database 101:
Designing Input Screens

Good input-screen design is a matter of using the limited space of a PC's display effectively, of making data entry as simple and logical as possible, and of making sure you break the data into enough bits and pieces as it's entered that you can later select, sort, and print records based on the criteria you need at that time—criteria, perversely, that you cannot be certain you know when you begin assembling the database.

Do a good job and the database will be a pleasure to work with. Do a sloppy job, and you may become so discouraged when you use the database that you soon give up.

Screen Layout Basics

It's easy to fall into bad habits, and hard to shake them. That's why, I'm convinced, so many PC users put together such terrible input screens with their favorite database programs.

I think lousy input screens also have something to do with the vast early popularity in the IBM PC community of Jim Button's fine shareware program, *PC File*. Both the instructions for using the program and its admirable, quick-and-easy style of working led many users into the trap of simply starting every field on a new line, at the left edge of the screen.

That kind of entry screen is quick to put together. It also offers some protection to the database neophyte, or the user who doesn't have much time to plan the database, in terms of potential field length. If more than one item appears on one line in a database input screen, an entry too long for the first space will have to be truncated . . . and most database programs make revising input screens to increase field size about as pleasant as a root-canal job. So by leaving an entire line for input, users don't need to think ahead very much about the possible length of typical field entries.

Unfortunately, working with a database assembled that way is a real nuisance. First, it's ugly—and no one, not even the most determined propeller-head among us, likes working for long with something so self-consciously unattractive. Second, it misses a chance to make better use of that input screen real estate—perhaps, for example, fitting all the fields onto one screen, rather than having to jump among several. Third, it fails to exploit our natural tendency to group and visualize related items as units, which can make for faster and more accurate input of data.

Instead of just stacking field names at the left side of the screen, one per line, consider using your display's real estate more creatively and intelligently, putting more than one field on some or all lines, leaving enough space after each field name for the longest entry you're likely to encounter. That takes a little planning. But the payoff can be substantial.

The Data Breakdown

In designing your own input screens for databases, follow these few simple rules for organizing them and breaking the data out into useful fields.

- **Group and order.** Gather database fields into clusters that reflect how we usually work and think about things. For example, entering *Mr.,* then *John,* then *Doe* in three successive fields called TITLE, FIRSTNAME, and LASTNAME is a lot more logical for most of us than entering *Mr.,* then *Doe,* then *John.* Going on to fill in ADDRESS1, ADDRESS2, CITY, STATE, and ZIP is plausible, too, because that's how we think about people's addresses. That way you've grouped items logically, and ordered them within the group.

  Some database programs (for example, Software Publishing Corp.'s *Professional File,* an exceptionally good flat-file database program) maintain their primary index on the first field in the upper left-hand corner of your input screen. Because indexed fields are much faster to search on, users of *Professional File* should probably begin their database input screens with the field they think they'll most often use for searching. If you think you'll be looking up people by their last names most of the time, for example, that field—unfortunately—should come first in your input screen.

- **Use the full width of the screen.** With just a little effort you can figure how much space you'll need for the longest plausible entry in each field. Remember to leave room for such details as hyphens or parentheses in telephone numbers, and the space the trailing hyphen and four additional digits add if you'll be using the new longer ZIP codes the Postal Service encourages.

While you can make good guesses on the amount of space you'll need for such things as last names, street addresses, and city names, consider adding a few extra spaces to those guesses now, rather than weeping later. (At the same time, don't be floored when, as you're entering the data, you run into the occasional too-long line, such as *7735 Quentianquahogaurum Boulevard Northwest,* or *Belle Arbors of the Palisades,* California. You can always use intelligent abbreviations near the end of such long lines.)

> *IMPORTANT: See the* Field Size Issues *section near the end of this chapter for notes on allowing space in these fields for inserting selection-criteria when working with the finished database.*

Over the years I've worked out some personal standards for typical field lengths in database entry screens. You won't need all these categories in every database, but before you discard something like "Country" or "E-Mail Address," consider whether you may really need those for a few entries. These suggested lengths won't cover every case—and you'll certainly still need to do some intelligent truncation of very long items at data-entry time—but you'll find them handy. (These suggested field lengths also appear on my personal cheat-sheet bound into the back of this book.)

FIELD TYPE	NUMBER OF CHARACTERS
Title	4
First Name	14
Nickname	12
Middle Initial	4
Last Name	20
Job Title	24
Company	24
Street Address	26
City	18

FIELD TYPE	NUMBER OF CHARACTERS
State or Province	5
Country	14
ZIP Code	10
Telephone	12
Telephone (w/ extension)	17
Fax	17
E-Mail Address	25
Telex	12
Telex (w/ answerback)	22
Secretary's Name	22
Spouse's Name	22
Age	3
Gender	2
Race or National Origin	10
Nationality	10
Social Security No.	11
Dates	24
Referred By (name)	22

- **Break data into small units.** You can never be sure just how you'll use the information in your database. No matter how certain you may be, for example, that you'll never need to break out names in any form other than *Mr. John Doe,* it's almost always a mistake to enter all three parts of the name as one data element. The most obvious problem is the need, later, to sort and select data by last names, which with most database programs is possible only if there is a separate last-name field for that sort-and-select process to examine.

But this idea goes much further than that. For example, if someday you're using that database to prepare a stack of fake personalized letters, you may want to use an informal, personal form of address in the salutation of the letter—*Dear John,* for example. For that, you'd need to have the first name of each person in the database in a separate field, for the mail-merge process. But let's say John Doe is universally known as Mac, and Ellen Markham is always called Ellie by her friends. Do you really want your "personalized" letters to revert to their formal given names in the salutations of those letters? Wouldn't you rather address them as *Dear Mac* and *Dear Ellie*?

That's easy if, in addition to the database convention of breaking names into TITLE *(Mr.)* FIRSTNAME *(John)* LASTNAME *(Doe),* you also add a field when you're beginning the database for NICKNAME. Enter *Mac* and *Ellie* there, and the data is available, in the right form, when you need to extract it for your word-processing program's mail-merge run.

- **Include a job-title field.** Using a JOBTITLE field following the names field in your database makes it easy to prepare more specific form letters, mailing labels, and other items from the database. You may want to address a sales letter to *Mr. Ed Hills, Vice-President for Manufacturing, Hollister Specialty Metals, 7650 Industrial Blvd. SW, Cleveland, OH 72727,* for example—but without room in your database to store Ed's title, you won't be able to print it on that letter, or on its envelope.

- **Don't forget a field for company names.** In databases built for business use, you'll usually want a company name field following an individual's name. I like to allow about 24 characters in this field, though I usually try to hold entries to 20 characters or so, to produce more attractive documents and reports from the database.

- **Use two address lines.** Allot two, not one, lines for the street addresses of the persons listed in your database. Call these lines something like ADDRESS1 and ADDRESS2. (They have to be identified separately, or your database program won't accept them as separate entities). You won't use both in every case, but when you need that second line, you really *need* it.

For example, an address such as *Ms. Gwen Howard, 3325 Maple St., Boulder, CO 12345* needs only one street-address line. But many addresses will be in the form *Ms. Lettice Smith, Landmark Office Plaza, Suite 454, 2200 Westover Parkway, San Antonio, TX 23456.* And for those, you'll be in trouble without a second address-line field for that *2200 Westover Parkway* entry.

- **Include fields for more than one telephone number.** A common and frustrating mistake for database newcomers is not remembering to include at least two fields for a telephone number when setting up the database—until, when they're entering data, they run into people with two or even more numbers.

You may want, for example, to have both an office and a home telephone number for someone. (That might also be expressed as "day" and "night" numbers.) Or you may want two office numbers: the company's main number, routed through its switchboard, as well as the person's direct-dial number. And what about a cellular-telephone number? It's easier to create fields such as DIRECTPHONE, MAINPHONE, HOMEPHONE1, HOMEPHONE2, and CARPHONE now than to try to rearrange everything later.

- **Remember the fax number(s)!** The ubiquitous fax machine is working its way into business databases. You'll probably want a field for the person's fax number—and in some case, a backup fax number—in your database.

- **Do you need an e-mail address?** If the person identified in this record in your database uses a third-party electronic mailbox, such as those provided by MCI Mail, AT&T Mail, SprintMail (formerly Telemail), or another e-mail outfit, you may want to include that e-mail "address" in the database. If they receive their e-mail on a local area network—perhaps a network inside your own company—you'll probably want to include their e-mail routing address, too.

  (For some, the idea of including electronic-mail addresses may sound pretty futuristic. Most businesspeople, of course, don't use e-mail now, and many think they're not likely ever to use it. But *database design should be predictive*, looking forward to what you may want to incorporate in this record at some future date. If you're really sure widespread e-mail isn't going to become a reality in the next few years, you can safely skip this field. But you'd better be awfully sure. . . .)

- **Use "screen layout zones."** Notice that everything we've discussed so far about this data-input screen, and the person it describes, can be gathered into a category we might call *who he is, and how to reach him.* That's a good example of the kind of logical grouping of data I suggested a moment ago—and here, of how the data can be most logically ordered within that group.

This field sequence follows the way most of us think about someone—who they are, where they live or work, how to reach them—and thus is going to be easier to enter than a more convoluted (or *ungrouped*) batch of fields. Which always translates into less expensive, more accurate data-entry.

To underscore that data grouping, consider adding a blank line at this point in the input screens—or if your program permits, draw a rule, or put a box around this section. Don't get carried away here; you can waste a lot of that valuable screen real estate on fancy formatting. But once you've grouped material logically, separating some of those groups makes for a more easily understood screen. Again: *anything that helps make that screen easier and quicker for someone to grasp will lead to more accurate input.*

That *who and how to reach him* opening for each record may be the most important part of your screen-design job. For no matter what detail follows, if you cannot identify or reach the person or company listed in the record, what use is all that detail . . . ?

We'll go on to the next part of input screens in the next chapter.

Field Size Issues

Though I've encouraged you to use your own judgment when determining field sizes, to make sure that you'll be able to enter the longest items you encounter in those fields—and I've included in this chapter and on the cheatsheet at the back of this volume my own customary field lengths, as a starting point for your work—there is another consideration that may cause you to add several spaces to the fields you set up in your databases.

This one has tripped up countless new database users. Some of those people have told me they were so disgusted that after they found the problem, and found that fixing it was almost impossible—because of the extensive work required to increase the size of so many of the fields in a database—they simply abandoned that database, and haven't tried to build one since.

Some database programs require that you enter sort-and-select criteria in the fields of your input screen when extracting data from the database. That means that in addition to allowing enough space for the data at input time, you may need to have enough space in that field to enter much longer entries—say, both start and stop dates when choosing records from a certain period of time—*and also the mathematical operators that define the selection criteria.*

If, say, you want to extract from your database all customers whose most recent orders fell between July 1, 1990 and June 30, 1991, and your database includes a LASTORDER field, you'll need to enter both dates, plus the appropriate selection codes, in that field. When you built your database you allowed a nice, safe-sounding eight characters for dates in that field, following the MM/DD/YY form (as in *10/12/90*). Now, though, you need to enter at least two eight-character dates, plus some connecting link between them to specify the range. That entry might look like this, depending on the database program you've chosen: `07/01/90->06/30/91`.

Thus a realistic, safe field size for dates in a program that works this way might be 22–26 characters.

You don't always need to allow so much extra space in fields. Say you added a "keys" field—such as a space to enter *M* or *F* for male or female. If you've used only two keys (as in the *M* or *F* example), you'll need only one or two spaces (depending on the program) later to insert as your selection criteria *F*, or *=F*, to find all females.

If the choice of keys is wider than the simple binary, one-or-the-other choice between *M* and *F*, though, try to imagine before setting the field size all the combinations you may want to use. Say, for example, that you use one- or two-letter keys to indicate race or national origin, and your choices include among others *W, B, H, A*, and *NA*, for *White, Black, Hispanic, Asian*, and *Native American*. At some point you or someone else using the database may want to select individuals from several groups in one pass. So your longest possible selection-criteria wouldn't be just the fairly obvious three characters—*NA* or *=NA*—nor even the very useful but less-obvious four characters in */=NA* for *not* Native American. Instead, it might be something as complicated as *B;H;A;W*, to select all persons whose records indicate *either* Black, Hispanic, Asian, or White in that field. And that would take an eight-character field.

You don't need to allow any extra space, of course, where it seems unlikely that you'll never want to make selections based on that field. But be careful with decisions like that. In database work, they have a way of coming back to haunt you. . . .

Naming Database Fields

Before we go on, let me add a note on the field-naming convention I've been using. You'll want short, succinct field names, because they take less space on-screen, and they're easier to fit into printout specifications. But don't make them so short that they don't make any sense to you (or to someone else) later, without referring to a separate explanatory file or note.

FIRSTNAME, for example, is a lot more intelligible than FIRNAM, 1NAM, NAME01, FN, or a whole flock of other substitutes I've seen. Abbreviations can quickly get out of hand, as when, for example, something like FAXNUM1, for someone's primary fax number, becomes 1FXNBR.

Using spaces in multiple-word field names can help, but is usually unnecessary and also wastes a space. Some old hands in the database business use an underscore or a hyphen to separate parts of field names, but I find that both unattractive and unnecessary. I'm not persuaded, for example, that FIRST_NAME or FIRST-NAME is that much more self-explanatory than FIRSTNAME, nor that OFC_TEL_1 or OFC-TEL-1 is better than OFCTEL1. But if you prefer spaces (and your database program will let you include spaces in field names), or if you like the look of word-fragments separated by under-scores or hyphens, feel free to use them as we continue.

I also like to type field names in all capital letters, rather than the more common upper- and lowercase combinations. I confess to a little ambivalence here: I think FirstName looks better on-screen than FIRSTNAME, and it's probably a little faster for the eye to read.

But using all capital letters for field names makes them stand out much better from the usual caps- and lowercase letters input on-screen. Thus a completed screen is much easier to take in at a glance than if it includes field names in upper- and lowercase letters.

The choice, again, is yours. There's no right or wrong way to do this.

The Much-Maligned
Notes Field

One of the most useful additions to a database is a notes field, where whoever builds the database can insert short notes about the other items in the record, and where whoever actually uses the database can add more background information on the person, company, or item described in the record.

Unfortunately, notes fields are also controversial; many PC database experts will tell you they dislike them, and some simply refuse to use them.

Why? It's a holdover from (and one of the many malign consequences of) the dominance in the PC business of the industry's first big-selling sort-of-relational database program, *dBASE II*. In *dBASE* (and in some other subsequently released PC-database packages), you couldn't search on a notes field when looking for records. Notes fields were (and remain) free-form text fields, and some PC database programs weren't smart enough even to be able to perform a word-processing-style character-string search—as when, for example, you'd ask the database program to find all records in a file that had the word "cheapskate" anywhere in the notes field.

If you think that a refusal to use notes fields simply because they're not searchable (a condition imposed by that one program, remember, and as a matter of chance, not in any way intrinsically part of database technology) is incredibly shortsighted, you're exactly right. "Computer experts" are often blind to real-world business realities, and not deigning to use something so valuable in business as a database notes field is a perfect example of that myopia.

As it happens, Microrim's *R:Base* broke the searchable-notes-field barrier several years ago, and now many PC database programs allow free-form searching on text-annotation fields. Yet even though most of that thin justification for turning up their noses at notes fields has been erased, some PC database gurus still raise their eyebrows at the idea of building those fields into the databases they design.

Just how might you use a notes field . . . and why are they so valuable?

Let's say you have a CLIENTS database for your office-furniture business. You put a 400-character NOTES field into that database's structure when you design it. A 400-character field takes up just five lines on an 80-character-wide screen, so you're not giving up much display real estate to provide space for those notes. Here are some of the kinds of entries you might find in that field after awhile:

```
talk w/ Jack Gulhorn when possible on new
orders: he controls the p.o. process
```

```
slow-pay sometimes; limit credit exposure by
staggering dely dates on big orders
```

```
Opening Cleveland ofc in Oct., will need new
F&F. John Wilkes sez contact them in July-Aug
re possible order.
```

```
loading dock closes at 3pm, make sure all our
deliveries arrive before 2pm
```

```
Mr. Mackey met w/ Bill Burns, their VP/Mfg, on
3-25; Mac sez Burns promised us another shot at
the acct after end of their 2nd quarter in May.
```

Isn't that *exactly* the kind of inside information you'd like to have available on your accounts . . . at the touch of a key? You'd never be able to plan enough conventional database fields to accept so many kinds of information. There's no need to; just use a notes field in your database design.

So what if you can't search on the contents of the notes field? Are you really going to ask the computer to find all the records that mention a loading dock in the notes field? Or that talk about purchase orders? Or all those that include a "Mr. Mackey"? Of course not. But that kind of informal, "inside intelligence" is just what you want your employees to have at their fingertips as they deal with your customers. And it's just the kind of benefit computers are supposed to deliver.

You may not need a notes field in every database you construct. But when you need one . . . you *need* one. Don't let self-appointed "experts" talk you out of using one.

Duplicating Database
Information Isn't Always
A Bad Thing

I often irritate database gurus (and other kinds of computer gurus too, for that matter) by suggesting that there are some real-world exceptions to their ivory tower Rules for Everything. A good example is my long-standing insistence that it's not always a mistake to duplicate information in database records.

I'm surely no fan of literal duplicate records; they just waste disk space and make the query-responses and reports you get back from the system confusing. But there are good forms of what the gurus would still call duplication, though I prefer to call it "second-vector data." That term is a little joke. I came up with it long ago in a panel discussion I participated in with a Famous Database Guru before a large audience at a computing society's national meeting. It took him aback: it sounded so properly academic, and so properly obscure, that he shut up for a few minutes so I could explain to the audience what I really meant.

What I mean by "second-vector data" is simply a second way of finding the same data, or a second, similar subset of that data. A few quick examples will explain the notion. And, I hope, lead you to start using dupli—oops, second-vector!—data yourself in your own database work.

Multiple Entries Mean Easy Look-ups

In my *Hot Line* contacts database (see *The Computerized Phone Book* in the **On the System Level** section), I actually *look* for ways to list the same person, or the same company, two or more times. For example, my plumber is listed four ways:

```
plumber SW PLUMBING .................... 338-4420
house: plumber (SW PLUMBING) ..... 338-4420
SW PLUMBING (Bob and Gary) ......... 338-4420
Willis, Bob (plumber) .......................... 338-4420
```

The idea is simple, and obvious: when I need a plumber fast, I don't want to have to worry whether I can remember the company's name, or the name of the guy there I deal with. So the information goes into the database in four different ways.

The same thing for my doctor. He's listed *six* ways:

```
Gordon, Jim (ofc) ................................. 454-1620
Gordon, Jim (home) ............................ 473-1729
Gordon, Jim (service) ......................... 452-8800
Gordon, Jim (lake house) .................... 928-1225
doctor JIM GORDON ........................... 454-1620
MD: Jim Gordon ................................. 454-1620
```

I'm not likely to forget *his* name, but I do need those several additional numbers for him under what I consider his primary listing. And someone who works for me might need to find him in a hurry, when I'm not around (or for that matter, if I'm unconscious, in the event of an accident). What would they look under? "Doctor," probably, or maybe "MD." So he's in there in those forms as well.

I often complain about the lack of duplicate information in another kind of well-known database: the book index. When I pick up a book on using DOS, for example, I might look for information on expanding the ENVIRONMENT area of the PC's memory in several ways: under "E" for *Environment;* under "S" for the *SET* command; under "C" for *CONFIG.SYS,* where the environment statement is inserted; maybe under "M" for *memory,* since I'm modifying the allocation of memory. I could probably think of another half-dozen ways to look for it, as well.

But book indexes usually list terms only one or, maybe, two ways. Usually that's not because the indexer was lazy, or because the publisher was trying to save on paper costs; but because the person preparing the index (who is almost never the author of the work) just didn't know enough about the field to know the kinds of synonyms readers might use when they're searching for the right entry.

(In this book, we've tried to provide the most extensive index and cross-referencing possible. I know we haven't absolutely succeeded—there are always going to be ways to look for an entry that we didn't anticipate—but this book's index is very consciously full of "extra," or second-vector, entries.)

Database Duplications

Let's go on to another kind of second-vector entry that can be really important. Say you're assembling a fundraising database of potential contributors to a cause, so you can send those people personalized form letters seeking donations. The typical name data would usually be broken into four fields: TITLE *(Mr.)*, FIRSTNAME *(John)*, MI *(F.)*, LASTNAME *(Merganser)*. If you were a really sharp database designer, you might also have included TRAILID for any trailing identifier, such as *Jr.* or *III;* and you might have provided fields for a spouse's name, with fields such as 2ND FIRSTNAME, 2ND MI, 2ND LAST-NAME. For our purposes, let's assume there happens to be a *Mrs. Ellen R. Merganser* living with her husband John, with the information on her inserted in the appropriate fields in our database.

But form letters addressed to John, or Ellen, or both of them, are going to sound pretty stuffy when they're addressed to any form you can assemble from those fields. The address line or lines on the envelope, and the corresponding inside-address lines in the letter itself, are going to be either

> *Mr. John F. Merganser*
> *1234 56th St.*
> *Somewhere, ST 99999*

or

> *Mr. John F. Merganser*
> *Mrs. Ellen R. Merganser*
> *1234 56th St.*
> *Somewhere, ST 99999*

and the "Dear So-and-so" salutation is going to look something like

> *Dear Mr. John F. Merganser and*
> *Mrs. Ellen R. Merganser:*

Not a very convincing "personalized" letter, eh?

Consider the effect, though, of adding to the database's information a field called CALLBOTH, which would have for this record the entry *Mr. and Mrs. Merganser.* It's a lot more certain to construct personalized letters using that kind of field's data; now with some Boolean algebra in the conditional statements used to extract the necessary data, the envelope and formal inside address can read

> *Mr. and Mrs. John F. Merganser*
> *1234 56th St.*
> *Somewhere, ST 99999*

and the salutation can read

> Dear Mr. and Mrs. Merganser:

(In fairness, that last form would be a little tricky to use, because of record-to-record variations in the actual data.)

Let's dig just a little deeper. What if, in addition to that very useful CALLBOTH field, we also added these fields to the database, with the indicated data in this record: CALLNAME *(Jack)*, 2NDCALLNAME *(Pinky)*, and CALLBOTHSHORT *(Jack and Pinky)*. Now a letter to either Merganser can begin

> *Dear Jack:*

or

> *Dear Pinky:*

and letters to them both can begin

> *Dear Jack and Pinky:*

Now *that's* a personalized letter that is going to be read, and will probably be seen by many recipients—well, at least by *some* recipients—as an original, one-of-a-kind communication.

And that's what I really mean by second-vector data: what may look at first like duplicate pieces of data, but that turn out upon closer inspection—and upon actually using the database!—to be enormously valuable *additions,* not duplications, in the file.

☙

VI

ON THE ROAD

The Traveler's Companion

Surviving on the road with a portable PC calls for a lot more than hauling that computer along on the trip. And no matter how small and light laptop PCs get, the size and weight of the stuff I have to drag along to actually *use* that computer on the road doesn't seem to get any lighter or smaller.

I'm currently traveling with a speedy 386SX-based laptop, which has a 40 MB hard disk, 3 MB of RAM, an internal voice/fax modem and a bright, sharp VGA screen . . . all packed into a box that's $8.5 \times 11 \times 1.5$ inch and runs about five pounds. Sounds great, eh? Except that the supporting cast I carry to make that computer really useful fills a case half again that size, and weighs half again as much. But like Karl Malden and his American Express card, I won't leave home without it.

The computer magazines are full of stories for traveling PC users about how to break into hotel telephone systems or how to scrape a little insulation off the phone wiring in airline clubs, so you can connect your laptop's modem to that line and check your e-mail box. (I know; I've written a lot of those stories. . . .) What they *don't* do is give you a checklist of the things you need to carry along in order to pull off those little tricks.

Here's my little list for surviving on the road—mainly, in hotel rooms—when traveling with a PC. And some notes on why I put up with this pile of junk in my suitcase.

- **25-foot AC extension cord** I got tired of discovering that the only AC outlet I could use to charge the batteries in my laptop (and to plug into for extended use in my hotel room to conserve battery life) was behind the headboard of the bed . . . which meant that to work at the computer, I had to sit cross-legged in the bed, PC balanced on a pillow. So I got the lightest-weight 25-foot AC extension cord I could find. Now I can plug it in wherever the outlet is, and run that cord to a point near a desk or table. And I've stopped tearing up my back by twisting into a pretzel just to use my PC.

- **25-foot telephone extension cord** Ditto. Even when I can detach the cord from the back of the hotel's telephone, the length of that cord still limits where I can set up the PC. (Why do hotels put such short cords on their telephones? Why do they think we always want to make calls sitting on the side of the bed?) Now I can use a double-female inline connector (see below) to connect this 25-foot extension cord to that cord I just wrestled out of the back (or likelier, the bottom) of the telephone, and run the phone extension cord to the same point to which I've run the AC extension cord.

- **6-foot telephone extension cord** Once I've run that long telephone extension cord over to a more civilized place to work than the nightstand, I still need a way to connect the telephone to the phone line. So I use this shorter cord to plug into the PHONE jack on the modem in my PC, and into the telephone.

- **6 to 8 double-female inline connectors** (See above.) I keep losing these —friends kid me that all across North America, hotel telephones are still connected to the house phone wiring through double-ended female connectors I've left behind. They're probably right. A friend at Tandy Corp., which operates the Radio Shack chain, tells me I contribute a substantial percentage of their annual net profits, through my purchases of these invaluable gizmos, which allow connecting two male phone-cord plugs.

- **2 3-foot telephone extension cords with clips** This is actually a 6-foot phone cord cut in half, with miniature alligator clips soldered onto the red and green wires at each cut end. The clips let me attach the cord to exposed telephone wiring—usually, exposed because I've opened a telephone, or taken a telephone wall-jack's cover plate off, or because I've carefully scraped the insulation off a couple of inches of phone cable. That kind of disassembly (read: vandalism) becomes necessary only when phones are truly hard-wired in place, rather than being connected at one or the other end of that cord with plugs and jacks. The other end of one of these cheater cords, of course, plugs into the modem in my PC (through a double-female inline connector and an extension cord, if necessary).

- **Duplex connecting plug** This is what technicians call a "Y" connector, because it has two phone jacks on one side, and a phone plug on the other. I attach it to the PC's end of my phone extension cord (through one of those ubiquitous double-female connectors) when I'm using two devices that need access to the phone line. That second device is usually a tiny traveling fax machine (see *The Traveling Fax Machine*) but once in a while it's a second portable PC brought along by a friend working with me; we leave both machines hooked up at a desk in the hotel room so we don't have to keep plugging and unplugging cords.

- **Leatherman survival tool** One of the few all-purpose tools you can really *use,* the Leatherman, from L.L. Bean, combines a pocket knife with several sizes of screwdrivers with both flat and Phillips heads, an awl for punching small holes, and an exceptionally good pair of wire-cutting pliers. It has replaced a half-dozen less-convenient tools in my traveling kit, and is the one item on this list I consider nonnegotiable: The Leatherman really is that good. (Warning: Leatherman also makes a minitool, which is much less convenient. Buy the standard model.)

- **CP+ Connection** It can be tough to get data calls out in hotels that use the latest electronic switchboards. Unlike earlier analog devices, electronic PBXs are full of traps. Rather than fighting them, I carry the tiny CP+ Connection (also sold under the name Konexx). A short cheater cord from the $3 \times 1 \times 1$ inch Connection box plugs into the handset cord's jack on the hotel telephone; the handset cord itself then plugs into one end of the Connection. Then I run a phone cord from the data jack on the PC's modem to the "data port" on the other end of the Connection unit. An override switch lets me choose between data and voice calls; in the latter position, the Connection is simply bypassed. For data calls, a second switch on the Connection can be set for *C* (standard one-line phone systems), *D* (electronic PBXs), or *E* (conventional, nondigital, multiline phone systems). You can't take those switch-position labels too literally; Northern Telecom's popular Meridian electronic PBX systems require that the switch be in the *C,* or conventional, position. But you won't harm anything by experimenting with the Connection box wired into the phone system, and eventually you'll be able to get out through even the most perverse phone systems. There's also a polarity switch that can be used when the system switch is in the C position, to solve phone-wiring problems.

- **Flat printer cable** This lets me use other peoples' printers when I'm traveling; I simply disconnect the cable running from their PC to their printer, then attach my own. (See *Why Carry a Printer?* in this section.)

- **Mini flashlight** When you have to crawl around under beds, among the dust bunnies, in search of telephone wall-jacks hidden behind thousand-pound headboards, a small one-cell flashlight will make your life easier. (Not a *lot* easier . . . but it helps.)

- **3 three-pin AC ground adapter plugs** I used to simply rip that third ground pin out of the end of my portable PCs' power cords. Then a friend's PC was fried when a hotel electrical problem sent a hefty pop down the power line. That wouldn't have happened if his system had been grounded, so now I try to be good and leave those ground pins in place. Which means I now also need a 3-pin adapter—or two or three of them, since like those double-female phone-cord connectors, I often forget and leave them behind in hotel rooms.

- **Electrical tape** A tiny roll of plastic electrician's tape lets me repair any damage I wreak on phone wiring in the name of making a connection. Hey, I'm not a *vandal,* right?

- **DON'T TOUCH sign** My biggest problem with using a PC in hotel rooms often has little to do with AC outlets and phone connections, but with well-meaning maids, who patiently unplug everything I've strung around the room, wrap up my cords for me—and thus lead me into another bout with those fierce dust bunnies under the bed. So now I carry a couple of small, 4 × 6 inch laminated signs, that say DO NOT TOUCH! I leave at least one sitting atop my laptop PC, often a second one next to it.

One item missing from this list is an acoustic coupler that can be used with a telephone handset, if all else fails. I used to carry a coupler, but the results were so unpredictable—and usually, so poor—that I finally gave up, and vowed to do whatever it took to make a direct, wire-to-wire connection.

If I did the Clark Kent number of dashing into a pay-phone booth, lashing my portable PC to the phone, and shipping a hot story off to the *Daily Planet,* I'd probably still carry an acoustic coupler and put up with its problems. But I don't do that very often . . . and I'll bet you don't, either. So why carry a coupler?

As you read over that list, I suspect you'll be struck, as I was, by how many problems facing traveling PC users could be eliminated if hotels just included "data ports" on their telephones—and a few more AC outlets. Recent hotel phones produced by Comdial (the new name for the venerable Stromberg-Carlson company) have separate RJ11-jack data ports right next to the handset. And some hotel chains, such as Four Seasons, are beginning to install those phones.

I deal with phone problems in two ways. First, like a lot of business travelers, I tend to stay in the same hotels in cities I visit frequently. Part of the litmus test in choosing those hotels is whether they have data ports on their phones. Second, when I'm heading to a city I haven't visited before, or one I haven't visited in awhile, my secretary calls the general manager of the hotel before booking a room, to make certain their telephones have easy data connections. Unfortunately, there's many a slip between a hotel manager's promise and reality . . . so I still carry my little survival kit.

If you carry a laptop PC, you should, too.

❧

Lost, Strayed, and Stolen PCs

I've been traveling with portable PCs since the first Compaq suitcase-size "luggable" appeared in 1982. Today the machines are smaller, quieter, lighter, faster, more powerful . . . but they still cost a bundle.

That cost, or actually that *value*, worries me.

A portable PC's literal replacement cost—the list-price figure the insurance guy growls over when you put in a claim—isn't the half of it. The value of the *data* stored on the hard disk in the machine (or in silicon memory, or on floppy disks tucked into the case with the computer) is usually far greater. Then there's the value of the programs, the time spent assembling and massaging all that data, the opportunity cost of doing *without* the computer until a new one is in hand . . . and, scariest of all, the possible value of all that data to someone else—say, to your biggest competitor.

So I worry about the consequences of lost, stolen, and strayed PCs when I'm on the road.

PC, Call Home

In 1985 I decided to try something to make it at least possible that if a portable of mine should walk off—or likelier, should *I* walk off and leave one on a plane or in a hotel room or on the back floor of a hurriedly returned rental car—I might get it back. When, a little over a year later, the trick worked for me, and a PC I'd foolishly forgotten in the overhead compartment of an airliner was quickly returned to me, I wrote about that surprising and delightful event in a column in *PC Week*. And passed the trick along, so that others might use it, as well.

I was almost immediately buried under an amazing pile of letters from readers, 80 percent of whom found my suggestion so hopelessly naive—"laughable," one reader wrote—that they questioned my sanity. No one in his right mind would *ever* believe, most said, that someone finding something as valuable as a computer would return it, rewards and other inducements notwithstanding. Did I, another wrote, "believe in the Easter Bunny, too?"

Well, no.

But despite the cynics' sneers, I do have a pretty high opinion of my fellow humankind. And my experience with strayed PCs has confirmed that view.

The trick is simple: put a sign-on message, seeking return of the computer, into the AUTOEXEC.BAT file on the hard disk of the computer (or on an otherwise-blank system disk you keep in the floppy disk drive when you travel, to protect that drive's heads against bumps and jars).

The premise is equally simple: someone finding a lost or stolen computer without visible sign of ownership is, sooner or later, going to turn the computer on. When they do, and look at its display, they're going to see that plaintive sign-on screen—and if they're the right kind of person, give you a call.

If you're of one mind with those who wrote me to tell me I was silly, read no further; if you don't already believe in people's innate good nature, I'm sure you've found ample evidence in this world that you're right, and I can't change your mind.

But if you're at least open to the possibility that someone finding your computer would do for you what you'd do if you found theirs (you WOULD return it, wouldn't you?), stay tuned.

Creating the sign-on screen is easy; I'll get to that in a second. But first I want to tell you about my two lost PCs that found their way home thanks to this trick. That's right: twice I've lost a PC, and twice it's been returned. I'm not proud of leaving one machine behind and having another stolen . . . but I feel awfully good about the people who returned those $3,000-plus machines.

The Forgotten PC

The first time, I left a nearly new Toshiba T3100 portable in the overhead luggage bin on a 727. I was making a very tight connection, had arm fulls of other carry-on pieces, and had brought the computer on the trip only as an afterthought, not sure it'd be used at all. So when I scrambled off the plane at O'Hare and did my clumsy jog to the connecting airline's gate, the computer was the last thing on my mind.

Which is probably why I left it on the airplane.

I made the connecting flight—barely—and was two hours into the long slog from O'Hare to Los Angeles when I realized I'd left the computer behind. I felt a sinking feeling in my stomach. There wasn't any critical information on the disk, but the Toshiba cost about $3,500, and I knew whose pocket *that* was coming out of. Worse, I knew I'd need the machine for a second trip a few days later.

This was before the days of Airfones, so there wasn't much I could do. I wrote a short note describing my plight to the airplane captain, asking that he relay my situation to his airline's operations office at O'Hare, and that they in turn relay the message to the first airline. But I didn't have much hope of seeing the computer again.

I vividly recalled putting that sign-on screen into the AUTOEXEC file on the machine . . . but that was, after all, a long shot. In this day and age, who's going to return an expensive computer . . . ? I anticipated a hasty and expensive computer-shopping trip at my destination, Los Angeles.

When I landed at LA I went to a pay phone and called my office. Was there by any remote chance a message about my . . . ? As a matter of fact, there was.

Turns out that one of the last passengers off the plane, a retired gentleman from Missouri, heard the flight attendants talking about this computer they'd just found in the overhead compartment. Because I was carrying it without a case, its AC cord looped through the carrying handle, the usual I.D. tag wasn't there, so the computer bore no marks of ownership. The flight attendants couldn't figure out who it belonged to, so they were going to leave it for the cabin cleanup crew to take to the airline's lost and found.

But my savior told them he thought anyone who was carrying such a nice computer on a plane must really need it, and so it shouldn't get swallowed up for days or weeks by the airline's lost-and-found system. He knew a little about computers; why didn't he go with them into the terminal, plug it in, and see if he could figure out from the files in it to whom it belonged? That guy must surely want it back right away. . . .

They consented, and one of the attendants walked with him into the terminal. They squatted behind the gate agents' counter, plugged in the machine, and waited for something to appear on the screen. My newfound friend told me later he thought it was an awfully long shot that he'd be able to find any useful clues on the machine's hard disk, but he used a PC himself, and thought just maybe he could make it work.

Then *boom*! That wonderful sign-on screen popped up—to his amazement, and to the collective surprise of the five or six airline personnel gathered around. One of them picked up a phone and called my office.

My secretary confirmed for them that the machine must be mine, asked if the airline could somehow forward it to Los Angeles for me on their next flight headed that way, and gave them the name of my hotel in LA. A helpful gate agent hand-carried the Toshiba to one of the airline's nearby gates, and put it into the hands of a flight attendant on an LA-bound flight leaving about an hour later. At Los Angeles she gave it to the airline's security people who, God bless 'em, had it delivered to my hotel.

When I called my office from the LA airport, I didn't know the end of this story yet, but I was hugely relieved to know the computer had been found, and was, in one way or another, on its way to me. I went to Century City, checked into my hotel—and a little while later the concierge called to say there was a man at his desk with "a radio or something" for me.

Close call; true story.

A daisy-chain of wonderful people had saved me from myself—but without that sign-on screen, they'd have been unable to help. At minimum, it would have taken far longer to get the computer back—and to put my mind at ease.

Whodunnit?

The second story is less interesting, and I don't know all the details. A second Toshiba laptop I'd been carrying on the road disappeared from my room in a very expensive San Francisco hotel—the kind of place where That Kind of Thing Doesn't Happen. Whoever took it grabbed only the computer; nothing else was touched. Two days later my office got a call from the manager of a PC store in Fremont, south of San Francisco. Someone had brought the machine in, trying to sell it to them as a used machine he no longer needed. They fired it up, saw the screen, and told the fellow he'd have to give them a couple of hours to check it over, to see what they could pay for it. The thief said he'd be back.

The store clerk called my office, learned the PC was stolen, and called the cops. The police spent the afternoon at the store, but the culprit (or his or her fence) never returned. Maybe he was spooked; maybe he just went on to his next nasty job.

But I got the PC back a day later.

The moral here is simple: Even if you know to a certainty that you're much too smart to ever leave a PC behind in a hotel or car or airplane *(remember, I thought I was, too)*, there's always a chance that that machine will be stolen.

An integral "please return" message costs nothing, takes perhaps five minutes to install—and could save *your* PC, too.

Here's how.

Personalizing Your AUTOEXEC

You want to make sure the sign-on is the very first thing that appears on-screen—or at least, as soon as possible after the DOS sign-on message, any message posted by your PC's ROM BIOS, and anything loaded by the CONFIG.SYS file. And you want to make certain that that message doesn't scroll by too fast for someone to read or copy down your name and phone number. Thus your message should be the first entry in your AUTOEXEC.BAT file, and should be followed by a PAUSE command, so it will stay on-screen until you (or the finder, someday) hits a key to clear the screen and continue.

Using DOS's EDLIN editor or your word processor, you add just a few lines to the beginning of your AUTOEXEC.BAT file.

To be on the safe side, you might want to make a copy of the AUTOEXEC file first, in case something goes awry as you modify it. You can do that easily by typing these lines at the DOS prompt:

```
C> COPY AUTOEXEC.BAT AUTOEXEC.XTR
```

That will stash a spare copy of the AUTOEXEC, under the name AUTOEXEC.XTR (for "extra"), in the root directory of the disk where the original is kept. Should your efforts to modify the real AUTOEXEC.BAT file go astray, you can always simply rename this .XTR version to AUTOEXEC.BAT and be right back in business.

Now, on to modifying the AUTOEXEC. Add these lines at the very beginning of your AUTOEXEC.BAT file:

```
REM
REM        If this computer is found, please call
REM        one of the numbers below for return info,
REM        and details on a REWARD for its return:
REM
REM           (217) 444-5555 (office, 9-5, M-F)
REM           (217) 238-8712 (home, anytime)
REM
REM        Thank You!
REM                            —John Smith
REM
PAUSE
```

Save the file, then turn your computer off, wait a few seconds, then turn it on again. When the new sign-on screen comes up, make sure it looks right. You may want to fiddle with the line spacing or otherwise tailor the message to your own tastes; just make sure the essential information is there. (Resist the temptation to provide your address; it's an open invitation for thieves to check out the rest of your possessions.)

Here's how that screen looks on your computer:

```
C>REM

C>REM          If this computer is found, please call

C>REM          one of the numbers below for return info,

C>REM          and details on a REWARD for its return:

C>REM

C>REM              (217) 444-5555 (office, 9-5, M-F)

C>REM              (217) 238-8712 (home, anytime)

C>REM

C>REM          Thank You!

C>REM                            —John Smith

C>REM

C>PAUSE
Strike a key when ready . . .
```

The "REM" word that precedes each line is part of the simple batch programming language understood by MS-DOS; it identifies programmers' comments, or REMarks, as opposed to executable code. Note that even blank lines must begin with REM. The PAUSE command causes the computer to stop and display the familiar DOS request to "hit any key to continue."

This is a very simple scheme; I can't guarantee that it will work. But I can promise that now that you've read this, if you *don't* put that file in the AUTOEXEC file on your portable PC, and someday that PC disappears, you'll wish you had.

Think of it as improving the odds a bit.

❧

LapLinking

Increasingly, the newest, lightest, and most innovative laptop PCs are forsaking built-in floppy disks. The resulting reduction in size and weight is substantial, and of course it also ends worries about damaged heads on floppy drives. If all things were equal—that is, if I could have a lap-portable of exactly the same size and weight that *did* include a floppy drive as one that didn't—I'd choose the machine with the floppy disk drive.

But in the real world, I've come to prefer, and to rely on for hard daily use, laptops *sans* floppy disk drives.

When I say that to PC power users, I often get skeptical responses: How can I put up with the nuisance of not having a floppy disk drive? How do I move files back and forth? Isn't that floppy-diskless PC really just half a computer?

My answer is almost always the same: Have you used *LapLink?*

My skeptical questioners usually say that well, yes, they've seen *LapLink*, and they know it works OK, but still, it seems to them that. . . . Ah-hah! They haven't *used LapLink*, only read or heard about it, or maybe seen a quick demo somewhere. And actually using the program yourself is essential, I've discovered, to appreciating just how fast and easy it is. Because *LapLink* makes going without a removable-media disk drive in your portable as close to painless as possible.

LapLink has several challengers in the laptop-to-desktop file-transfer-utility market. And in truth, some of those competitors (such as *Brooklyn Bridge* and *FastLynx*) are almost as good as *LapLink*. But this is a category Travelling Software pioneered, and *LapLink* is the leader all the others are chasing. *LapLink* uses your desktop and laptop PCs' serial or parallel ports to transfer data at speeds once thought impossible. Your serial port, normally limited to 9,600 bps or 19,200 bps (depending on the vintage of your PC, and thus the type of UART serial-controller chip found inside), is pumped up to 115,000 bps.

The *LapLink* package even includes the cable you need for those transfers, so you don't need to make a second trip to the computer store for the right cable. And it's the *right* cable, because it has three connectors on each end: 9-pin serial, 25-pin serial, and Centronics parallel. That hydra-headed cable can connect any DOS PC to any other DOS PC, as long as each has some kind of serial port, or both have parallel printer ports.

The most recent versions of *LapLink* will even automatically copy the program onto a newly connected machine, if necessary, as long as *LapLink* is installed on the machine at the other end of the cable.

Smart Software

One of the two most common complaints I hear from those who haven't actually tried *LapLink* for desktop-portable connectivity is that it would be such a nuisance to have to turn your desktop PC around and hook up that cable every time you want to swap some files. Right: it *would* be a pain. That's why nearly every regular *LapLink* user I know leaves the cable permanently connected to a serial port on the back of his PC, with the other end of the cable trailing out under the desk or otherwise easily accessible. That way it's a snap to sit down, pick up that loose end of the cable, plug it into the lap machine, and go to work.

Turn both machines on, type LL3 (for *LapLink* Version 3.0, or the appropriate command for the version you're using) on each machine, and the two computers link up. That's it: the connection process is completely automatic. *LapLink* shows side-by-side on each PC's display listings of the current directories on both machines. You can control *both* machines from either's keyboard, so you don't need to switch back and forth from one keyboard to the other.

Just make sure you're in the right directory on each machine, then tag the files or programs you want to transfer, tap C for Copy, and *LapLink* will quickly move the files over to the other machine. The program uses a proprietary error-correction protocol, so as it moves each block of data, it checks to make sure the transfer was perfect, and confirms on-screen that the transfer was, in *LapLink's* own terms, "100 percent perfect."

The second complaint I hear about *LapLinking* and floppy-less portables is that it's awfully hard to load software on them. How, in fact, *do* you get programs from the software publisher's distribution disks onto one of these floppy-diskless marvels? *LapLink* to the rescue again. *LapLink* can treat any disk drive on your desktop PC as a "local" drive on the portable, so you just shuffle your original program disks through that floppy drive on your desk-bound machine, and let *LapLink* install the software on your floppy-less portable's hard disk. The process is essentially invisible to the software; I've never found a program I couldn't install on one of my portable PCs in this manner.

Indeed, *LapLink* has become such a standard in the portable-computing world that makers of laptop PCs are starting to include it with their machines, burned into a ROM chip in the machine. It's easy to see why: it makes using a floppy-less portable a joy. You'll hardly notice that drive isn't there.

Except, of course, every time you pick up the machine and pack it in your attache case for a trip. And marvel again at how light it is.

❧

Portable Cheat Sheets

I use a very few software programs a great deal, and several more only once in a while. I suspect that matches your pattern of PC-use, too. Most of us rely on a short list of programs we use very frequently, and thus come to know pretty well, and a somewhat longer list of those we use less often and thus know less well (and, if the truth be told, perhaps hardly at all).

But even with programs I use nearly every day, I still can't remember every trick and command and subtle difference from other programs. *(Nora? Tell me again how I can get a nonbreaking hyphen in Microsoft* Word*?!?)* So I rely on cheat sheets of my own devising. At my desk, a bizarre accumulation of these notes—compressed onto the front and back of a single 4 × 6 inch index card, printed in small type with lots of almost-illegible annotation—lives under my keyboard. Ever at the ready, it bails me out when I can't remember how to do something I do only once in a great while in one of those keystone programs. And it's invaluable in helping me remember that much broader set of only-dimly-remembered commands and tricks in my less-used software library.

I've learned that if anything it's even more important to also keep a photo-copy of that cheat sheet tucked into the case of whichever portable PC I'm carrying at the moment. Because the traveling version is subject to a lot of wear and tear, which would smear its laser print into illegibility very quickly, I protect it inside a plastic sleeve. I use a 4 × 5 inch photographic-transparency sleeve, and trim the card a bit on the ends, simply because that sleeve was sitting on my desk the day I decided to make up my first traveling cheat sheet. I could as easily use clear contact paper, a cut-down vinyl sheet-protector of the sort usually tucked into three-ring binders, or simply cover the card in a protective cocoon of Scotch tape.

(I don't similarly protect the card at my desk, because that would keep me from adding squiggly little update notes from time to time. And by using a plastic sleeve on the traveling card to do the opposite—*keeping* me from changing the one I carry on the road—I force myself to make new, updated traveling copies once in a while, lest I find myself on the road without my latest and greatest additions to the one at my desk. Amazing, the little tricks we play to keep ourselves honest. . . .)

Now, when I'm sitting in the hotel room in Chicago, and I can't remember that trick in MCI Mail to see who else received an incoming message I've just read, when it smells to me like the electronic equivalent of a form letter, I look up the answer on the cheat sheet.

Often colleagues and clients traveling with me have seen me dig out the cheat sheet and look up some obscure detail. Many of them have kidded me about it—and you're supposed to be an *expert?*, they say—but it's amazing how often I find out later that they've done exactly the same thing.

Actually, in doing this we're all stealing a page from the book of that savviest but least-appreciated member of the office team: the experienced secretary. It's hard to find a good secretary who doesn't have, slipped under the keyboard of her PC (or typewriter), a cheat-sheet list of a few dozen things she needs to know right away, but can never remember: the telephone number of the boss's kid's dorm at State U., how to get *WordPerfect* to accept *WordWhizzer* files, the name of that wonderful woman in accounting who gets expense-reimbursement forms through even when they've got some funny-looking figures in them.

No matter how PC-savvy you like to think you are, I'll bet an old floppy disk that a similar cheat sheet system could help you, too.

At your desk, sure. But even more, on the road, when you can't call out *"Nora . . . ? How do I . . . ?"*

Why Carry a Printer?

I really like the little Kodak/Diconix portable PC printer. A tiny, tough, reliable device about the size of an elongated hardback book, it fits easily in the attache case that doubles for me as a portable-PC case (see *Bag It!* in this section). The Diconix's ink-jet print head produces perfectly acceptable output on almost any kind of paper, and because it uses the ubiquitous Epson/IBM Graphics Printer command set, I can find a printer driver for virtually any application I have.

The ink-jet design also means it's quiet, so when I'm sitting in a hotel room at 2 A.M., I don't worry about setting the guy in the next room's teeth on edge—nor my own!—with the whine of a dot-matrix mechanism. I don't often use it with its built-in batteries, because I don't often need to print something when I'm not near an AC outlet. But it's reassuring to know I *could* run on battery power, if I needed to. It's a swell tool, one I've learned to trust.

I've also learned to leave it at home when I travel.

The idea of a truly portable printer long seemed wonderful to me, but the perfect machine eluded me for a long time. I had a short dalliance with Hewlett-Packard's clever little ink-jet printer, but it was just a bit too large to be easily portable. When I found the Diconix, I thought I had the ultimate answer.

But I must be getting smarter, not just older, because after a year or so of travel with the Diconix, I found the best answer of all: Don't carry a printer. Do without, or, when necessary, use someone else's printer. More recently, I've found an even sneakier alternative.

Excess Baggage

One thing I noticed when I was traveling with the Diconix was how little I really used it. It probably has enough miles on it to earn its own frequent-flyer card, yet in the years since I bought it I've probably printed fewer than a thousand pages on the machine—as much as I like it. What I found was that when I'm traveling, I really don't *need* printouts most of the time. Want, yes, sometimes; really need, not often at all.

When I carry a PC on a trip, I'm typically trying to get in some extra time working on large projects that can wait until I get back to the office. Or I'm writing messages I'm going to send from the road, via MCI Mail or another electronic-mail service. Or I'm working with a client on files I'm going to save to a floppy and leave with that client. So why bother with printouts?

The Invisible Printer

Sometimes, of course, those conditions don't apply, and I find I really do need a quick printout of something I've been working on. It was in trying to figure out how to handle those occasions that I discovered how nice people are about letting someone, often a complete stranger, use their printer.

Before long, I began carrying a printer cable instead of a printer. Since IBM-style PC parallel-printer connections are marvelously standard at the printer end, all I needed was a cable with a Centronics-style D-connector at one end, for the printer, plus the DB25 connector at the other end for my portable PC.

I found that when I had the cable along, people were even happier to let me use their printers. Before I stumbled onto that idea, and just asked if I could unplug their computer and plug mine in for a moment, I got some skeptical looks. Some people were clearly worried that when I was through, their computer setup would never work properly again. But I quickly figured out the reason: they saw me messing with things on the back of their PC, where all is mysterious, and where dangerous gremlins must surely lurk. (I also found myself crawling through the dustballs of America, through forests of tangled cables and accumulated trash and dead insects. It's not a pretty place behind most PCs—perhaps including yours?)

So instead I now simply hold out my portable PC, printer cable already connected, and ask if I can please plug that cable into their *printer* for a minute, to print a page or two. I'm not asking if I can fool with their PC, so the worry factor for my newfound helpers is far smaller: they associate those dreaded P-C P-R-O-B-L-E-M-S with things at the computer end, not at the printer end, of that connection. I also do a lot less crawling around under desks, counters, cabinets, carts, and the other things we use to prop up our PCs, which helps my back, my temperament, and my dry-cleaning bills.

I think it's a wonderful comment on human nature that literally *no* one I've asked has ever said no when I asked if I could use their printer for a moment.

One additional step is necessary: now I load onto the hard disk of my traveling PCs a much wider range of the printer drivers provided with applications packages. Though I still find I use the Epson/IBM driver most often—even many small printers that don't explicitly support that command set use something so close to it that for common settings, they're effectively Epson-IBM compatible—I also usually put on a few Okidata drivers, and others for H-P LaserJets and printers from Diablo, C. Itoh, NEC, Alps, Tandy, and Texas Instruments. Some programs also have what amount to generic printer drivers—often called something like PLAIN or TTY, or WHEEL; I put those on the disk, too. Storing these extra drivers on the hard disk takes an insignificant amount of additional space, but lends a substantial amount of confidence that I'll be able to find something that will make my new colleague's printer work for me.

Often, these Good Samaritans are simply amazed, and not a little charmed, that MY computer will work properly with THEIR printer. They didn't know it worked that way. PCs are still a Black Art for many otherwise-sophisticated people, so don't be surprised if you run into that reaction often, too.

I've borrowed printers this way at airline ticket offices, airport clubs, travel agents, dozens of offices, a couple of banks, zillions of hotel desks, newspaper offices, a pharmacy, two hospitals, academics' offices, a trade-show check-in counter, and even a couple of computer stores. Without exception, I've met friendly and helpful people in the process, and I recommend it highly.

I know: it'll be hard to ask the first time, and you'll feel a little foolish. Tell 'em it was my idea.

Carry a Cable, Not a Firehose

One more trick to make this even easier: Carry a light, compact flat cable, not the usual round, heavy-duty number. These so-called ribbon cables were never meant for the rigors of the road, but for a much gentler existence inside a PC's system box, connecting output ports to motherboards, disk drives to controllers, and so on. But they're remarkably tough and long-lasting. I've replaced two—at a cost of maybe $10 each—over the years I've been carrying them, and neither of *those* had given up yet. They were just looking a little frayed and ragged, and I didn't want to push my luck.

A standard 6- to 8-foot parallel printer cable weighs three pounds or more, and is impossible to carry except in a big, clumsy coil. By comparison, my little 6-foot ribbon cables, with connectors (which are the heavy parts), weigh about eight ounces, fold flat, and can almost be hidden in the palm of my hand.

Even Sneakier...

I mentioned that lately I've found an even more convenient solution to the occasional need for a printer when I'm on the road. This one won't work for everyone, and I still carry that ribbon cable in my computer case. But often it's the fastest and easiest way to get a printout on the road. Credit where credit is due: I owe thanks for this sneaky trick to Borland's Philippe Kahn, one of the great originals and also one of the wild men of the PC business.

Here's the trick: If you're an MCI Mail subscriber, just send yourself a fax of the material you need printed.

If what I need is simply to get some text or numbers down on paper—and that's usually the limit of my traveling printing—I just save the document or spreadsheet or whatever to disk as a print file, then log onto MCI Mail through my portable PC and send the file to myself, addressed to the fax machine at the hotel or office or other location where I'm working. Within a few minutes, the fax arrives, crisp and attractive. (Unlike a lot of not-very-good-looking PC-fax material, MCI uses a special, high-legibility typeface, and the fine-resolution fax-transmission standard, when forwarding faxes that originate as MCI Mail messages. Thus almost no matter how old, beat-up or out of alignment the receiving fax machine, the incoming printed pages will look good.)

One more step makes this just about perfect.

Most fax machines use thin, curly, thermal paper that's hard to write on. But the whole reason I need a printout in the first place is that I need a decent-looking piece of paper to put in someone's hand. So I often photocopy those faxed pages on a decent Xerox-type copier. *Voila:* great-looking hard copy, at little cost in effort, time, or cash.

MCI Mail charges me just 50 cents for the first half-page, and 30 cents for each succeeding half-page, to send those faxes—including telephone-line charges. Most hotels, airline clubs, and other, similar locations charge guests only for sending faxes, not for receiving them; and of course when I'm working in an office there's no charge at all for receiving something.

Quick, cheap, elegant, and very easy. Thanks, Philippe.

The Traveling Fax Machine

For many of us, faxes have become such an integral part of our working style that forgoing them when we're traveling can hurt. I fax an awful lot of stuff to staff, colleagues, and clients, from clippings I tear out of local newspapers to expense-account minutiae to "please take care of this for me" requests. The last item could be handled through electronic mail—but the first two can be done only with fax.

If you're as hooked on using faxes as I am, you may decide to look into an internal or external fax modem for your portable PC. My suggestion: *don't*. Experience has taught me that adding a fax card to your portable may be the *worst* way of handling the need to send and receive faxes when you're on the road.

First, PC fax cards, whether installed in deskbound PCs or tucked away in laptops, all suffer from the same problems. See *PC Fax: Yes, But . . .* in the **PC Communications** section of this book for my generalized case against PC fax units. Briefly, I find using PC fax cards of whatever sort is usually a nuisance, with generally poor results. And my experience has been that those problems are magnified when I take PC fax modems on the road.

The complications of PC-faxing from your hotel room or other temporary quarters can be infuriating. There's the inevitable search for an RJ-11 telephone jack to plug into. Endless problems getting through switchboards. Uncertainty about whether the fax got through properly to your addressee.

And that's just for *sending* faxes. What about the complications of receiving them via a laptop's PC fax modem? How are you going to print them out? (Remember, the fact that faxes are instant hardcopy—you can make marginal notes on them, send them on to others, file them away, have a copy at hand without turning on a PC—is a large part of their usefulness.) Do you really have enough room on the relatively small hard disk in your laptop PC (or worse, on floppies) to store those big incoming faxes until you can get home and print them for your files? What about screen resolution? Faxes are hard enough to read conveniently on a full-size desktop VGA-level monitor. Is that squinty LCD display on your portable PC really up to showing you incoming faxes?

There are several alternative methods of sending faxes when you're on the road—all better, I'm persuaded, than adding PC fax capability to your laptop.

Truly Portable Fax Machines

The easiest answer, of course, is to simply use someone else's fax machine. In hotels and offices that's easy. If you're worried that using someone's fax machine will mean you'll have to print out your files first, then invest in a tiny portable printer: you'll get a lot more use out of it than you will out of a laptop fax unit.

The next obvious path is to simply carry a fax machine with you. In the past, that would have been crazy. So-called portable fax machines, such as the early Medbar units, were only marginally portable. You had to really *want* to send a fax to justify carrying them around. But today's portable fax units—machines built specifically for portability—are remarkably small, light, and easy to use. And if you're worried about the lack of confidentiality of faxes given to the bellman for transmission by a hotel, you'll love the direct, point-to-point communication possible with your own portable fax machine.

If you're interested in portable fax machines, I strongly recommend Panasonic's KX-F80, which will fit into just about half of your attache case. It has a "fine" resolution option, one-touch dialing, and auto redialing. It also offers three great advantages over the other portable units I've seen: it includes a complete built-in speakerphone, so you won't have to go back and forth between the hotel-room phone and the fax machine. It includes a copy function, so in a pinch you can make acceptable (if still wispy and curly) copies via its thermal-paper printing mechanism. And it includes an easy-to-use answering machine, which is a lot more reliable for message-taking than most hotel switchboard personnel. All that functionality costs just $500 or so.

Fairness requires me to acknowledge that connecting a portable fax machine is about as much of a pain in the neck as connecting a portable PC with an internal or external fax modem: all involve finding an AC outlet and running a cord to it; finding an RJ-11 phone jack and running a cord to *it;* then figuring out how to dial out through the hotel's switchboard.

If the idea of carrying your own fax machine around sounds wacky, keep reading—yet another option is coming up—but you should know that such savvy businessmen as Bill Magowan, the founding genius behind MCI, carry machines with them constantly when they travel. (And in Bill's case, it's not something he palms off on a traveling staff, because he doesn't take a staff with him when he travels; the fax machine goes in his briefcase. And he uses it virtually every day he's on the road.)

Fax From E-Mail

Finally, if you subscribe to one of the mainstream third-party electronic mail services, such as MCI Mail or AT&T Mail, you can direct messages you send through those systems to be delivered, as faxes, to any standard Group III fax machine in the world.

I use MCI Mail's "Fax Dispatch" service frequently. The service uses a special type font designed for the limitations of faxing, and it ships your faxes out at fine resolution, so they often look better at the receiving end than a typed or printed letter you'd scanned into a traditional fax machine. Sending an e-mailed fax is easy with MCI Mail: You just type (FAX) after the addressee's name, and the system asks the necessary questions about the fax number to use, the number of retries it should attempt . . . and even generates and appends a cover page to the message.

MCI Mail's fax service is cheap, too: currently just 50 cents for the first half-page, plus 30 cents for each additional half-page. The cover page is free, as are repeated retries if the receiving machine is busy or turned off; and a free confirmation of receipt (or nonreceipt) report is sent to your MCI Mail mailbox. That's not much more expensive than a fax sent from a standard fax machine would cost, and it's far less than the usual highway-robbery rates hotels charge for sending guests' outgoing faxes. (Of course, you still have to find an RJ-11 jack, dial out through the switchboard, etc., etc. . . .)

Those are the options. Clearly, there are elements of frustration and fiddle-factor in all of them. Which answer works best depends a lot on just how important faxing is to you when you're on the road, and whether you mainly send faxes, or also receive them. And how important confidentiality is in those faxes.

☙

Bag It!

There's just one thing wrong with most portable-PC carrying cases: they don't work.

It's amazing that companies with enough savvy to build lap-size portable PCs—acknowledged technological wonders—produce such sorry means of transporting them. Almost without exception, when I get an evaluation unit of a new, about-to-be-released world-beater lap portable—tucked neatly into its black nylon or leather case, of course—my thought as I open the case and the computer falls out and hits my feet is "Did the guys who designed this thing ever *use* it?"

The biggest problem? Not enough room to carry what you need to really *use* the computer.

Lap portables are wonderful tools. But you don't go on the road with just the *computer,* do you? There are floppy disks, power cords, transformers for recharging the unit's batteries, perhaps extra batteries, maybe an external modem, long and short telephone cords, probably a telephone "cheater" kit to allow modem connections in hostile environments (such as $200-night-and-up hotel rooms), probably an AC extension cord . . . and oh yes, the computer itself.

Plus assorted paperwork: printouts of some of the files on the disk, other documents, maybe a software cheat-sheet or two. And if, like me, you like to have one hand free as you run through airports and fend off muggers, you also need to tuck into that carrying case the stuff that would otherwise travel in the attache case you had to leave back at the office: airline tickets, passport, itinerary, calculator, sunglasses, extra glasses, Tums, pens, pencils, a few file folders of Important Papers, a company telephone directory, this morning's *Wall Street Journal,* car keys, and a few dozen other traveling-on-business necessities.

I won't even mention the possibility of a portable printer. . . .

Have you ever seen a laptop carrying case that acknowledged that we actually use these machines in *business,* and thus need to carry a few things besides the computer itself?

Actually, there are a couple of ways around this mess. As bad as the computer was itself, the gray nylon carrying case for IBM's PC Convertible was very good. It was also heavy, bulky, and looked like something you'd take on bivouac with a Marine platoon . . . but it was roomy enough to hold almost any manufacturer's lap portable plus the required accessories and business necessities. Maybe you can find one sitting forlornly in a corner of a computer store. Maybe they'll throw in a PC Convertible for free if you buy the bag. . . .

A second good answer is a bag from Targus, a company that makes a variety of fairly large, somewhat clumsy but amazingly roomy laptop cases. Don't buy one by mail; you need to haul all your stuff along to a computer store and spend a while trying to pack it into their various-size cases to get the right one. Targus cases are available in fabric and leather; the leather bags are expensive but classy and durable.

Finally, the best (if most expensive) answer may be to look for a soft-side leather attache case that's the right size and shape for your PC and gear, then dedicate it to just that purpose. I finally did that, settling on a gorgeous brown leather Scully case from Italy. One side houses the laptop of the moment, along with all the computerish accessories it requires. The other side holds my business stuff, and in a pinch can even accommodate a fresh dress shirt and a pair of socks. (I have to be careful which side I open in meetings. . . .)

Unfortunately, the Scully cost about $350—a steep price for a computer bag.

Of course, as laptop machines get ever smaller, we're starting to able to carry them in regular briefcases or shoulder-bags. Bags from Land's End, Orvis, L.L. Bean, and other makers of casual and sports luggage can make great carriers for the NEC Ultralite, TI Travelmate, and other new "notebook" PCs. But they don't do much for users of older, bigger portables.

Why don't computer makers themselves turn out appropriate bags—or rather, contract with good bag makers for custom-sized bags for their individual models?

At least one did: Compaq hired Athalon to produce a stunning black leather case for the clumsy Compaq Portable 386. The case was a masterpiece of design engineering, with zippers everywhere, inside and out—a biker's delight—and magically expanding gusseted sides and pockets that opened or closed as needed, depending on whether you had Compaq's ungainly expansion unit, or tape backup unit, attached to your Portable 386.

The Compaq/Athalon case had that boxy, square-miniduffel look of a very expensive gym bag. Which was its downfall, I'm told: most people who bought them (billing them to their companies, of course) quickly stopped using them as computer-carriers, and instead tucked their racquetball racquets, cans of balls, gloves, shorts, shoes, T-shirts, and foot powder into them. And corporate America decided it wasn't so excited about buying its employees $300 gym bags.

Oh yes, one other thing: once you put the computer inside, even that Compaq marvel had no room for accessories, business papers, and so on.

It's a crazy business.

Tapping into Your
Desktop PC
From the Road

When PCs were uncommon business tools and only a few of us were lucky enough to have them on our desks, life was a lot simpler. Today, though, when many businesspeople have not only a deskbound PC, but also a laptop, or have PCs both on their desks in the office and in their dens at home, or all three, things can get pretty complicated.

Say you're in San Diego on a business trip, toting your trusty lap-portable PC. You suddenly realize you need a *1-2-3* worksheet from the hard disk in the PC on your desk back in Hartford. You *meant* to copy it onto the hard disk in your portable before you left, but. . . . How to get it? You can call the office before everyone's left for the day (remember that three-hour time difference), ask someone to boot up your PC, navigate through your files, find the one you need, copy it onto a floppy, and send that disk to you by overnight courier. Well, maybe . . . but it's a lot of hassle, and you probably don't have the extra day to wait for the disk to come.

If you use Lotus *Express* and MCI Mail, a communication software/e-mail service combination that can handle binary file transfers, you could call the office, ask someone to boot up your PC and send you that file as an e-mail message. After awhile, you could log on to your MCI Mail box and see if the file came through.

But there are easier ways to access files and programs on distant PCs. A whole class of programs known as "remote computing" software makes it easy to log on to another PC over the phone. You can exchange messages with the other PC; you can transfer files between the two machines; you can even (though with some pretty severe performance limitations) run a program on that distant PC from your local PC, watching it execute on your screen.

These remote computing packages were first used for technical support within the PC industry, and then within large companies. By installing a copy of the program on each modem-equipped PC in the company, staffers in a company's PC-support office can respond to cries for help by logging on to the user's PC, in effect taking it over and running it from their own PC's keyboard. Since everything that happens on that worried user's PC appears more or less simultaneously on the help technician's screen as well, the expert can try his bag of problem-solving tricks directly, without the frustration of coaching the user through a long series of commands and instructions. *("Now hit ENTER. OK? OK? Right. Now, hit the down-cursor key two times. No, DOWN. OK? OK? Hello . . .?")*

Dialing Up Your Printer

As useful as that kind of remote-control computing can be in a tech-support setting, it's even more helpful as a way for the individual PC user to get to his "other" PC. In fact, once you install remote-computing software on your office PC and any other PCs you use, you'll find you can turn that greater complexity of today's PC environment to your advantage.

Networks are a good example. When you tap into your networked desktop PC from a portable while you're on the road, you can go a step further and connect that desktop machine to the local area network. Suddenly you have access not only to those programs and files resident on your own desktop, but also to all those resources connected to the network, such as programs and files resident on the network's servers, reference material on networked optical disk drives, and fax servers and printers.

Even if your desktop PC isn't hooked into a local area network, you can still perform some neat tricks, such as transferring a file you've just written with the word-processing software on your portable PC back to the hard disk of your desktop PC. Then start up the copy of that same word-processing program that resides on the desktop machine, and tell it to print the file on the printer connected to the desktop PC. When you return to the office, the printed copy is awaiting you.

(In a pinch, when I've been traveling and needed a printout of something but couldn't borrow someone's printer, I've used this trick to print a copy at my office, then asked someone in the office to fax that printout back to me at the hotel where I was staying. It's a roundabout way to get a letter printed, but it works.)

There are at least a half-dozen widely distributed remote computing programs. I prefer *pcANYWHERE IV* from DMA, but I've also used successfully DCA's *Remote2* and Microcom's *Carbon Copy Plus.* Triton's *Co-Session Plus* and Norton-Lambert's *Close-Up* also have good reputations.

When you're shopping for remote software, remember that you'll need copies for both the office PC and the remote machine. Publishers of remote computing software price their offerings differently; with some packages you'll have to buy separate programs for each machine; with others, you get both versions, or a single version that works at either end of the connection, for one price.

Remote2 and *pcANYWHERE* are particularly economical, at less than $200 for both ends of the connection. Both are also easy to use and reliable. Both packages can also get through your office's switchboard, if necessary, en route to your PC and modem, by allowing you to place the call in voice mode, then flip to data mode once your call has been put through to your desk and you hear the whistle of your desktop PC's modem. The automatic file-compression routine used by *pcANYWHERE* is nice, too: the program compresses the file at the transmitting end, then automatically decompresses it at the receiving end, thus speeding up file transfers by as much as 50 percent.

A Few Precautions . . .

Using remote computing software does involve some trade-offs. For example, your desktop PC and its modem must be left on at all times. That really isn't a problem—your PC will probably last longer if you never turn it off than if you keep switching it on and off every day. But if that idea worries you, you can buy little relay-controlled devices that connect to your modem and PC and, on receipt of an incoming data call, wake up your PC. If you want to be able to print at your desktop machine from a remote PC, you'll need to leave your printer turned on, too. (These problems disappear for LAN users, of course, whose PCs, and all connected devices, are typically kept running all the time.)

You'll also want to protect yourself against accidental lock-ups of the desktop machine due to crossed connections. And you'll want to make sure someone in your office can't accidentally foul up a remote session if they should notice your unattended PC merrily working away, and start fiddling with it. Most of the better remote-computing programs have features to handle these situations.

The leading remote computing software packages also have means of ensuring the security of your desktop PC, though none of these measures is going to be as convenient as you'd like.

A common system, for example, involves a callback routine. You place a call from your remote PC to the PC on your desk, the desktop machine answers, and you enter a password. The desktop PC immediately hangs up, and looks up that password in a file you've left on its hard disk. In that file, the password leads the computer to another telephone number—in theory, the number from which you just called—and the desktop computer then calls that number. The auto-answer modem in your remote PC answers, and presto, you're on-line again.

The idea is to keep miscreants from calling up that desktop PC, logging in, snooping around, and wreaking havoc. And callback systems work pretty well if you always call the central machine from a fixed remote location. If you just want a system that allows you to access your office PC's files from your home PC, for example, this should work well.

The problems arise when you'll be calling in from the road, and don't know in advance the numbers the desktop PC will need to call back. You could, of course, set up a whole string of passwords on your desktop machine, each associated with a different city you visit and the hotel there where you usually stay. But then those callback data calls would have to get through your hotel's switchboard to your room—which isn't going to happen.

And what about when you need to call in from other cities, or from other hotels? Or from clients' offices?

Alternatively, of course, you can disable the callback security feature of remote computing software. But then you're vulnerable to hackers. Like most computer-security questions, this one involves trade-offs you'll have to weigh for yourself. Are the power and convenience of unfettered remote computing worth risking a break-in by a hacker? Are there any really sensitive files on your PC? What if a malicious caller did something really vicious, like reformatting the hard disk in your PC? Is the security of a callback system perhaps worth the limitations it places on your access to the office computer?

Don't let security issues scare you away from the convenience of remote computing. But think about these issues before you open the door, so to speak, to your PC to any caller clever and patient enough to figure how to break into your system.

TIME OUT III

Power Users Be Damned

I wish I knew who came up with the phrase "Power User." I'd go for his throat. It's not that I hate the phrase so much: I use it myself. What I hate is the baggage that has come to be associated with the term. And how many people succumb to an exaggerated and often dangerous sense of self-importance when they think they've become Power Users.

For example: In many companies, "PC Power User" has become one of the tags hung on people who know so much about PCs that they no longer have time to learn much about their jobs.

For example: In many companies, there's a widespread perception that since Power Users clearly (think they) know all there is to know about PCs, they think everyone should use the same software and hardware they use. Whether it fits their needs or not.

For example: In many companies, self-appointed (should I say "self-annointed"?) Power Users love to lord their status over those people who pay more attention to the bottom line than to the bottom disk drive. And that does not win them Mister or Miss Congeniality trophies.

Let's put it plainly: It's swell to be a "power user" (no capital letters) kind of person, if you really enjoy working with a PC. I like PCs; I enjoy the notion of being a power user. But when you cross that line to (drum roll, please) "Power User" status, and start thinking your facility with small computers makes you a great manager, a great boss, an automatic fast-tracker, and maybe even someone who ought to be telling everyone else around you What They're Doing Wrong, you commit what can be a fatal mistake.

Short-term, it can feel pretty good. It's always nice to notice that you're good at something, and to have your peers acknowledge that ability. Short-term it can probably help your career: people who master a lot of skills important to their jobs get noticed. And short-term it can help you actually do your job better, which is even more likely to get you noticed.

But long-term, going around rippling those PC Rambo muscles is a great way to knock yourself off the fast track, abrade relationships with your colleagues, waste a phenomenal amount of time . . . and persuade your boss you're not as smart as he or she thought you were.

Which is a good way to become a Power*less* User overnight.

Dealing with The
Guys from DP

Once upon a time, the Data Processing Department was one of the real, if sharply bounded, centers of corporate power. If the people who ran DP centers didn't often ascend to the very top of their companies—they *were* a little weird, and didn't exactly take a global view of the business, their CEOs said—they were nonetheless well paid, and senior management usually left them alone. Running a DP shop might not have been a way station en route to the top, but it was a comfortable sinecure. DP bosses were backed up in their decisions, even when that alienated other company managers; and their budget requests usually got quick if grudging approval.

After all, the DP shop's dark warnings of "possible system slow-downs," and "running out of capacity" certainly sounded ominous. Who wanted to be responsible for bringing the company to its knees by denying DP's request for a few more disk drives? Or a new processor? And besides, who knows when they're telling the truth? Who *understands* all that stuff?

About two decades ago, that forbidding reputation of the DP shop, and the general fear but respect for DP managers as priests of black arts, began to change. Data processing was out; "management information systems" were in.

Unfortunately, for many data-processing executives that transition in American business from the DP era to the MIS age was reflected mainly in their wardrobes: better suits, button-down shirts, and no more clown ties. Running a Management Information Systems department certainly sounded a lot better than being in charge of Data Processing. But the job was still a lot like running a gas station, though you didn't have all those grease stains on your clothes when you went home at night. You still ran an internal service bureau.

Except that a great percentage of MIS managers forgot the essence of running a gas station well: giving good service. Internal "clients" got tired of hearing about the legendary—and sometimes all too real—"24-month backlog" before their request for a new kind of system, and sometimes even for a new print spec for a new report from existing databases, could be handled. MIS Knew Best; the rest of us were supposed to remember that There Are, After All, Priorities Around Here.

PCs have gone a long way towards making that kind of MIS shop obsolete. Managers who've built a PC database or two themselves know it isn't that hard to spec a new database report—and in any case, they need the information by the end of the day tomorrow, or it isn't going to be much use in the tumultuous markets in which they compete. Analysts who've built a profit-forecasting system in *1-2-3* or a foreign-currency-positions tracking system in *Paradox* know that asking those COBOL retreads in the MIS department to help develop an account-profitability system means endless flow-charting meetings before they can even see a prototype. By which time the accounts whose profitability seems so important are likely to be some *other* company's accounts.

MIS people like to complain that PC-oriented business people, and PC-oriented business systems, pay too little attention to such important issues as data integrity and system security. The PC people respond that MIS people live perpetually two years behind, while they must manage in a world based on quarterly results and shaving a day off average receivables.

But those MIS people can still stick a powerful stake in the wheels of progress. Luddites they may be; but they're a force to be dealt with, nonetheless. And the hotshot departmental manager who wants to build a new strategic system to track just-in-time inventories on an hourly basis—and get that system up and running in 90 days—can get blindsided when MIS decides that *this* time he's gone too far.

Just as fast-rising corporate stars know you manage up as well as down— you manage your boss as surely as you do those who report to you . . . and *he* knows that, and judges you on how effective you are at that game—the savvy line manager today knows that while he can get results a lot faster by working with the PC-level development resources in his company, he's wise to keep looking over his shoulder, too. Benign relationships with the MIS shop are useful; they can help buy freedom.

Especially if a new PC-based development project is likely to be a big effort or a long-range one, is likely to offload work from the MIS shop's mainframes, or is likely to be a highly visible *succès d'estime* within the company, a smart manager makes sure he has at least neutralized MIS before he begins his crusade.

That said, it's certainly a mistake to assume the MIS troops can't possibly be helpful in developing those new systems, or that their professional backgrounds don't have much relevance to the development of a new generation of distributed client-server systems. Especially among the newer breed of MIS managers, there is a growing understanding that MIS must either become an active, enthusiastic partner in the current "downsizing" of a company's critical systems . . . or must get ready to turn out the lights.

And while the historical emphasis on centralized control in traditional glass-house-focused MIS shops dismays and worries managers who want to develop new kinds of systems for delivery on PCs and LANs, there are aspects of system control, system administration, and system maintainability to any new system. In your company, the only repository of that kind of expertise is likely to be the MIS shop.

If you're a hotshot manager with an innovative idea for a new system, by all means protect yourself, your ideas, and your people from a subtle, perhaps masterful disemboweling by the "Old MIS." But also remain open to the possibility that the people and systems of the "new MIS" may hold answers to questions you haven't even asked yet . . . answers that, if sought early, may let you turn those ghosts of DP into important allies.

Dealing with The Office PC Junkie

A lot of us like PCs. Some of us really love them. And then there are the people who *live* for them.

Those are the PC junkies, the people who've become so captivated by personal computers that they live for little else. You wonder what they did before PCs came along; clearly, these people must have been looking all their life for something, anything, to give them some identity. The NQ (Nerd Quotient) is high here: these people take first dates to user-group meetings, and tell jokes in hexadecimal.

And I'll bet you've got one sitting next to you in the office . . . right?

While we may joke about PC junkies, we should also tell the truth: we rely on them. When PC Support isn't answering the phone and *WordPerfect* throws you a curve, who're ya gonna call? PC Buste—er, the office PC Junkie. Because as weird as they are, and despite those fascinating two-hour stories they like to tell—like the one about how George Tate and Hal Lashlee had so much fun naming dBASE II, even though there had never been a dBASE I *(Get it? Hah? They called it TWO, even though it was really ONE! Isn't that marketing genius for you! Amazing! GREAT industry!)*—they know what they're talking about. And they know how to get *WordPerfect* to print boldface superscripts.

The problem dealing with people who are walking repositories of the history of the PC industry, and who actually CARE about all that stuff is, of course, getting them to shut up once they've told you about boldface superscripts. *Which reminds me of the wonderful story about how Alan Ashton—he was this professor out in Utah, see—and this other guy got together to start up Word-Perfect. In those days they called the company SSI, you know, but WordPerfect was their big product. . . .*

Unless you do shut them up, you'll still be sitting there at your desk the next morning, watching the sun come up through pupils the size of peppercorns. *You know, it's funny, there: that same company, of course, did DataPerfect, which you'd think would be a big hit too, especially because it used the same idea of a lot of function-key assignments for the basic stuff. But it's never become a big hit, has it? No—and this is really interesting, huh?—but just think what would have happened if old George Tate and Hal Lashlee had been out there in the Utah desert, y'know? They could have called it DataPerfect TWO! Hah! Now that reminds me of. . . .*

I don't want to be a hypocrite here, because I've told my share of computer-industry war stories, too. But the trick is to tap the expertise of these guys without opening the door to funny jokes about memory chips and a social history of DIP switches. Three tips:

First, visit PC junkies on *their* turf, at *their* desk, end the conversation there, and return alone to your own office. Asking a nerd to come sit down at your PC for a minute to look at something is like getting your phone number on a list of contributors to worthy causes: you'll never be lonely again.

Second, try to get very specific answers, which you make clear you need for an important piece of time-sensitive work. Ask not "How do I get boldface superscripts in *WordPerfect*?" but "I'm in the middle of this letter I've got to get out in the next ten minutes, and have this sentence that's boldfaced. No problem in *WordPerfect* on the boldfacing, but I've also got a couple of super-scripted numbers in that sentence. Can you tell me in a hundred words or less how to get those superscripts to print bold, too?"

Third, don't go out for a drink after work with a PC junkie. Do that once and you've started a long and intimate relationship. And I hope you enjoy those evenings in front of the fire, as you chuckle through those hilarious tales about Mitch Kapor and the early days with *Tiny Troll . . . which of course he wrote before he wrote 1-2-3. Well, I mean, of course HE didn't write 1-2-3, Sacks did, but . . . .*

VII

ANALYSIS
AND PERSUASION:
PC Graphics

The One-Minute Overhead

If you've never used any form of PC graphics, you're missing out on a lot of the power—the *leverage*—of a PC. I want to give you a quick taste of just how easy it can be to create high-impact graphics with the tools you already have.

Let's say you have to give a short presentation to the quarterly meeting of the executive committee tomorrow morning. You'll be reporting on the progress of the development and marketing plan for your new product, the XR-10 pollution-control device for car owners to install on their vehicles. If the company keeps the funding flowing, the product's going to be finished on time, hit the streets on time, and become a big moneymaker. And you're going to be a star.

On the other hand, if management gets cold feet and slows down the funding—or worse, kills the project—you'd better dig out the name of that corporate recruiter who called a few weeks ago.

Your presentation should be short and sweet, with enough detail to make the committee comfortable—but even more important, with enough crisp structure and such a profound sense of momentum that they're reassured your product will be a winner. So you sketch out your notes on the progress on Project XR-10 since your last report to them.

The project is on schedule. R&D has signed off on the new chemical process. Production has begun planning the line to build the XR-10. The Sales people are well into working out the distribution decisions, and have developed a tentative price schedule. Marketing has developed a promotional tie-in with another of the company's products. And the outside ad agency people should have their first presentation on concepts for a campaign ready in two weeks.

The bad news: production is worried that the new polymer needed for the XR-10's housing may be in short supply; they're trying to get leads on more reliable suppliers. The new suppliers may charge more, which will change the equation for pricing, narrowing the estimated gross margins on the line, maybe requiring a price increase. And there are going to be some messy negotiations with your counterpart in the Automotive Trim Division: production says they'll have to limit possible near-term future expansion of Trim's production capacity if they're to free up the space for your new XR-10 production line. And after earlier assuring you that you were home free with the name "XR-10," Legal is now backpedaling, saying they're worried that other trademarked names may be a bit too close for comfort; maybe you should think about changing the product's name.

That's a lot of information to convey. You can help express both the facts at hand, and what you intend to do about them, with a few simple overhead transparencies. By projecting the overheads as you speak to the group—and by handing out paper copies of those overheads first, so committee members can make notes on your verbal elaborations—you can show that you're on top of things. Of course, since by using overheads you literally have your outline for your comments right in front of you—though no one is likely to realize that—you'll be a lot more confident and secure as you deliver the news.

That's the *right* kind of corporate gamesmanship: not bluff or bluster, but concise, candid reporting. And it's what will both get you that additional funding and also mark you, to the executives in that room, as someone to keep an eye on.

Quick, Clean, Persuasive

What are the main points? How can they be grouped? That's what goes on your overheads.

Here's the first one:

XR-10: On Schedule

R&D
- Signed-off

Production
- Manufacturing planning
  underway

Sales
- Distribution plans underway
- First pricing model ready

Marketing
- Promo tie-in in place
- Ad agency presentation
  due next week

And here's the second:

```
Rough Spots

Production Capacity
  • working with Trim group
Materials
  • securing alternative
     sources for polymer
  • costs may be higher,
     changing pricing
     and/or margins
Legal
  • 'XR-10' in some doubt
     as product name
```

Add a third one, to wrap up the schedule and compare plan with actual, so far:

```
Status
```

	ORIGINAL PLAN	CURRENT ESTIMATE
Prototypes	3/15	3/12
Packaging	3/25	3/25
Sales training	3/28	3/28
Production units	5/2	5/1
Roll-out	5/25	5/25
Retail pricing	$79	$79-89
Print ads break	5/22	5/22
TV ads break	5/24	5/24

You've broken out the core of your report into concise, articulate categories. You've given a terse summary of the status of each category; in the meeting you'll elaborate briefly on each point. You've shown the positive, reassurance-building points first; then gone to the current exceptions list; then closed with a summary showing just how close to the original plan the project is at this moment.

And you've done it all on three simple overheads.

Your Turn

What do you need to produce those overheads? Forget graphics programs, desktop publishing programs, even those weird programs intended to turn out overheads. Just boot up your word processor, enter that text, format it to print in large type, and send the job to your laser printer. Load the printer with three sheets of acetate, or simply hand-feed them; then run off enough copies on paper for everyone at the meeting, plus a few extras to cover the inevitable *who-are-THEYs?* who always materialize in the back of corporate conference rooms during budget-review meetings.

If your laser printer can't provide large type for those overheads, and you don't have soft fonts available on your PC or on the network, buy a large-type font cartridge for the printer. The best and easiest to use big-type cartridge I know is Headlines in a Cartridge, from Pacific Data Systems. It has both Helvetica and Times Roman in 18, 24, 30, 36, and 48-point sizes, and italic versions of those two typefaces in most of those sizes, too. It's cheap, easy to use, and produces high-quality results.

I used Microsoft *Word*, a LaserJet II printer, and Headlines in a Cartridge type fonts to produce these three sample overheads. Total time from turning on the word processor to snatching the finished overheads from the printer tray: just under eight minutes. I used bold Helvetica type for these: 48-point for the headlines, 36-point for categories, 30-point for the individual items. Those overheads will be easily readable in the average conference room. And they look reasonably good, too: not elaborate, not design-y, just clean and crisp.

Which is good design, too, remember.

OK. Now tell me why *you* can't do those overheads just as fast as I did. Don't have a special overhead-transparency program? Neither did I: I used an ordinary word-processing package. Don't have a laser printer attached to your PC? *Someone* in the department does; borrow theirs. You *are* an up-and-comer, aren't you?

Did it take just one minute? Of course not. But what really took time was the *thinking:* how to break the report into logical sections, how to sequence items, whether there should be a summary and what form it should take. That's not computer time, though; that's time you'd spend wood-shedding anyway, pulling your presentation together. Of course, knowing that you were going to have to distill the report down to a few key points to put them on overheads may well have helped your thinking along. . . .

Gilding the Lily

You could, of course, go much farther. Maybe you should make an overhead of a timeline for the period between the meeting and the product roll-out date, and perhaps also a second timeline, showing the product's projected performance during its first 90 days on the market. A map might show nationwide distribution points; a pair of pie charts might show how much market share you expect XR-10 to take away from competitors during its first year. A bar graph of projected sales for that period could also project when the product will turn the corner and the company will begin earning a return on its investment; you might even prepare two or three different projected-revenue graphs, showing the estimated impact on volume and profitability of varying pricing strategies. . . .

But not this time.

Save the embellishments until you have a little more confidence and experience. You don't want to spend the last seven hours before that meeting working away at the computer, trying to get things right. You want some quiet time to think about what you're going to say. And too *many* visuals are even worse than too few or none; rather than impressing your audience you just confuse them.

Keep it simple. Use one-minute overheads. Just a few of them. And knock 'em dead.

It's MY Y-Axis, Sir!

One of the more troubling complaints I hear about business graphs is the suggestion that their creators have fiddled with the vertical axis, or *Y-axis*, of graphs. I find these remarks frustrating not because I doubt the potential for graphs to lie—in fact, graphs can be very effective lies—but because more often than not, I find myself wishing someone *had* fiddled with a graph's vertical axis.

The complaint, usually, is predicated on the notion that the vertical scaling was adjusted in an effort to distort the true meaning of the data. Certainly that's possible, and it's not hard to do. If you want to make the argument that the Dow Jones Industrials average is going through wild gyrations as it fluctuates between 2,650 and 2,750, just construct a line graph of daily closing prices for the period of that fluctuation, with the vertical axis scaled from 2,600 to 2,800. The huge daily zigzags up and down will make it look as if the economy is about to collapse. Rescale that Y-axis from 0 to 3,000, though, and you'll get almost a flat line for the daily trading range, leading to the opposite conclusion: a highly stable market.

So we should begin by accepting the idea that graphs can as easily distort information as they can present it accurately and in context.

But my experience, in hundreds and hundreds of hours spent in corporate conference rooms, looking at thousands of PC-generated graphs, has been that rather than trying to deceive by changing axis scaling, presenters much more often fail to use the useful tool of rescaling the vertical axis to present their information and their arguments in ways that make the data more meaningful and thus more understandable.

There are three basic kinds of adjustments to the scaling of the vertical axis in graphs that can be useful in preparing business presentations: using a limited-range scale; using a logarithmic scale; and using a broken scale. Here's a checklist to help you decide when to use each.

- **Limit the range of values.** If the values you're examining in a graph vary widely, but only within a relatively narrow part of the range from zero to the largest value you want to show—and especially when that zero-to-maximum-value range is very wide—consider plotting your values over just a limited part of that range. The securities-price fluctuation example above is a good illustration of this principle.

  Other examples: quarter-to-quarter variations in corporate earnings per share (say, between $3.20 and $3.45); daily maximum-temperature variations during summer between 92°–98°; audience-share ratings for a television network that vary over the course of a 39-week season from 15.7% to 16.3%.

  In each case, your audience would be better served if you limited the range of the vertical scale of a graph of those values. The quarterly EPS graph might use a selective vertical scale from $3–$4, for example; the daily highs chart might range between 70°–100°; the audience-share graph could range from 10% to 20%.

  In every case, the person using the graphics would have an obligation to note that limited scale—verbally, in a stand-up presentation with the graphs shown as slides, and by clearly marking the vertical axis itself in printed handouts of the graphs, perhaps also adding a lower left-hand-corner note alerting readers to the scaling selectivity. And certainly anyone using a selective-scale approach is always open to complaints of data distortion.

  But consider the alternatives. Scaling the EPS chart from zero to, say, $10 would be meaningless and confusing: was the presenter suggesting a $10 per share quarterly earnings goal? Scaling daily temperatures between, say, 0° and 100° would be ludicrous: who expects references to subfreezing temperatures in a summer-highs analysis? And plotting audience-share on a 0% to 100% scale would trivialize the substantial impact on a network's revenues of even tenth-of-a-point variations.

  Even worse, in each case the resulting almost flat-line graph would make the fluctuations seem much smaller than they really are. In other words, they would distort the *meaning* of the data.

- **Use a logarithmic vertical scale.** Nearly all of the major PC business-graphics software packages allow the user to choose a logarithmic scale. Those scarred by memories of using log tables in high school math may be scared away from that option, and many people simply don't understand what a logarithmic scale is. But log-scaling is wonderful when you have very low values mixed in with very high values. And PC graphing software that offers logarithmic scaling handles the conversion from linear to log scale automatically.

In scientific research, for example, it's not uncommon to find values clustered at the very low and very high ends of a range, with almost no middle values. A researcher studying airborne pollen distribution might find the various kinds of pollen detected in one area present in the following parts-per-million concentrations: 6, 2, 9, 4, 1,689, 2,213, and 1,945. Plot those on a standard scale and the low values are going to virtually disappear into a kind of messy "noise" at the bottom of the scale. But go to logarithmic scaling, which in effect opens up the low end of the scale without moving the high-end values into the stratosphere, and they'll be highly visible.

Logarithmic vertical scaling is more appropriate when the audience for a graph can be expected to have some scientific, technical, or mathematical background; unless you're accustomed to working with log scales, they can be confusing. But for audiences familiar with log displays, and with data points clustered around very low values and much higher values, log scaling can be invaluable.

- **Use a broken scale.**   When one or two values in a chart are wildly out of line with the majority of values shown, it can be a great help to use a so-called "broken" scale. In graphs of this sort, the vertical bars representing the out-of-range values are visually cracked, or broken, to show that the scaling of those bars is not the same as for the others in the graph. Then those bars (and, usually, *only* those bars) are labeled with their absolute values, so the reader can see how they relate to the other values shown.

Let's say, for example, that you're plotting a vertical-bar graph of the length of time each of a group of PCs takes to complete a complex calculation. For the seven PCs, the times are 2.3, 4.2, 3.6, 1.9, 2.8, 3.1 and 64 seconds. If you simply feed those numbers into a PC graphics program, it's going to scale the vertical axis from zero to 75 or so, in order to accommodate that one high value. And in the process, those much more important low values are going to disappear into mush at the bottom of the graph.

Clearly the 64-second time is an aberration; that PC is broken, or has a fundamental flaw in its design. There was a good reason for assembling this group of machines (we presume), so you don't want to simply throw that one out; yet you don't want a graphical representation of its anomalous performance to obscure the more relevant but much smaller values from the other machines.

The answer: scale the vertical axis of the chart from zero to 5 seconds, then break the vertical bar for the 64-second machine, and add a label to the top of that bar with its absolute value (for example, *68 sec.*)

It's been hard to find PC graphics programs with the sophistication to handle that kind of treatment, but graphics-software publishers are listening;

before long you can expect the "break, truncate, and label" option to be a standard menu choice in high-end packages.

Boardroom Machiavellis will note that instead of using this kind of intelligent adjustment of the vertical axis to present information in a more accurate context, that distortion provided by full linear axis-scaling can also be used to make a point—in other words, using the theoretical neutrality of a linear axis to effectively distort data, in the name of winning an argument.

I leave the propriety of that kind of gamesmanship to your good judgment.

❧

Less *Is* More:
Fewer Fonts

Nice, all those fancy type fonts you have these days in your printer. Or stored as soft fonts on your PC's hard disk. So of course you're tempted to use a lot of them in your work. A lot of them in *all* of your work. With the result that your graphics look like something pasted up by a kid in kindergarten from letters and numbers clipped from the morning paper.

One of the keys to effective graphics is keeping down the visual clutter, the "background noise" that distracts us from the message the graphic is supposed to convey. There are many forms of graphical clutter, from needless background grids in bar graphs to little arrows and notes and other annotation spilled all over the image. But probably the most egregious example of visual clutter is the use of too many typefaces in a graphic.

"Too many" typefaces, of course, is in the eye of the beholder. But when you use a sans serif headline on a graph, a serif typeface for the subheadline, a different serif typeface for the labels on the X-axis, yet another sans serif face on the Y-axis legend . . . I think we can safely assume you've gone too far. Unfortunately, the proliferation of readily available typeset-look typefaces for PCs today encourages that kind of overkill. Especially for those with PostScript printers, which typically have 35 or more fonts built into them, it's easy to get drawn into wretched excesses.

Avoid that temptation towards typographic overkill. If you're new to producing PC graphics, adopt one typeface—say, Helvetica, perhaps in light, standard, bold, and extrabold weights—and stick with that one typeface, or typeface *family*, for your graphics. Graphics professionals call that kind of design "monotypographical harmony"; the word *harmony* is the key.

Using different-weight typefaces from one type family can produce stunning results. Indeed, I'm convinced Apple and Adobe would have served us better when they first crafted that *de facto* standard for multifont PostScript printers if, instead of throwing in so many different typefaces, they had given us more weights and variety from a couple of the typeface families in that set. For example, such unattractive faces as Bookman and New Century Schoolbook, which are found in virtually all of those printers, could have been replaced with Helvetica Black (a very heavy variation) and Helvetica Light (a thin, elegant ultra light-weight version). With these added to the regular and bold weights of Helvetica already present in the printer—and with italic versions available in each weight—we'd have a much richer palette of typefaces, with correspondingly better results. (Of course, you can create that extended range of weights yourself for those PostScript printers, by augmenting the built-in fonts.)

If you're a little timid about using type—if this is new to you, but you want to give it a try—this notion of using a variety of weights, instead of a variety of typefaces, is a particularly good one, because it forms a safety net under your first efforts.

In a typical vertical-bars graph, for example, you might use Helvetica Black for the headline, standard-weight Helvetica italic for the subhead, and Helvetica Light for the axis and value labels. Add standard-weight Helvetica "Roman" (that is, nonitalic) type for the legend identifying the source of the data, and you've got an extremely attractive basic slide.

Or for "word charts" used as overhead transparencies, use Helvetica Black italic for the headline, and Helvetica Bold in both Roman and italic forms for the text, for a clean, professional-looking chart.

In the hands of those without at least some training in graphic design, mixing typefaces is likely to produce a less attractive, less *effective* graph without the simplicity, directness, and power of a monotypographic look. Don't worry that your slides will be too plain, or too primitive. Many Fortune 500 companies have graphics standards that *require* the use of just one typeface in their internal business graphics . . . even when those graphics are produced by full-time design professionals who presumably know what they're doing. (FYI, more often than not, that typeface is Helvetica.) So you'll be in very good company, indeed.

The famous epigram usually attributed to Mies van der Rohe but actually first written by Andrea Del Sarto in 1855, is exactly right: Less is more.

Three Powerful But Overlooked Graphs

Most of the PC graphics you see are pretty much the same. Line graphs, bar graphs, pie charts (ever wonder why no one calls them pie *graphs*?) are The Big Three of PC graphics. Toss in all-text "word charts" and you've probably covered in excess of 90 percent of the business graphs produced on PCs. If you get really exotic—hi-lo graphs of stock-price movement, scatter-plots, the occasional area graph—then you've probably covered 99 percent of the graphs in use.

That's not a bad range of options; certainly you can display most kinds of business data in one or another of those forms. But most of us never venture beyond The Big Three simply because our "graphing vocabulary" is so limited: we haven't any direct experience with other graphical representations of quantitative information.

I want to recommend three special business graphs I find immensely useful—but that fall outside that Big Three. Not all of them can be produced by every PC graphics package, but all of them can be produced on PCs . . . and I think you can reasonably expect these more sophisticated kinds of graphs to appear in all of the mainstream PC packages before long.

These three little-known gems are stacked 100 percent bar graphs, bar-in-pie graphs, and my all-time favorite secret weapon in PC graphics: the bubble chart.

The 100 Percent Solution

While there's nothing unusual about vertical or horizontal bar graphs (sometimes also called vertical or horizontal column graphs, when the bars are given drop shadows for a 3-D effect), "stacked bars" are something else.

Normally, of course, each bar in a bar graph represents the whole of something, and the cluster of bars represents a group of wholes. You might, for example, prepare a vertical bar graph showing each regional office's gross sales for the last fiscal year. Each bar would represent the sales of each office; the group of bars, taken together, all the sales offices.

But what about a look at the sales *within* each regional office, by product line? Changing to stacked bars would let you represent not only the total sales for each office by the height of the bars; you could also show the relative percentage of sales by product line within each region by dividing each vertical bar into several slices. Thus a stacked-bars graph not only shows the absolute performance of each office, and the relative performance of every office against every other office; it also shows the breakdown of sales by product line within each office. That's a way of getting "3-D information" into a single easy-to-produce, easy-to-understand graphic.

But let's take the notion of stacked bars further. Say you want to look at the relative weekly audience shares of each of four imaginary national television networks in the U.S., for four consecutive weeks. Total audience size would fluctuate during those weeks, of course, but as a programmer for one of those networks, you're not interested in total audience size, only how you did against the other guys. That's a common form of business analysis: What percentage of the market do we have, and what percentage does each of our competitors have? And most important of all, how did those percentages change over time?

That's when you need 100 percent stacked-bar graphs. The bars are of constant height all across the graph, because each bar represents 100 percent of the total television-viewing audience for each week. Within each bar, the height of each section represents each network's market share. It's easy to tell in a quick look how each network did in each week against its competition. And it's easy to sweep your eyes across the graph, and note—again, because the height of the bars does not vary—the trend: who's doing better, and at whose expense.

Though you can get more information on the page by varying the height of each bar, to represent fluctuations in total viewership, that additional information is often less useful than the relative-movement information that pops out of a 100 percent-size-bars graph.

This is a remarkably information-rich type of graphic, yet it still looks good and is easy to read. We could get the same market-share data for any one week, of course, with a pie chart; but to get the third dimension—the change over time—with pie charts, we'd have to have four side-by-side pies, which would get awfully confusing. And it would be a lot harder to read the changes from pie to pie in that form, whereas in a multiple-bar 100 percent-stacked-bars

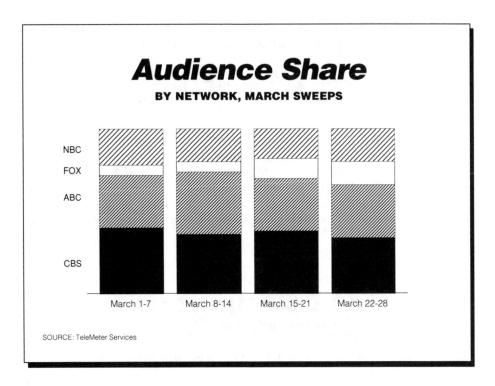

graph, the eye can easily and naturally trace horizontal lines across the graph, making it easy to spot week-to-week changes.

Hidden Data Revealed

I love that opportunity to get a third dimension of data, or a second or third layer of information, into a graph that remains easy to construct and easy to figure out. Another favorite of mine, which offers that same kind of multilevel detail-within-detail information, is the bar-within-a-pie graph.

Pie charts are very good at showing percentages of a whole, but of course they don't provide any information about the details within a wedge of the pie. It's possible to "explode" a pie wedge by moving it out from the main circle, then subdividing that wedge into skinny colored or patterned wedges, but those thin wedges can be very difficult to read. And quite understandably, people often don't realize that the exploded wedge is supposed to be showing another level of detail: they think those skinny slices are simply thin wedges of the same kind and level of detail shown in the whole pie.

Rather than exploding a slice of a pie to get at the details of that part of the whole, I prefer to append a small vertical bar graph to that wedge of the pie.

That way both the relative weight of the slice of the pie and also the relationship between that wedge and its underlying detail become clear.

Readers with a good eye and quick mind will realize that this is really a variation on the 100 percent-stacked-bars idea. I'm interested in both cases in showing both the relative shares of a whole, and the absolute shares within a part of the whole.

Let's say we want to plot the percentages of the customer base of XYZ Computers by kind of buyer. Separate pie wedges might be drawn for individual buyers, corporate customers, government agencies, and educational institutions. But within the government-agencies segment, I also want to show the breakdown by sales to federal, state, and local-agency customers. This is an ideal situation for the bar-within-a-pie form. The resulting graphic is self-explanatory:

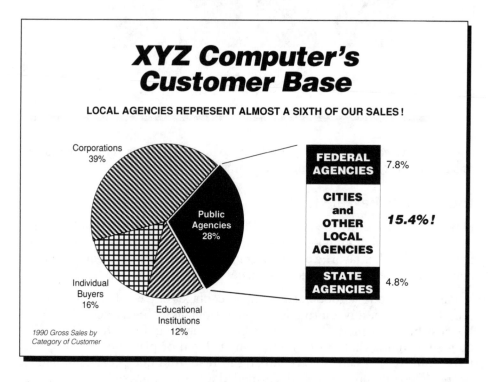

You may be tempted to take this a step further, by breaking separate little vertical bar graphs out of two or three pie wedges. Resist the temptation; with more than one bar, the graphic becomes too cluttered, and both legibility and readers' comprehension of its meaning start to plummet.

The Mysterious Bubble Chart

Actually, what I find most mysterious about bubble charts is why more PC graphics programs can't produce them. The only package I know of that can handle them is Lotus's *Graphwriter II.* That's unfortunate, because once you've seen bubble charts, you immediately start finding perfect applications for them. Maybe we should start a letter-writing campaign. . . .

Bubble charts are sensationally useful, because they show relative volumes, or weights, as well as two-axis positional data. That's a mouthful, but easy to understand when you see a bubble chart.

Say you want to construct a graph showing the absolute and relative prices and absolute and relative sophistication of a group of products in a market, and also their respective market shares. That would be extremely difficult to accomplish with any other "flat" graphic. With a bubble chart it's easy. The scatter-plot aspect of a bubble chart handles the distribution of each product on the X axis (for price) and Y axis (for sophistication); the size of the bubble for each product represents its market share:

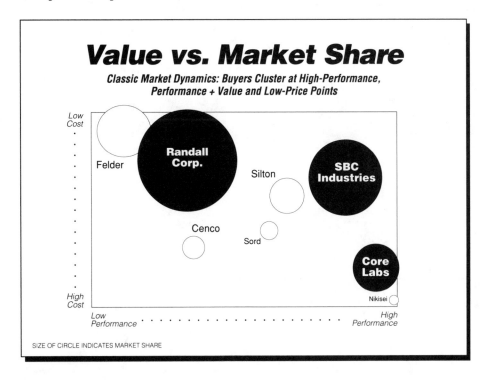

In my experience, it's always a good idea to take a few seconds to explain how bubble charts work, the first time you show one to a group. Though people catch on to them quickly, and many of the people in a group will understand how to read them without any explanation, there are usually a few for whom the explanation is necessary.

But fair warning: once you begin using bubble charts, you can expect people to start sidling up to you after your presentations to tell you how wonderful those charts are, and asking how you *ever* came up with them? It's a good feeling, and rewarding to know that they're so impressed. But it's a nice little test of your character, too: Will you let these people go away believing you've just invented a new kind of graph? Or will you gracefully accept the praise but 'fess up that bubble charts have been around for a long time . . . ?

❧

Where Did the Numbers Come From?

How often have you looked at a graphic on a printed page, or at a chart someone was projecting, and wondered just where those numbers came from?

Were this year's revenue numbers actuals or projected? Was that annual-inflation modifier guessed at, or did it come from a government agency? *Which* government agency? Were those results for the last three quarters audited, or in-house numbers not yet blessed by the accountants? Did those Middle East oil production figures come from OPEC, or from last week's *Time* magazine?

It's so simple to establish as a standard component of a graph a "SOURCE:" credit in the lower left-hand corner of the visual. And if there's any question about how recent numbers are, add the date, too.

SOURCE: U.S. Commerce Dept. Estimates, 1990, or *SOURCE: Q1, Q2 Audited Results; Q3, Q4 Projected* annotations can make audiences feel so much more confident that your numbers are correct, up to date, and meaningful—and can avoid contentious questions.

A simple rule: If it's quantified, it's got to be attributed.

❦

Don't Narrate Your Slides . . . And Other Tips For Effective Presentations

One of the most common gaffes committed by speakers using 35mm slides—whether produced with the help of a computer or not—is to fail to *speak to the audience.*

Instead, they turn sideways or look over their shoulder, stare at the screen, and read the slide to the audience. Then they pause while they change to the next slide, and start reading to you again. Then they . . . I know: it's goofy. But recall how many times you've endured a slide presentation in which Mr. Smooth simply *read you his slides.* Did he think you couldn't see them?

The problem, usually, is that somewhere during the preparation of the presentation, Mr. Smooth got confused about just why he was using slides. Slides exist to underscore the high points of presentation, to provide a kind of background emphasis for the speaker as he addresses his audience. Slides are only support, just means to an end—the effective presentation—but not the presentation itself.

But when they have more than three or four slides, many speakers begin speaking to the screen, constantly looking back to see what's there and reading the lines from the slide to the audience.

It's painful to watch.

I use slides often—and see others use them even more often—and I've become convinced the best way to use slides is to NEVER look at the screen, but only at the audience. And I never wait for a slide change, but instead discreetly change slides while I'm talking and looking at the audience. If I can hit the ADVANCE button on the remote control when I'm right in the middle of a phrase, so much the better: I want those slides coming up behind me, or off to my side, as if by magic. I want the audience's attention focused on what I have to say, not on a slide show.

When I teach this technique to executives, they often say that the reason they keep looking at the screen is that they're deathly afraid of the wrong slide coming up as they speak, which they'd find terribly embarrassing. I understand that fear; anyone who's worked with audio-visual presentations knows the chance of things going wrong—wrong slide, wrong tray, wrong sequence, upside-down and backwards slides—is always greater than we'd like. But that's part of the game: *If you're afraid to play, don't use slides.*

The trick I use, and teach others, is a simple one. I carry a small, round makeup mirror with me, and before I speak—usually during the rehearsal, or at least during the break just before my talk—I mount it on the podium, using its wire-frame base. I put the mirror where the audience can't see it, but I can; and where, by glancing down as if at my notes, I can see a reflection of at least part of the screen behind me.

The image is reversed, of course, since I'm in effect looking over my shoulder via the mirror. But I know my slides well enough—and you should, too—that I don't need to see every word on them to know what's up there. A quick glance at the mirror reassures me that the right slide is on-screen. And since I can't see the whole screen, and refuse to look at the screen during the presentation, I'm never tempted to read the slides to the audience, nor to pace my presentation to the rhythm of slide changes.

Sneaky Tricks for the Podium

A few more speaker's tricks: Buy a small travel clock, with a white face and large, legible numbers and hands, and stick it in your attache case when you're going off to deliver a speech. Mount it behind the front lip of the podium, out of sight of the audience but easily visible to you. (I carry a tiny roll of duct tape, so I can make sure both the clock and the mirror are really stuck in place, and won't come crashing down on my feet as I speak.)

With that clock always in easy view, you won't have to worry about spotting your host in the back row of the audience for a "time to quit" signal, or looking around the room for a clock, or sneaking glances at your wristwatch. But you *will* be in command of your time slot, confident that you're on schedule (or early or late), that you're leaving enough time for Q&A afterwards, that you'll be able to wrap up right on time. Meeting planners will love you: no one *ever* ends a speech on time, which is why schedules at meetings and conferences slip further and further behind during the day.

You might also consider buying and carrying with you your own radio-controlled remote control for slide projectors. With a radio system you're completely free of the entangling wires of most remote-slide-advance units. You simply hold a little device about the size of a garage-door opener—the transmitter—in your hand as you speak, and (invisibly to the audience) push a button on it to change slides. A second unit mounted on the projector—the receiver—plugs into the projector's remote-control jack, and does the actual work of advancing slides. Since virtually all projectors use the Kodak-standard remote-control jack, you don't have to worry about carrying a set of oddball cords and adapter plugs.

Good quality radio remotes cost less than $200, and can help make you a presentations pro, with a reputation among your audiences for confidence and style at the podium.

Using a clip-on (or lavalier) wireless mike system can help your reputation—and your self-confidence—a lot, too. A tiny lapel mike clips to your tie or collar; a thin wire runs from it to a transmitter about the size of a cigarette pack, which is clipped to your belt, or hidden under your jacket. Again, a receiver located at the sound board or plugged directly into the room's PA system picks up the signal.

I love wireless mikes, because they let me wander away from the podium. One of the most effective techniques a presenter can use is to stay behind the podium for the first third to one-half of a presentation, then at just the right dramatic moment, step away from that podium—across stage, or down towards the audience. If you're wearing a wireless mike, you can move anywhere, in any direction—even out into the audience, *a la* Phil Donahue—without worrying about mike cords, sound drop-outs or screeching audio feedback.

Finally, if you're tempted to do some pointing at the details of a slide or two—if I can't persuade you to act as if that screen isn't there, and never look at it at all—consider buying or renting a small laser pointer. Early units were big, heavy, and clumsy; today you can buy a compact, hand-held, battery-powered laser pointer for $300–$500. But don't use it constantly; pointers of any sort are most effective when they're used sparingly, and certainly not on every slide or to underscore every point.

The test: Could your audience make just as much sense of a slide if you weren't pointing? If so, don't use the pointer on that one.

All this may seem to have little to do with PCs. But if you're going to consider producing slides on your PC, then it's important to know how to make the most of them, too—in other words, how to make effective presentations.

Which surely starts with *not* narrating your slides. . . .

☙

LCD Projection Plates:
The Poor Man's
Video Projector

So-called "projection plates"—those odd, neither-fish-nor-fowl devices that sit atop an overhead projector and throw onto a big screen images generated by your PC—can be incredibly useful tools. But they've been surprisingly slow to catch on. The earliest projection plates had real problems: projected images would turn dark; individual pixels in the LCDs would burn out and stay dark; the units' electronics would overheat; and sometimes the translation from the PC's color image to the LCD plate's monochrome image was very poor, resulting in murky projected images.

But projection plates have improved rapidly. If you took a look early on but didn't like what you saw, it's time for a second look.

I find projection plates among the most powerful PC presentation tools. The problem, I'm convinced, is that too many people who looked at them brought the wrong set of expectations to them. Among the complaints I think reflect a fundamental misunderstanding of the role of projection plates:

- **They don't show VGA (or EGA, or CGA) colors.** Right. They're either monochrome devices, or false-color devices. The latter substitute their own very limited palette of colors—usually shades of orange and purple—for the gorgeous, vivid colors you see on a PC's video display. So what? Color LCD plates are available, but at prices that start around five grand. For a lot less than five grand I can rent a color video projector when I want true-color images. Heck, I can *buy* some of the smaller portable color video projectors for that price.

But ninety-nine percent of the time I don't need color for what I do with LCD plates, any more than I need color overheads ninety-nine percent of the time I use *them.* View LCD projection plates as monochrome (or false-color) systems and you'll love them. Compare them to the image on that 27-inch Sony in your living room and you'll be disappointed.

- **They're too low-resolution.** For what? I was initially disappointed with my first LCD plate, because it used CGA-level resolution. I got those big, blocky letters on the projection screen, and thought that was something of a throwback. Then I moved up to an EGA-level projection plate. Wow! And then I discovered that the skinnier if sharper letters of an EGA display (and of a VGA display, for that matter) are actually *less* effective for small-group projection than those wonderfully big, blocky, *legible* characters of CGA resolution!

  The moral: Stay with CGA. It works better for your audience.

  Remember, too, that since we usually drive these projection plates from a portable PC, your PC has to be able to support those higher resolution levels. Some do, but many still deliver only a CGA-level-resolution image through their external-monitor jacks.

- **It's a nuisance to use a projection plate when your PC doesn't simultaneously show the same image on its own built-in screen.** Right. With portable PCs, which turn off their own displays when you attach something to their external-video connectors, you'll have to sit oddly screwed-around in your chair, looking one way at the screen, then another at your PC . . . and then maybe in a third direction, at your audience. But this isn't the projection plate's problem; it's your *PC's* problem. And it would work exactly the same way if you were feeding that video signal to a $100,000 color video projector. So stop complaining about projection plates and write your PC manufacturer to ask why they didn't provide a full-time live display in the PC.

If you can get past that kind of nonsense, I suspect you'll find projection plates useful tools for a lot of your presentations. I find corporate people use them primarily for two purposes: presentations that involve direct manipulation of computer data on-screen during the talk; and canned presentations, where for one reason or another the presenter prefers not to use slides or overheads.

Encouraging More Informal Presentations

An example of the first category is software training. If the PC support staff is helping your coworkers learn a new version of a software program already in wide use at the company, they probably don't need to hold formal classes in

PC-equipped classrooms. If most of these people already know how to use the program's basics, the job is to present to them the delta: the differences in the new version. So simply running the new version of the program, and showing not only the results achieved by using its new features but also a step-by-step walk-through of how to get those results, can be a very effective form of training.

In some companies, this is seen as a classic training classroom/video projector job. If you get hooked on using a video projector, you'll probably take that perspective, too, since it's so effective to be able to project the work you're doing on your PC on a large screen in front of others. But since few video projectors are portable—and once you've installed one of those big ceiling-mounted GE or Electrohome video projectors in a training room, and finally gotten the screen alignment right, you're not *about* to move it again—that addiction to big-screen projection could lead you to adopt a "training center" attitude. In other words, even though teaching people how to use this new upgrade isn't really a training-classroom job, those PC-support people are going to be inclined to handle it that way, scheduling a series of classes in the training center.

But what if, instead, they made this process a lot more relaxed and informal, and in consultation with the managers (or high-profile PC users) in each department set up classes in those departments, not on the support department's turf? They could then use conference rooms in each area. They could do several smaller (and thus probably shorter) classes. It would be a lot more convenient for those coming to these sessions, and it would take a lot less of their time than if they had to trek over to your PC-training room. Which means they'd get a much better turnout.

It's not necessary to give up the advantages of video projection to run these "distributed classes"; just use an LCD projection plate, a portable PC, and an overhead projector. Those audiences will never miss the sharper type and pretty colors of the video projector. But they *will* appreciate the courtesy and convenience of popping into a quick demonstration of the upgrade's new features, right in their own department.

The Projected Desktop

Of course, on-location training sessions are hardly the only uses for projection plates. The second major category of presentations I see on them are sometimes described as "desktop presentations," or "PC slide shows." Sometimes these are nothing more than a series of text screens (which always makes me wonder why the presenter didn't just print the material as a series of overhead transparencies). But sometimes they use animated sequences, or such effects as rapid dissolves from one image to another or split-screen displays, which really do use the power of the computer.

The best of these projected "slide-show" presentations often jump out of the canned sequence to a short "live" segment consisting of real-time data manipulation—for example, a quick flip to a *1-2-3* worksheet, with some real-time analysis for the audience of the financial impact of the options the presenter is discussing.

Remember, too, that one advantage of preparing a presentation for delivery on a projection plate controlled by your PC is that you can quickly change the presentation—changing the order of the visuals, or assembling different subsets of images from a large "library"—to suit an audience. You could to this with a slide show or overheads, too, of course. But rebuilding a slide show is a nuisance at best, a disaster when you start getting slides in the tray upside-down and backwards. And anyone who's worked with overheads for long knows how easy it is to get them out of sequence; most of us write little numbers in the upper right-hand corner of overheads, out of the projection area, so we can keep them in sequence. Fiddle with that sequence, and those once-useful numbers get *very* confusing.

You can deal effectively with many questions by preparing extra graphics in advance that address specifically the Q&A points you think you may encounter. Anticipate those key questions; construct appropriate, data-filled "slides" to respond to or counter them; and store those slides on your PC's hard disk. Number each, and keep a little cheat-sheet of those key-numbers in front of you as you make the presentation, so you'll be able to find the right Q&A-response image immediately when you need it. The second or third time you respond in part to a question with a detailed, obviously thought-out-in-advance graphic, your audience is going to decide you have this down cold: you've thought through all the objections and alternatives, and your conclusions must be right.

(But don't fall into the trap of answering every question and quibble by saying "I've got a slide here that answers that," then flipping to that slide. Questioners don't want to be referred to the computer for answers in a live presentation; they want to hear what *you* think. Use these visuals as support for your arguments, not as the arguments themselves, unless you want to antagonize, rather than reassure, your audience.)

Putting LCD Plates to Work

Though I see LCD plates primarily as personal tools—if you make very many presentations as part of your job, you can easily justify buying one—scattering a few around your company as shared tools can subtly encourage your colleagues to increase the effectiveness of their presentations, too.

If your conference room doesn't have a video projector, consider equipping it with a far less expensive, far more reliable LCD projection plate. If, as I suspect, you already have slide projection and overhead projection options available there, that moves "computer projection" into its proper perspective as just another option for presenters. (It also encourages presenters to choose the most appropriate medium, rather than reflexively going for computer-image projection. If all they're doing is in effect showing you a few static over-heads, they're going to look pretty dumb if they show you the data on the LCD projection-plate system. They'll only do it once; no one will have to say a thing.)

Projection plates are a particular delight when you have to haul a presentation around the company—or around the country. If the advantages of computer projection are important to you, don't forsake them when you're making that presentation away from your home turf; and don't go through the hassle of making sure there's a PC and a video projector at each location, or renting one or both. (Or worrying about whether the conference-room PCs that run the systems will have the right size floppy-disk drives; and whether they have enough memory; and whether your application or "slideshow" presentation software is loaded on them; and whether you'll have time to copy your data onto the hard disk of that machine; and . . .)

Instead, just bring a hard-disk-equipped lap-portable PC and an LCD projection plate as you travel. Load the software and files you need onto that PC and you'll be able to rehearse your presentation to your heart's content, *using the same equipment you'll be using for each presentation,* right in your own office. Just ask for an overhead projector and screen at each location—they'll already have them, or be able to rent them easily—and you're set.

Intelligent use of LCD projection plates can make you a more effective presenter. They're not always the right answer—and using one when it isn't appropriate can make you look foolish—but once you've added one to your personal arsenal of PC tools, you'll be amazed at how much mileage you get out of the device.

&

Repetitive Graphics
Made Easy

One of the satisfying and yet also often frustrating aspects of working with PCs is that with something over 20,000 programs now available for MS-DOS machines, there's specialized software for almost every need. My shelves of weird-but-wonderful PC programs include a hog-feeding-management program and a program that uses measurements made with sonograms to predict the sex of a baby long before it's born. Nothing about those programs seems weird to hog farmers or perinatal specialists, of course . . . and that's just the point.

I always enjoy finding oddball programs that do things the clients in my consulting practice tell me they need done, but that cannot be accomplished by any program they've been able to find. Sometimes, I don't find a special program for a job; I just unearth a little-known feature buried away somewhere deep in the menus of a program designed for more general tasks.

That happened a couple of years ago, when the secretary to the CFO at a steel distributor in the upper Midwest asked me for help. She had to prepare the same set of nine complicated graphs over and over again, every week, and was getting tired of the drudgery.

Graphical Drudgery

Her boss had developed a series of cross-linked *1-2-3* worksheets that calculated financial ratios he thought were especially relevant to the steelyard business. He had designed nine pie and bar charts that displayed those results graphically, and that he handed out at the management committee meeting every Tuesday morning. The CFO didn't intend to update those spreadsheets every week *himself,* of course, let alone spend the time and effort required to rebuild the graphs. He handed that off to his secretary, who overcame her initial timidity about *1-2-3* and soon became proficient at entering the data, then going back and reconstructing "those darned graphs."

It took her most of Monday every week to turn out the graphs. Her boss wondered how it could take so long; after all, *he'd* already done all the hard work, hadn't he, when he initially set up those worksheets and graphs?

I was spending a couple of days at the company, looking over their plans to install an inventory-tracking system, when the secretary called me aside and asked if I could I find her a program that could automate the production of that same set of graphs—using the new numbers every week, of course. The inventory system turned out to be a bear to construct, and took us forever, but the answer to *her* question was easy: "Get a copy of *Graphwriter II.*"

Because it turned out that while she thought she was the only one in the world stuck with that dumb, repetitive job, the need to produce a fixed set of graphics at regular intervals is fairly common. I've heard her plea often. Lotus's graphics-software team heard it too, not long after it bought *Graphwriter* (and *Freelance*) from the company that developed them. Lo and behold, an autocharting feature turned up in the next release of the package.

Though I like *Graphwriter* for its ability to produce bubble charts (see *Three Powerful But Overlooked Graphs,* in this section) and a few other uncommon graph-types, the program is hardly a state-of-the-art PC graphics package. Yet intelligent product design, such as including bubble graphs and building in auto-charting, has kept *Graphwriter* alive in the face of stiff competition from more sophisticated programs. (Which poses an interesting question: Is sophistication in PC software a matter of putting in all the newest features, running under a glitzy graphical interface . . . or is real sophistication a matter of meeting even your customers' smallest and oddest needs?)

Autocharting

Graphwriter II's automatic-charts feature relies on the program's tight links to *1-2-3* worksheets, and its fill-in-the-blanks approach to chart building. One way in which *Graphwriter* is a little behind the times in the PC world is that forms-based chart-creation style. Unlike newer graphics programs, which allow users to build graphs interactively, *Graphwriter II* asks you to first fill out a form onscreen specifying the chart type and style, and optionally, to provide the information the program needs to link up to a specified *1-2-3* worksheet and get the values for the graphs. It then produces the graph, which can only be changed by calling up the form once again.

(To underscore the program's goofy attachment to the way we used to do things when the mainframe was king, the *Graphwriter II* package even includes a pad of preprinted chart-specification forms on paper, so The Boss can scribble down instructions to his minions on how he wants his charts to look; then they can, *harrumph*, execute those instructions at their PCs. That's exactly how computer-generated graphics were once produced—in an era that at most companies is now, happily, only a dim memory.)

To use *Graphwriter II*'s autocharting feature, you simply fill out an electronic form on-screen for each individual chart. Those individual graph's filenames are then entered into a master Autochart File List, which for our purposes we'll save as TUESMEET.

When you're ready to produce each batch of charts, you first load *1-2-3*, enter the new numbers in the worksheets associated with those charts, and save them (under the same filenames you used for the original worksheets). Then change to your *Graphwriter II* directory and type at the DOS command line a simple instruction:

AUTOCHT TUESMEET

Graphwriter II will automatically load each chart in the order listed on your Autochart File List, go out to the updated *1-2-3* worksheet file, get the new data, redraw the chart—then send it to your printer (or plotter, or other output device). All *Graphwriter*-supported output devices can handle Autochart output, though of course they'll need automatic sheet feeding (or some patient hand-feeding) for successive pages, which eliminates most pen plotters.

All in all, it's a slick feature, unduplicated in any other PC graphics package. And, unfortunately, it's buried away in a little-known—if nonetheless enormously useful—program.

The moral: No matter what you want your PC to do, someone somewhere has probably written a program that can do exactly that. Just keep looking. . . .

❧

Quick! Grab that Screen!

It's sometimes desirable to capture, write to disk and then later print a screen image from one of your programs. You might, for example, be putting together a teaching guide to help new users of the program get up to speed with it quickly. Or you might simply be preparing a one- or two-page handout to show someone else how to perform some specific task within the program—showing an aide or temp how to fill in a database entry screen, for example.

In the days of all-text PC displays, that was fairly easy. The problems of getting an accurate representation of how a text screen really looks onto paper, especially when that screen display uses the oddball IBM PC Extended Character Set, are dealt with in *Getting Those Odd PC Characters from LaserJets*, in the **Printer Madness** section of this book. But text-only displays are becoming increasingly rare in the PC world: today the chances are good that the programs you work with use graphics displays. Which means ordinary "screen dumps" of text screens often won't be much help, IBM character-set or no.

When you need to print an accurate representation of a screen, you need a special class of PC graphics program called a "screen grabber." These packages pop up over the application you're using and allow you to set a large number of parameters. Then they disappear, freeze the screen, capture and write to disk a digital snapshot of that screen. When they're through, they more or less gracefully return control of your PC to your program.

There are two good commercial screen-grabbing packages for PCs running under DOS (or DOS plus Microsoft *Windows,* which presents its own special set of problems): *Hotshot Graphics,* from SymSoft, and *Pizazz Plus,* from Application Technologies, Inc. I've used both, and prefer *Hotshot Graphics.* It has a few convenient features lacking in *Pizazz Plus*—for example, the ability to draw a hairline box around the captured graphic, so that when you print it, it's separated from surrounding text, for greater legibility and a more polished look.

Hotshot Graphics also produces slightly crisper text, to my eye, in its screen images.

But I mainly prefer *Hotshot Graphics* because of its superior image-editing tools. The program makes it easy to highlight part of a screen, or add a drop shadow; you can also annotate screens with little text boxes, and draw arrows and other symbols. I find the ability to add those touches to captured screens essential, because most often I'm capturing screens for use as tutorials for others; being able to easily add highlighting and annotation right on the screen image itself often eliminates the need to write separate text passages to accompany the screen images. The result is a more concise tutorial document.

Hotshot Graphics also takes up about a third less memory than *Pizazz Plus* —about 25 KB, rather than 38 KB—which is critical for a pop-up program, which by definition will be used with another program loaded after it into memory.

A few tips for successful screen grabbing:

- **Unless you really need color images, capture color screens in the screen-grabbing program's black-and-white mode.** The problems in capturing, then accurately reproducing, color screen images are legendary among computer-magazine editors—I speak from long personal experience!—who have spent thousands of hours and a small fortune developing special color-output screen-grabbing software. If you can possibly live with black-and-white output, do so.

- **Set your application program to produce monochrome screens, if at all possible.** Both *Hotshot Graphics* and *Pizazz Plus* offer routines to remap a complicated color screen to a series of grays. *Hotshot Graphics* works better than *Pizazz Plus*, but with a lot of time and fiddling, both are capable of good results.

  A better answer is to force your application program into its native monochrome mode before starting to snap those screen shots. The program's developer has already worked out the best way to translate those hues and shades of color into black-and-white tones; don't try to reinvent the wheel.

- **Be wary of using too many gray steps.** Desktop laser printers can only handle four or five steps of gray (dot) patterns with clarity. Many screen-grab programs will allow you to choose a much wider scale of grays for translation from color screen images. If you wind up with gray values too close to one another, you'll get a mushy, ambiguous screen snap, with little or no differentiation between some adjacent "colors."

- **Watch out for solid black backgrounds.** It's hard to reproduce a large solid area of black on most laser printers; the technology just isn't up to it. Lots of things can help, such as using a fresh toner cartridge, stopping the printer to remove and shake the cartridge from side to side between every page, and turning the print-density dial to the darkest possible setting.

  But it's better still to simply avoid those large solid-black fills by reversing the colors in your captured screens, so you have black or dark-gray type against a white (e.g., clear) background. That kind of change usually has to be made at the time the image is captured, so keep this in mind as you work—and the first time you grab screens from a new application, make a few quick print tests while you're still in screen-grabbing mode, so you can adjust your basic settings to produce that reversed-screen effect.

- **Capture screen images to disk; edit and print them later.** Screen-grabbing software often allows editing and printing of images one-by-one, as each is captured. But it makes a lot more sense to capture those images to disk, then exit your application, reload the screen-grabbing program, and do any necessary editing. Save those images to disk, then move on to printing.

  Often enough, you won't be printing captured screens from within the grab utility, but from within your word-processing or desktop-publishing program. Even if you do plan to print screens to paper from within the grabber, you'll find it makes for a better, more logical workflow to complete all your editing before moving on to printing.

- **Use a laser printer for captured screens.** Even if you normally work with a dot-matrix printer, you should buy, borrow, or steal a laser printer to print captured screens. Though the screen-grab programs do offer support for a wide range of printers, these programs are really optimized for laser-printer output.

  And when you're working with captured screen images—especially if you make them smaller on the page, as is usually the case—you're right on the edge of having enough resolution: those screens weren't all that sharp to begin with. Exploit the crisp output of a laser printer to save as much of that resolution as possible.

- **Use TIFF files when in doubt.** The output format you choose for your screen shots will depend to a large degree on how you'll be using them. If you'll be printing them through a word-processing or desktop-publishing document to a PostScript printer, you'll probably choose the EPS (or Encapsulated PostScript) format, for best results. Screens destined to be folded into Microsoft *Word* files will be saved in the .IMG file format;

for *WordPerfect,* they'll need to be in the .WPG form; graphics headed for output in programs that run under *Windows* (or for exchange via the *Windows Clipboard*) will be in .PCX or .CLP formats.

But when you're unsure what to use, chose your grabber's TIFF (or .TIF) output option. Screen shots saved in TIFF (Tagged Image File Format) files will generally reproduce best, anyway; and if you're uncertain which format you'll need, you'll find TIFF will probably work with your target program, once that decision is made.

- **Don't reduce the image size too much on the printed page.** This is partly because of possible problems with image quality as you shrink the image; but it's mainly because a screen snapshot much smaller than about 3 × 4 inches is going to be awfully hard to read. Computer screens can be incredibly helpful (and professional-looking) additions to a document . . . but squinty, hard-to-read screen images are infuriating.

Not as easy as you thought it would be, eh? And you're surprised? Remember, these are *PCs. . . .*

❧

Forget About Pen Plotters

One of the earliest tools of PC-graphics mavens was the pen plotter. Hotshots seemed to go into every meeting with a few brightly colored overhead transparencies, and invariably wowed the crowd. These people were really hip; clearly fast-trackers. They understood how to use *Lotus 1-2-3*—maybe even those "macro" things, too—and you could tell they *really* understood graphics, because they turned out these nice *1-2-3* graphs on their trusty plotters.

That was a tough act to follow . . . in the early 1980s.

Hewlett-Packard's six-pen 7475a plotter soon became a standard tool for most business users. We used it to crank out zillions of overheads and color handouts. They were colorful, but boy, were they *ugly*.

Today, pen plotters have gone the way of the daisy-wheel printer. They're slow, taking up to a half-hour to turn out a single graph or chart. They use ugly "stroke fonts," which produce letters that look like a first-semester drafting student's homework. They often (and quite inexplicably) screw up, scratching odd lines across a plot, rendering it useless and requiring you to start from scratch. The tiny pens used in plotters are hard to find, are expensive, run out of ink too soon and without warning, and get scratchy, tearing the plotting paper long before they're used up. Oh yes: you have to use special, expensive, hard-to-find plotting paper, or you'll get nasty-looking "bleeds" where the colored ink starts to spread. Unless you want to turn out overheads, of course, in which case you need special, expensive, hard-to-find acetates and matching no-skip plotter pens.

Sounds great, eh?

In spite of all this, some corporate people still swear by—as well as *at*—their plotters. Usually, it's because they've been told Color Is A Must For Effective Presentations.

I like color visuals as much as the next person, and given a choice between two otherwise identical graphics I'll usually take the color one, thank you. But with the proliferation of high-quality, low-cost laser printers in business today, we're no longer talking about "otherwise identical" graphics. There's a better way.

In fact, in *every* way, laser-printed graphics are preferable to plotted graphics. With the printer you get better-looking type, sharper lines and lettering, much better solid-fill areas, far faster operation, far fewer mechanical hassles. It's quick and easy to turn out a sufficient number of exact-duplicate hand-out paper copies with a laser printer; turning those out on a plotter would take days.

Ditch the plotter. It's not capable of producing work up to the standards expected today. Pen plotters still have a place in drafting rooms, though before long they'll be replaced there, too, by electrostatic plotters, whose prices are dropping steadily.

But plotters have no place in the office of the 1990s.

PC Slide Shows:
Ready for Prime Time?

One of the hot new buzz-phrases to come into circulation in computing over the past couple of years has been "desktop presentations." Like so many other PC terms, this one is widely misused—or at least, used very differently by different people. Some say it refers to the process of designing graphics, such as 35mm slides and overhead transparencies, on your PC; others say it means using a PC to present those graphics to an audience, in what are often now called "PC slide shows."

The first idea is great; the second, half-baked and at least for now, hobbled by the present state of the art.

PCs make superb workstations for producing graphics. DOS PCs or Macintoshes running programs such as Aldus *Persuasion* or Microsoft *PowerPoint* are powerful and remarkably flexible tools for laying out graphics, producing bar graphs and pie charts, setting type, dropping in colored backgrounds. Connect your PC to a laser printer and you'll get superb black-and-white overheads, plus crisp black-and-white paper handouts of your material for "leave-behinds." Hook it up to a slidemaker, or link it to a service bureau through a modem, and you can get professional-quality 35mm slides and color overheads.

So there's nothing farfetched about using PCs as presentation-graphics-preparation workstations: they fit the role very well. It's when you contemplate that next step—using the PC to show the finished work to your audience, instead of using slides or overheads—that things begin to go downhill rapidly.

Perhaps PC slide shows won't always be so inconvenient. Perhaps screens will get brighter, sharper, larger, and flatter, so that more than two or three people can watch the presentation—and so even those two or three hardy souls won't have to elbow their way into an odd little group, squinting at your PC's screen. Perhaps portable PCs with large, bright color displays will become widely available, at affordable prices, and will be small and lightweight enough to carry easily when we travel.

Perhaps, heck: someday those dreams *will* come true. But until then, showing PC slide shows is usually a bad idea. If your company has equipped its conference rooms with those huge, expensive, and ungainly Mitsubishi 37-inch color video monitors, driven by PCs or Macs, your case may be the exception. Or if there are high-quality video projectors mounted in your conference rooms, and, again, a PC stands nearby to feed it images, you may be one of the Elect. Both situations can handle internal presentations well. And if you take your PC slide shows on the road, you might even find a portable PC with an LCD projection plate useful for some presentations. (See *LCD Projection Plates: The Poor Man's Video Projector* in this section.)

For the rest of us, PC slide shows mean too many compromises. In image quality, for example, where both 35mm slides and overheads are sharper and brighter, and give you much better colors. Or in convenience, where it's easy to count on finding a working Carousel projector, or overhead projector, at a site where you're supposed to make a presentation, rather than having to request, or rent, or haul along your own computer and projection system. Or in audience size, where 35mm slides can deal effectively with an auditorium full of people, instead of two or three people hunched together, peering at your portable or desktop PC.

For now, for most PC users, PCs serve a lot better as production tools for graphics than as projection systems. Someday, though, someday. . . .

❧

Overheads or Slides?

People often choose the wrong medium for a presentation, because they're using the wrong basis for their decision. They may decide that 35mm slides would be too expensive, for example, while laser-printer-produced overhead transparencies are affordable. Or that the easy portability of overheads makes them a better choice than the somewhat bulkier Carousel slide tray. Or that time constraints make a big newsprint pad, used as a flip-chart, a better choice than overheads. Sometimes people opt for the flashiness of video projection—even when the primary attributes of video, moving images, and synchronized sound aren't used.

Cost, portability, turnaround time, and razzle-dazzle all count. But I'd argue that the primary factor in choosing a presentation medium should be the audience's needs, and the size of the room in which you'll be making the presentation.

Ever sit in an auditorium full of people, trying to see what some bozo presenter had on the overhead transparencies he was projecting down there in front? (He made it worse, probably, by producing those overheads from typed pages . . . thus guaranteeing that no one past the second row had the slightest chance of reading the overhead.) If so, you'll know immediately what I mean about matching the presentation medium to room size: overheads are *awful* in really big rooms.

Every medium has its optimum audience size, room size, and application. Slides, for example, are great for relatively formal and unchanging presentations, where you have enough time to turn them out, and enough budget to pay for them. But even more important, slides are absolutely the medium of choice for large rooms, where only the power of a 35mm projector—perhaps an extra-bright projector with a souped-up light source—can punch that image through to the front of the room.

Slides can only hold a limited amount of information, of course, which can be an asset, since it forces us to break information into small bites, using more rather than fewer slides. And slides give you bright, attention-getting colors, plus the option to include color photographs among your images.

Overheads, on the other hand, are hopeless in large rooms, but ideal in small settings—such as the typical conference room. Slides are OK in spacious conference rooms, but can be overwhelming in a smaller room. And remember some people's tendency to nod off when the room is darkened.

The theoretical advantages of using overhead transparencies aside, one very real gain is that you can work in a fully or partly lit room, where the light level and peer pressure will keep people from snoozing out on you. Overheads also encourage spontaneity: Bring along a Vis-a-Vis felt-tip pen—the best of the erasable felt-tips for writing on plastic sheets—and scribble right on your overheads. Or just make checkmarks as you move down the points on each overhead, so your audience knows where you are.

Since PC-produced presentations generally fall into those two areas, the choice often seems to be limited to those media. But there are other forms of presentation materials you can produce on your PC, too.

For one of my most popular seminars, for example, I use a series of large, mounted posters. These were originally produced in *PageMaker,* as a series of pages in a single document. The standard 8.5 × 11 inch laser-printed pages from that *PageMaker* file were sent out to a local photostat shop, which blew them up 4.7X to a little less than 40 inches wide by a little more than 50 inches tall. The resulting high-contrast "line-art stats" were then drymounted onto .5-inch-thick GatorFoam, a remarkably tough backing material.

Each of the 15 or so posters in that group cost about $50, and they've proved quite a bargain.

I could as easily, and certainly less expensively, have printed those *Page-Maker* pages onto overhead transparency film, and used an overhead projector. In fact, that's what I *did* do in the first few test-runs of the seminar, until I was certain I had the copy for those posters down pat. But each one stays up in front of the group for a long time, and I wanted to work in a fully lit room, rather than spending the day in the depressing half-light that works best with overheads.

I prop the posters up on an easel at the front of the room, where everyone can see them. The image is even larger than it would be with an overhead projector throwing them onto a typical 40 × 40 inch or 50 × 50 inch screen, and also a lot brighter and sharper; I find they work well. In fact, people in that seminar often get up, walk to the front of the room, and start speaking to the group themselves, pointing to the current poster—and sometimes even dig back through the stack to pull up and use an earlier one.

As a presenter I *love* that kind of response. Indeed, I often simply sit down when that happens, so the person who's gotten up to speak has the stage, so to speak, to him- or herself. It is a *very* effective technique. And it's a good example of the kinds of presentation media we can craft when we begin with a PC. But it would never work in a larger room, with classroom-style seating; people sitting past the first couple of rows wouldn't be able to read the posters.

The point here is simple: Consider the advantages of each of the possible forms of presentation media . . . but pay the closest attention to the audience's needs and the room size. Match your presentation media to those and your presentation will seem to fit naturally into the setting.

The Importance Of Leave-Behinds

No matter how flashy and persuasive your graphics are when you make a presentation, they aren't enough. Overheads aren't enough. Slides aren't enough. Flip-charts aren't enough. *Ever.*

Because no matter how impressed and convinced the people in that room are when you're through, your message hasn't finally clicked until they've taken it back to their staff, superiors, engineers, sales forces, or other constituencies. If you expect them to be even half as persuasive as you were—and to get it right when they retell your story for you!—you need to arm them with the tools they need to make your case persuasively.

You need "leave-behinds": copies of your graphics, and probably also a summary of your case statement, conclusions, and recommendations. And you need a set of those leave-behinds for every member of your audience.

Using a PC to prepare materials for a presentation makes that easy. Virtually every graphics program that can turn out overheads or slides can also produce crisp black-and-white copies of those images on a standard laser printer. Programs such as Microsoft *PowerPoint,* SPC *Harvard Graphics,* Lotus *Freelance,* Aldus *Persuasion,* and Micrografx *Charisma*—the five leading presentation-graphics packages—make it easy to create graphics in one form, then convert them to another. With *Persuasion,* it's particularly simple to start in, say 35mm slide format, then automatically convert your visuals to paper-based leave-behinds, thanks to its AutoTemplate feature; but the others are easy enough.

You don't need to give your audience copies of *every* graphic in your presentation. If you use "builds," for example, in a series of slides or overheads—progressively revealing one bulleted item after another in a four- or five-point list—don't give people copies of each page of the build, just the last one, with the whole list.

If color is really critical to your graphics—if, for example, you've used color to differentiate adjacent horizontal slices in 100 percent-stacked-bar graphs —but don't have a color printer, make sure the program you use has a "black-and-white" setting that converts those colors to a series of monochrome patterns (cross-hatches, dots, stripes, etc.), so the different slices are still clearly distinguishable. And even then, don't trust the program's savvy by blithely sending a stack of images to the laser printer and then heading out to lunch. Run an actual test page of each of those graphics, to make sure the choice and progression of black-and-white patterns is clear and not subject to misinterpretation. Only after you've seen and OK'd each of those test pages should you send the full-run print job to the printer.

Note that if you use a service bureau to produce 35mm slides or overheads in color, it can usually provide relatively inexpensive Xerox or Canon plain-paper color copies of your images. So unless the audience is a sizable one, you may be able to give everyone color handouts that exactly match your projected visuals. In many areas, local quick-print shops can also make inexpensive plain-paper color copies of your color originals.

Even if you only use a word processor for your graphics, it's still important to produce those extra paper copies of your presentation, so each person in your session can go away with his or her own "summary kit" of your argument.

Remember to number each page in the series of images you use as handouts. You probably won't do that for the originals you project. You know their order: numbering would only add a confusing element to the graphics on-screen, and you might want to use the graphics in different sequences for different audiences. But make sure *every* set of leave-behinds you hand out has correctly and boldly numbered pages.

Beyond your graphs and charts, consider whether you need a one-page summary of your concept, its development, and your conclusion and recommendations. If all those points are covered on one of your graphics, that may not be necessary . . . but if they are, it makes me wonder how legible that one do-all/tell-all graphic can be!

More typically, presentations have the premise, facts, arguments, summary, and recommendations scattered across several slides or overheads. Preparing a concise, one-page statement of those points to use as a cover or closing sheet in your leave-behind package will make certain the members of your audience can distill all that into their *own* concise statement of your case, as they internalize the information and then present it to others.

It doesn't take long to prepare a set of leave-behinds. But those few minutes can be a powerful lever, increasing the effectiveness of your presentation and extending its reach. If it's not worth taking that extra step to assure that your message has the fullest impact, maybe you ought to ask whether it's worth making the presentation in the first place.

So You're a Mouse-Hater?
Try a Trackball

Often our reaction to new tools is more visceral than intellectual, more emotional than rational. When we know how to use Tool A well to do Job A, and someone comes along to suggest we really ought to try Tool B, which will not only do Job A better but may lead us into doing Jobs B through G as well, we suspend our critical faculties and reach deep down inside for a primitive reaction: *NO!*

What's wrong with the old way, the old tool? And who the hell says I now have to do all those other things besides? I don't *want* to do them. And I don't want to use your new tool either, damn it!

That was, in loose paraphrase, how one of the best corporate executives I know told me he first reacted when a PC support person in his company suggested he put a mouse next to his keyboard. Not only would he have to learn to use the silly thing, as he'd thought; but the impudent kid had also gone on to suggest that if he put the mouse on his PC to use with *1-2-3* (the only PC program he'd ever used, or ever *wanted* to use), he'd soon find himself using graphics programs too, to turn out colorful drawings and graphs. And maybe, before long, he'd even consider replacing his PC with one of the Macintosh computers that were slowly percolating into the company.

Draw pictures? Learn another program? Dump his genuine, true-blue, IBM computer? "No, I don't think so," he muttered, and walked off.

It was four years later—by which time he'd become something of a computer whiz in the company, using several programs at a high level of expertise—before he got around to trying a mouse. He'd seen Microsoft *Excel*, liked it, had a copy sent up, and quickly discovered *Excel* (and its underlying *Windows* environment) aren't very usable without some kind of external pointing device. In other words, a mouse.

Which he liked at once. When he actually *tried* it.

I offer this story as an example of how easily we can be dissuaded from trying new things simply because of how they're presented to us. And also to suggest that putting a small rodent next to *your* computer might not be such a bad thing.

Mice are simply essential in a graphical screen environment. You've got to be able to point at objects on-screen, draw rectangles to select objects, and click on commands to run the program. While there are keystroke equivalents for nearly every mouse point-and-click command, most are so hopelessly clumsy that you'll wonder if the development of those keystroke-alternatives wasn't secretly funded by the CIA. Mouseless PC users soon either give up on the application altogether, or surrender and get a mouse.

So why not be smart, and use one from the beginning? Or even better, why not be smarter *still* and get a trackball?

A Logical Extension

As much as I like mice on computers, they have their drawbacks. The biggest is that even the best of them require a fairly large clear area to move around in, to the right (or for the left-handed, to the left) of the keyboard. My desk often isn't very clear anyway, and when it gets bad, papers start encroaching on that workspace on either side of the keyboard mighty fast. A good and virtuous person might see that as a sign from above to start cleaning up, but too often I usually just let the paperwork pile up until it's hard to find even the keyboard itself. Your desk may not be that messy—but do you really want to surrender another 70 or 80 square inches of desktop real estate to yet another computer gizmo?

Mice also require mouse pads, little putting greens on which they can roll around without skipping. Do you really want to put a small, square putting green next to your keyboard?

And mouse cables tend to get incredibly tangled. Sure, if I kept my desk neater, my mouse might never get tangled up at all. But by the time I've traced the mouse cable back to where it wrapped around the pencil cup, got stuck in the jaws of the stapler, and was pulled tight under the corner of the computer itself, I'm hardly of a mind to recall that cleanliness is next to godliness, and that Neatness Counts. Instead, my instinct, resisted only with great effort, is to rip the mouse cable out of the back of the computer and throw the whole thing at the wall. Where there are still a few dents from the last time I ripped. . .

Trackballs: Mice for Grown-Ups

With a trackball you can eliminate all the nuisances of a mouse while retaining all its point-and-click advantages. There are other major advantages to using a trackball, and I'll get to them in a moment. But if trackballs only reduced the amount of real estate necessary for proper operation, helped keep your work-space free of clutter, and eliminated tangled-cable problems—all of which they do, effortlessly—I'd still be a big fan.

Think of a trackball as an upside-down mouse.

A mouse consists of a plastic housing with a ball sticking out of the bottom. A cable runs from the housing to the back of your PC. You hold the soap-bar-size plastic housing in your hand and move it to and fro, forward and back-ward across the desktop (or mouse pad), causing the ball underneath to roll in the direction you move the mouse. Those moves are detected by the mouse's internal mechanism, which translates them to absolute movements of the cursor on the computer screen. When you want to do something, you click one of the two or three buttons at the front of the mouse.

Trackballs, by contrast, leave the housing in place on the desk, with the ball on the top, sticking partway up out of the housing. You simply rest your finger-tips or occasionally the palm of your hand on the ball, roll it back and forth, and produce exactly the same kind of movements of the cursor on your com-puter's display. With a much greater economy of motion, in less space on the desktop, without a cable flopping back and forth constantly looking for ways to get in trouble. Large, comfortable buttons that perform the same clicking functions of mouse buttons lie beside the ball on the trackball house, right under your fingertips.

I not only prefer trackballs to mice, I like *big* trackballs. I've long used a Kensington Microware Expert Mouse on both PCs and Macintoshes, and I didn't realize how important the large ball (a little over two inches) of the Kensington units was to me until Apple brought out its klutzy Macintosh Por-table. It has a one-and-a-quarter-inch ball, located at the right end of the key-board. The first time I tried it, I hated it: I had to squinch that smaller ball around with my fingertips much of the time. Even with experience, I disliked it. My fingers never adapted to the touch and motion of that tiny ball. The sure, even rolling motion of the Kensington trackballs was utterly missing; surely this was a joke. Logitech, which produced the Macintosh trackball mechanism for Apple, soon introduced its own oddball trackball system for IBM PCs, using that same small ball. And DataDesk, upon whose keyboards I absolutely dote, also used that small ball design in an otherwise-wonderful modular keyboard called the Switchboard.

Perhaps this is only a question of taste. I'll concede that I have fairly (but not exceptionally) large hands; maybe that's why I dislike the smaller trackballs. If you don't think trackball size makes much difference, try a large one, then a smaller one. I'll be surprised if you don't agree that the smaller one feels uncomfortable after using the larger one.

Hardware and Software Issues

Software compatibility may be an issue for some PC users who are considering a trackball. In the past, the software drivers supplied with many trackballs (as well as the drivers provided with many mice) were not fully compatible with the drivers developed by Microsoft for its famous Microsoft Mouse, the acknowledged industry standard. Because the driver is the essential link between the mouse or other pointing device and users' application programs —virtually all of which expect to see a device compatible with the Microsoft standard—PC users sometimes had trouble getting non-Microsoft pointing products to work correctly.

Those problems became particularly evident with the introduction of graphical environments, such as Microsoft *Windows,* and then OS/2-*Presentation Manager.* And the regular introduction of new versions of *Windows,* each with niggling incompatibilities with earlier versions, and with pointing-device drivers, made the problem worse.

Finally, the introduction of *Windows* 3.0 in mid-1990—itself a milestone for the PC business, since *Windows* 3.0 solved all the important problems of earlier versions and finally delivered on the promise inherent in *Windows* for years—brought pointing-device-driver incompatibility problems to a head. No mouse or trackball manufacturer could afford to be left out of the boom caused by *Windows* 3.0; because *Windows* virtually demanded a mouse or trackball for efficient use, it provided enormous impetus for the pointing-device market.

As a result, much greater attention was paid to compatibility with the Microsoft Mouse-driver standard, and now virtually all of the major suppliers' trackballs are fully compliant with that standard.

Indeed, some even go beyond Microsoft compatibility in useful ways. For example, some trackball drivers allow users to adjust the relationship between the distance the cursor moves on-screen and the distance the trackball is moved. In many cases, that includes what is called "ballistic control": the faster the ball is rolled, the greater the distance the cursor moves on-screen for each unit of trackball movement. That's especially important with today's trend towards larger, higher resolution screens. Since higher resolution screens by definition include more dots, or pixels, and cursor movement is measured in pixels, a higher resolution display can mean a lot more mouse or trackball movement than users may be accustomed to. By adjusting the ballistics of mouse or trackball motion, users can fine-tune the relationship between the pointing device and their choice of display system. (Ballistic control is now provided in the software drivers supplied with many computer mice, too.)

When trackballs weren't quite so popular as they are today, some PC users had physical-interface problems as well. Mice are typically available in two versions: one to plug into a serial port on the PC; another to plug into a provided interface card, which takes up one expansion slot inside the computer. In the early days of trackballs, manufacturers usually provided only one form or the other: either the serial-port or the bus-card interface.

That was a problem for PC users, who when considering adding a pointing device had already faced a difficult decision: did they prefer to lose a serial port (of which *no* PC has enough), or an expansion slot (of which few PCs have enough)? At least with the Microsoft Mouse, and most other computer mice, they could have it either way. But the far smaller market for trackballs made producing two different models economically impractical for most manufacturers, so you simply took what was available.

Now that trackballs have gained popularity, most are available in both bus and serial models. Many even go so far as to use the special connector introduced in 1987 with the IBM PS/2s and the new version of the Microsoft Mouse that appeared shortly thereafter.

The net effect of these changes, on both the hardware-interface and software-interface levels, has been to remove compatibility concerns from buyers' agendas: choose a mouse or a trackball from a major supplier and you can expect full compatibility with DOS, *Windows*, or OS/2-*Presentation Manager*, and your application programs.

I don't hate mice; I thought they were a great advance when they were first introduced. And I used the Microsoft Mouse happily for a long time. But once you become accustomed to a trackball—which takes perhaps five minutes— you not only don't want to use a computer again without a pointing device attached; you want a trackball, period.

If I've provoked you only enough to get you to try a mouse, that's still great. You'll be more effective at the computer, and won't regret the decision.

Unless you subsequently try a trackball, too. Then you'll wish you'd purchased the *right* pointing device in the beginning.

VIII

PC COMMUNICATIONS

E-Mail Etiquette

If your PC is connected to a network of other PCs at work, or perhaps to a network of several different kinds of computers, you're probably a regular user of electronic mail, or e-mail. In offices without networks, PC users often have access through modems to external e-mail systems, such as AT&T Mail, MCI Mail, or Sprintmail.

Computer-to-computer messaging is highly addictive: try it once or twice, and you'll be hooked.

But as you become used to the speed and convenience of e-mail—especially, to the way it keeps you out of "telephone tag" loops with your coworkers—you also begin to notice that communicating by electronic mail isn't just a computerized replacement for paper-based messages. The spontaneity of e-mail—the quick on-line answer, such as *"Joe: Do it!"* to a long incoming note that would otherwise not get touched for hours or days—encourages a much less formal style than those long letters (and, especially, those wheezy intra-office memos) we used to exchange.

New e-mail users are often unsure just how quick and breezy they should be. What's the proper etiquette for e-mail writing style? Is a "Dear Bill" required at the beginning of a message? Or is it OK to just plow into the body of the note? Are such written-communication no-no's as sentence fragments, all-lower-case lines, and two- or three-word replies OK? What about a close: is a "Cordially" needed, or will a quick "—Jack" be sufficient?

My prescription: Make e-mail messages as quick, spontaneous, skeletal, and informal as you can. The more we use e-mail as a replacement for quick passing-in-the-hallway exchanges, or for scribbling a quick reply in the margin of a written letter and returning that letter to its sender, the better we exploit its speed and convenience. The message headers provided automatically by even the simplest e-mail systems include all the sender, date and time information the recipient needs . . . so why put that in again?

One of the worst traps new e-mail users fall into is reading their mail on-line, then jumping off-line to compose long, detailed, thoroughly corrected and spelling-checked replies—then going *back* on-line to send those long-winded answers. That's a profoundly antiproductive move, in my view. It can take even more time than reading an incoming letter, then dictating or writing a reply!

Avoid that temptation. Avoid formality. Avoid verbosity. Make your e-mail messages brief and spontaneous, and you'll encourage others to do the same.

E-mail isn't for the ages, but for the moment: use it that way, and you'll use it well.

When Cracking Wise Isn't

There's more to effective use of e-mail, and "e-mail etiquette," than quick answers, though. Be careful, for example, about excessive informality. Brevity and directness are one thing; flippancy masquerading as informality is another. Just using PCs and e-mail is enough of a shock to many people in a business setting; getting e-mail messages that cross the perceived line of respect for superiors—reading things on-line they know wouldn't be tolerated if said aloud—can push these people into pushing back.

Another problem: be wary of cracking jokes on e-mail systems. Without the wink, nod, and grin you see when someone makes a funny or sarcastic remark to you face-to-face, it's easy to lose the idea that something *is* a joke. What seems funny to me may offend you . . . simply because you didn't realize I was trying to *be* funny.

E-mail regulars sometimes try to overcome this by adding little e-mail conventions, such as typing <grin> after a remark meant to be funny, or even typing a silly little happy-face lying on its side, like this :-), into the message. If you're comfortable with adding those little cues, do so . . . but know that a lot of your e-mail correspondents are going to think that's an awfully juvenile touch.

When it comes down to offending people by making remarks that may be misunderstood, or looking like a kid with a computer game, the best choice may be to simply skip the funny comments.

PC Fax: Yes, But . . .

I never cease to be amazed by the incredible surge of interest in fax machines. Just a few years ago, facsimile transmission was seen almost universally as a "bridge technology"—something to get us through the late 1980s, until nearly everyone had, or had access to, a PC. By then, the reasoning went, standard electronic mail would have taken over, and faxing would have become about as retrograde a method of communicating as possible: in a three-way tie, perhaps, with telex and the U.S. Postal Service as bad memories businesspeople would rather forget.

Instead, fax roared to the forefront. Around 1989 the number of fax machines installed began doubling every year; stories about delis accepting faxed orders for take-out food moved from apocryphal to true to so-what; yuppies began putting fax machines in their homes; the phrase *"What's your fax number?"* became commonplace.

Wait a minute: what happened to modems and electronic mail and bulletin boards? Well, the simple answer is that they were blind-sided. While we were pooh-poohing the idea that anyone would really be intimidated by a keyboard, or would simply choose not to have a PC around, the world noticed how incredibly easy it is to drop a couple of sheets into the input bin of a fax machine, tap in a telephone number, and walk away. No fuss, no muss; just fast, easy, cheap communications.

And you could send the *whole document,* too, not just a text-only summary or excerpt, so when not-so-little details such as letterheads, office forms, graphics, sketches, and so on were important, they weren't lost, as they invariably are in character-based electronic mail. In fact, maybe electronic mail is really just a bridge technology, to get us through the early 1990s, until nearly everyone has, or has access to. . . .

No, no, no. It won't work like that, because the two are completely different approaches. PC-to-PC electronic-mail (sent, of course, through an intermediary system, whether the Compaq LAN server down the hall, or perhaps MCI Mail's VAXes in the Washington suburbs) is still great for quick back-and-forth questions and the exchange of documents in editable form; while fax is ideal for the exchange of documents *as documents*, with the look and feel of the original intact. It isn't that electronic mail should be afraid of fax, nor that fax should be afraid of electronic mail—but that Federal Express and the other overnight couriers should be afraid of *both*.

Fax and computer-to-computer electronic-mail are going to coexist for a long time. In the end, a converged form of the two will edge both aside. But that's still a long way off.

The Logic Behind PC Fax

The boom in PC fax cards has been a clear sign of our eagerness for that still-distant convergence. The premise is so appealing: since many of the documents we fax back and forth across the planet every day begin in someone's PC, as a letter or proposal or filled-in form or CAD drawing or whatever, why then add the external process of printing out that document, carrying the printout down to a fax machine, scanning it in, and sending it on its way? Wouldn't it make a lot more sense to simply fax the document directly from its creator's PC? Since printing is a kind of "out-scanning," and running the document through a fax machine is a kind of "in-scanning," couldn't we also get better quality at the receiving end by avoiding both of those resolution-robbing steps?

And what about security? One of the huge advantages of PC fax ought to be that there are no prying eyes peeking at the message on its way from sender to recipient. In most offices, a fax machine sitting in an unused alcove or distant hallway chugs out incoming messages all day long. A couple of times a day, an office runner stops, picks up the stack of faxes from the machine's in-basket, sorts through them to try to find which pages go together, and to whom . . . then leisurely reads the more interesting messages. Eventually those messages find the way to their addressees' desks—or at least, to their secretaries' desks. But it's hardly a very direct—or private—pathway from sender to recipient.

Of course, nosy office runners aren't the only ones who get to see your incoming faxes. Anyone in the office, in the guise of looking to see if an important fax they're expecting has arrived, can paw through that stack in the machine's in-basket, reading the juicy ones along the way, of course. Or just feeding them back through the fax machine and hitting its COPY button, if they'd like their own personal copies of your best stuff.

In practice, messages sent from one fax machine to another are hardly confidential. That may not matter, most of the time. But once in awhile, all of us use faxes for sensitive material. So PC fax transmissions—from my screen to yours—ought to provide very high security, right? And perhaps on that basis alone justify the purchase of PC fax cards?

PC Fax in the Real World

Well, sure. And PC fax *does* make sense—in some cases. If all you want to do is create a rather plain-looking text document, and quickly transmit it to someone else, and you're not particularly concerned how it will look at their end, PC faxing certainly can make sense. It's when the document gets a little more elaborate that things get touchy.

Say you want that document to appear at the receiving end on your company's letterhead. Well, if you have a high-resolution .PCX-file scan of that letterhead, and know how to insert into your document the codes to tell your PC fax card to find and attach it before transmission, then you're probably OK. Of course, getting that letterhead positioned on the page the addressee of your message receives is a little tricky, but. . . .

And what if you want your signature to appear at the bottom? Same story: if you've got a scanned image of your signature already stored on your disk, and you know how to tell the PC fax card to find that signature and insert it at the right point, then things may work as you expect. Of course, if you want to fit that signature neatly between a typed line that says "Cordially," and another a bit further down that says "Otis Zapp, Vice-President," then you may have a little problem. You'll probably get it right, eventually, especially if you're willing to spend a long time sending practice faxes to that real fax machine just down the hall, trooping down there after each is received to see how close you're getting to what you intended.

What if you want the document to appear at the other end in that attractive Times Roman typeface everyone in your office began using a couple of years ago, when you all got those new laser printers?

Well, Bunky, this is going to take a while. First, get out your fax card's manual. . . .

The Joys of Receiving PC Faxes

But Wait! As the man selling Ginsu knives on late-night television says: *There's More!* We haven't talked yet about receiving faxes on a PC. Isn't that a big improvement over the old fax-to-fax system? And a lot more secure?

Well, maybe. Let's go back and see what's really involved. First, configure your PC so that the software that controls your fax card runs all the time, in the background. (Otherwise, it won't be able to receive a fax unless you have the fax program running at the moment.) That will take a certain amount of RAM out of your precious 640KB, but hey—this is *productivity,* isn't it? Who cares whether you have enough room left for those few pop-up utilities you use all day, or for your network-linking software? Memory for your *applications?* Oops, sorry; forgot about them.

Now call up your company's telecommunications manager and order an additional direct telephone line, outside the company's block of shared lines, installed and run to your desk. (Otherwise, incoming faxes are highly unlikely to get through your modem pool or other shared-line situation.) He probably won't mind at all, and isn't likely to point out just how much that's going to cost, or in how many different ways that violates both company policy and his own personally-developed-at-a-huge-cost-to-the-company telecom plan for the enterprise. When the guys arrive to knock little holes in the wall of your office, and yell back and forth as they pull wires through the ceiling, just ignore 'em. Maybe it's a good time for that long weekend on the Cape that you've been promising Muffy or Biff and the kids.

When the phone line is in, hook up everything, and have some postcards printed for everyone you communicate with—coworkers, branch-office staff, customers, prospects, and so on. Make sure your boss gets one, too, and *his* boss, as well. The card should explain carefully why they're not supposed to send faxes to you any more at the company's fax number—you know, the one in the ads, on your business card and letterhead—or the one listed for your department in the company telephone directory. No, instead they should send them to this new direct fax-line of yours, the number for which is . . . umm, wait a minute . . . I've got it here somewhere. Your coworkers, branch-office staff, etc., will all be *very* impressed: you must be mighty important to have set up your own telecommunications domain. I'm sure they'll go out of their way to remember and always use your special number.

Finally comes that moment of truth, when your first fax arrives. You'll be sitting there working on a *1-2-3* spreadsheet, or meeting with a client, or maybe just talking on the phone, when a beep and a flashing message at the bottom of your PC's screen alerts you that you have a fax coming in. You'll hurriedly quit whatever you were doing, close the *1-2-3* file, exit that program, and load the other program that lets you read incoming faxes.

Hmm: Still coming in: this must be a big file.

As you soon learn, it is: your PC handles incoming fax files as graphics files, which means they're often *verrrrry* big—200 to 300 KB is common. No matter; you've got lots of room left on your hard disk, don't you? The transmission is complete now, so you can load and read that hot fax . . . on your screen. It's a little squinty, of course, but as you scroll down, and maybe sideways, through that big file you actually get to see what someone sent. Amazing.

Actually, so you can read it more easily, you'll probably print it out. No problem: issue the commands, wait while that big file works its way over to the printer, and *zip!* There it is, coming out of the printer right now: *an actual paper copy of your incoming fax!*

Technology triumphs again.

Zealotry vs Productivity

The truth is that PC faxing is still in its infancy. And like any technology that's still in its infancy but proposes to overthrow a well-established technology, PC fax demands a revolutionary zeal from its followers. Backsliders in the cadre will soon remember fondly how easy it is to just print out that damned letter, toss it in the bin of the fax machine, and know that it's going to arrive in good order.

Things will get better. I promise. But not soon.

In the meantime, we should consider using PC fax for the few things it does better than conventional fax, and not waste our time arguing that PC fax is anything like a reasonable replacement for a fax machine. An extension of faxing power, sure; a replacement for standard fax machines, hardly.

If that sounds like heresy in a book about "PC productivity"—which many people will inevitably think means putting as many programs and tasks on your PC as you possibly can—then I haven't made my case, nor the case for this book, very well.

Productivity simply means working smarter: getting more done, more effectively. It has nothing to do with pushing work onto a certain tool, but everything to do with choosing the *right* tool. Which isn't always, I'm convinced, a PC fax card.

PCs and Broadcast Fax

Despite all its hassles, there is one function PC fax can provide that really is more productive and convenient than using most standard fax machines: sending the same fax to many addressees. That kind of "broadcast" faxing is becoming much more important these days, as many companies use fax broadcasting for frequent distribution of updated price lists, memos to branch offices, alerts to customers of the in-stock status of critical parts, sales reports, and many more items sent with some regularity to fixed distribution lists. Anyone who's had to send a multipage document to a long list of addressees will recall with a shudder the frustration of standing at a regular fax machine, endlessly feeding the document into the machine over and over again, and gradually checking off names and phone numbers on the list of addresses as each transmission is completed.

High-end fax machines—the big, console-size ones that look more like high-speed copiers than fax machines—have built-in broadcast capability. You can stand at the machine and tap on the names and telephone numbers of everyone on your distribution list, name that list, then save it on a hard disk inside the machine. Then you scan in your document, which is also saved on that disk, and tell the machine to start sending—or likelier, tell it to send the faxes overnight, when long-distance rates are cheaper.

The keyboards on those behemoths are usually abysmal, so entering all that data error-free is often quite a job. But not many offices have these mega-fax machines, which presents the perfect opening for PC fax cards.

Despite the inconvenience of readying anything more than the simplest document for transmission via PC fax, if that document is going to a long list of addressees, PC faxing is worth the trouble. Especially when there are going to be regular fax transmissions to that list—and inevitably, there will be other multiple-address faxes on some cyclical basis—the time and effort to master PC fax becomes insignificant.

The software provided with even the most primitive PC fax cards makes it possible to enter addressees' names and telephone numbers at the PC, store those names and numbers, and group them into distribution lists. Once the document is ready to go, the user simply chooses the appropriate list and lets the PC fax card go to work.

If You're Still Not Convinced . . .

With the incredible rate of improvements in PC products, recommending one "best" product in any category is a perilous notion. By the time you read this book, another, even more impressive product may have appeared. But at this moment I'm reasonably confident in recommending Intel's SatisFAXtion board as the one to buy. By using its own on-board (80186) microprocessor to manage fax transmission and reception, the SatisFAXtion card minimizes its demand on your PC, so you can continue with other work. The accompanying fax-management software—and the even better special software available to SatisFAXtion users who use Microsoft *Windows* (by request, through Intel's Personal Computer Enhancement Operation)—is the best available with any existing PC fax card.

Intel has encouraged applications software makers to support the CAS technical standard for sending faxes—a standard developed by Intel and promoted by them in cooperation with communications-hardware giant DCA. The idea behind CAS is brilliant: we should be able to simply pop up a window while working in any PC applications package, and with a couple of keystrokes send a perfect-looking fax of the document on-screen to anyone on a previously stored list of fax addressees. Unfortunately, support of CAS so far by applications software publishers has been thin to nonexistent. Half-hearted CAS-standard utilities are available from Intel for *WordPerfect* and *1-2-3* users. Both work, but not with anything like the speed and convenience possible with full, *built-in* CAS support in applications.

Even if better CAS support from software publishers is slow in coming, the Intel board and its subsequent hardware and software upgrades seem likely to remain at the top of the PC fax heap.

I'm obviously still skeptical about how many PC users really need PC fax cards—and about how many of those who buy one will find they're actually *using* it, a couple of months later. But if you're in the market, and especially if you like the idea of fax broadcasting, the SatisFAXtion is probably the fax card for you.

One-Line Sanity

If you're lucky enough to have a direct outside telephone line for your PC's modem (see *The Evils of Modem-Pooling*, in this section), but then decide you want to add a fax card to your PC as well, you're probably going to have a tough time convincing the telecom department to give you a second outside line that bypasses the company's PBX system. But without that separate second line, you may only be able to use your new PC fax board to send faxes, not receive them.

Since I'm not much of a fan of receiving faxes on PC fax cards, but use them mainly to *send* faxes, that wouldn't worry me. But it would seriously worry a lot of people for whom the ability to receive a fax was part of the justification for investing in fax cards.

Some PC fax cards with on-board or piggy-back modems can automatically detect the difference between incoming fax calls and incoming data (modem) calls, and will correctly route the call right on the card. If yours can perform that function, you're in luck. If not, you'd better start lining up support for your requisition of that second line—or looking into a fax-data switch.

Fax-data switches, which allow civilized, full-featured sharing of one phone line among voice, data, and fax applications, are for sale nearly everywhere these days, often for as little as $50. I've tried many of them, and have found few that were both reliable and convenient. Two that have served well deserve mention.

The first is Technology Concepts' TCI FLM-203. This external box has an input jack for your phone line, and three output jacks for a fax card (or separate full-fledged fax machine), a modem, and a standard single-line telephone. It's a very smart device: it detects incoming fax or data calls, routes them to the right unit, and locks out interruption of the fax or data transmission by someone accidentally picking up that connected telephone; or it decides this is a voice call, and keeps the fax and modem out of your way.

The TCI box also has a jack for an answering machine, which functions in the usual way on incoming voice calls.

Choosing the right fax-data switch—and appreciating just how well the TCI box works—requires a little background on how incoming calls can be handled. Incoming fax calls present a warble tone to the system; incoming modem calls, a whistle tone. Voice calls, of course, have neither. Sophisticated systems such as the FLM-203 automatically detect these differences, and use them to route the call. Other systems (such as the Rainier device described below) are less automatic; they require that you record a short message on the machine, asking callers to press one button on their telephone for voice, another for fax or data, to say a word such as "fax," or to simply wait while the system times-out after a few seconds and directs the incoming call to the fax machine.

Systems that require a human caller to listen to a message and respond can mislead callers into thinking they're talking to an answering machine, with uncertain (and often unhappy) results. In any case, this type of system is much less automatic, and thus less convenient, than those such as TCI's, which handle the switching transparently.

The TCI system also offers "barge-in" protection, so that accidentally picking up the connected phone won't garble a fax or data transmission; but extending barge-in protection to extension phones using the same line requires adding additional, inexpensive TCI lock-out units to every protected extension.

It also works fine with most PBXs.

The TCI FLM-203 costs about $175; a simpler model, the FLM-202, which handles voice plus either (but not both) a fax machine or a data modem, costs about $125.

The second system I can recommend from long and happy personal experience is more complex, and not suitable for very many offices. But it's wonderful at home, and since so many fast-track PC users have home PCs as well these days—or carry portable PCs back and forth—it's worth mentioning. Rainier's TB-201 has to be installed where the telephone lines come into your house (but inside, out of the weather). The Rainier system requires recording a message for incoming callers, instructing them to dial "3" for a voice ring-through, or to wait until the unit "times out" and provides a fax-receive tone. (If the call is coming directly from a fax machine, of course, the connection is made without human intervention.)

The advantage of the Rainier system, in return for requiring that message, is that it automatically extends barge-in protection *to every extension in your home*, without requiring that any additional devices be added to those telephones.

That is, just one TB-201 installed on your phone system locks out every telephone in the house when you're sending or receiving with your fax card or modem. Anyone with teenagers will immediately appreciate the importance of not getting knocked off the air, so to speak, by someone who picks up the phone elsewhere in the house.

Installing the Rainier box isn't difficult, but for nontechnical types, it's a job probably better left to a phone installer. The TB-201 costs about $250.

There. Now you're armed with two good answers that can help preserve your sanity if you're working in a situation where you need the equivalent of two direct outside lines . . . and that request for a second outside line for your PC gets turned down. As it will be.

What? *Me?* A cynic? No way . . . I've just worked with a lot of telecom managers.

❧

There's No Such Thing As An Anonymous Fax

One of the stranger aspects of the fax craze sweeping through business these days has been the boom in joke faxes. I'm not talking about transmitting a page of stand-up comedy routines, of course, but rather the penchant for sending everyone you know who has a fax machine a funny cartoon you've clipped from the morning paper, or a mock ad you've written . . . or worse.

One of the silliest examples of this is actually more than two decades old: the bare-bottom fax. In the mid-Sixties, young secretaries and junior clerks working late at night would sometimes doff their pants and sit atop their offices' then-new Xerox machines. A push of the button and they'd be the subject of a truly bizarre rear-view electronic snapshot that could be surreptitiously—and entirely anonymously—circulated around the office. Or kept for private distribution. (Except, of course, when you missed that one copy you inadvertently left in the machine's output tray.)

Funny or stupid, hilarious or profane—take your choice. Either way, the key to the game was anonymity: no one knew *whose* bottom that was smiling up at them among the paperwork in the IN tray.

Unfortunately, we're now seeing that bare-bottom-Xerox game extended to distant sites through fax machines. But those who send these curious messages often forget that they're no longer anonymous. A neat line across the top of each page of the received copy identifies just when, and from whom—or at least, from whose office—it was sent.

You don't have to fax bare-bottom Xeroxes across the country to fall prey to the lack of anonymity of fax transmissions. I know a corporate PR department head, for example, who was fired after someone on her staff faxed to a dozen friends in the press advance copies of an unflattering story about the company's CEO . . . each copy, of course, bearing the XYZ Co. Corporate Communications Dept. header on every page.

Maybe the midnight character-assailant thought none of those media people would let their copies drift back to the CEO. But *someone* sent him a copy the morning it was received. The PR head was gone that afternoon.

As I travel the U.S., Europe, and Japan working with clients, I keep hearing unsettling stories about people thinking they could fax messages or artwork— whether low-grade porno or low-grade insults—without leaving their fingerprints on the job. Increasingly, perhaps because of the ease of broadcasting a PC fax to many addressees at the touch of a key, those stories tell of messages originating in someone's PC.

A word to the wise, the old saw goes, is sufficient: don't join the ranks of the self-indicted.

Fine and Superfine:
Marks of Civility

This one's easy: Use the "fine" or "superfine" resolution settings on your fax machine when you're sending messages, to make them easier to read at the recipient's end. And if you use a PC fax card, set it at the fine level and leave it there.

Faxes are hard enough to read as it is. Standard fax resolution produces marginal results . . . when everything works right. When things are less than perfect—which seems to be about 90 percent of the time with fax machines and fax cards—standard-resolution messages can be hard to read.

Nearly every Group III fax machine, and every PC fax card I've seen, offers a solution: the higher-resolution "fine" fax standard. The message takes slightly longer to transmit but, at the receiving end, it comes out much clearer and more legible.

Many fax machines—but sadly, no fax cards I've yet seen—also offer the option of the even-higher-resolution "superfine" standard. That additional resolution may be overkill—often I can't see the difference between faxes sent at fine and super fine settings—but it's nice to know the option is there if you need it.

If you doubt that the difference between standard-resolution and fine-resolution settings is so tangible, send the same document from one fax machine to another, once at each setting (or just use your fax machine's "copy" function at each setting), to see how the transmission looks at different resolutions. You'll be amazed at the difference.

Especially for PC users who print correspondence, reports, etc., in a type-set-look typeface such as Times Roman on their laser printers, then scan those printed pages into a fax machine, the difference is well worth it. Frankly, if you're going to send outgoing faxes at standard resolution, you may as well stay with the old familiar 10 characters-per-inch typewriter-look Courier typeface. It will survive the jungle of noisy phone lines and ill-adjusted fax machines far better at standard resolution.

Fine or superfine resolutions are also helpful when you're sending order forms or other documents that have a lot of fine lines or small boxes, and when you're transmitting small-type documents, such as tiny-type spreadsheet printouts.

Use a PC fax card? Since most PC fax cards turn your output into the equivalent of a page printed by an Epson dot-matrix printer, you may think the difference isn't worth the trouble and slight additional cost of using higher resolution settings. It is: set your PC fax card on fine and *leave it there.*

And if you're among the hardy souls who create documents using typeset-look Postscript typefaces, then run those files through a PostScript interpreter before sending them with a PC fax board, you *really* need fine resolution from your fax board. Otherwise, all that effort is largely wasted; you might as well have stayed with the usual ugly, Epson-look, fax-card output.

The Evils of Modem Pooling

If you're a PC user in a large company, and you presently have a modem connected to your PC, I have some bad news for you. Someday soon your company is going to convert (if it hasn't already) to an all-digital PBX and telephone system.

You'll know it's happening when you start getting progressively more enthusiastic memos from the telecom manager, each one proclaiming more loudly how much you're going to enjoy the wonders of the modern all-digital telephone system.

You'll get another memo on the schedule for classes on how to use the new system's features, and you'll probably also get a little cheat-sheet to keep under the phone, since there isn't a chance you'll remember what's taught in that class . . . if you bother to go. There may even be a memo about the separate classes on the wonderful voice-mail system you'll have access to as you come to enjoy the wonders of the modern all-digital telephone system. You'll probably get another cheat-sheet for that one, too, because the telecom manager knows you didn't go to the first class, and have probably already lost that first cheat-sheet.

And then, one fine day shortly after the system is installed and everyone's complaining about it, you're going to get a visit from someone who's going to take your modem away. Don't worry, this vandal will tell you: he giveth as surely as he taketh away. He's going to run a cable from one of the many available serial ports on the back of your PC to a connector on the back of your new telephone. And then, he's going to tell you proudly, you'll be able to use one of the lines into the wonderful new modem pool, which is hidden somewhere in the telecommunications wiring closet.

There's no need for your own dial-out line any more—and thus, of course, you have no need for that modem. Instead, you can enjoy the wonders of the modern all-digital telephone system, which can deliver anything you want over that single cable running to your telephone.

There's just one little problem: you'll probably never have reliable dial-out modem access again. And if you now sometimes call into your office PC with a remote communications program when you're traveling, or log onto it at night when you discover you forgot to bring home a file you want to work on in your den . . . well, you'll soon find you have no dial-in modem access anymore at *all.*

This Is Progress?

Telecom managers love to pull out PC users' modems and put the company into modem pooling. They have swell arguments about how cost-efficient pooled modems are. Just drop a few rack-mount modems into the telecom system, route your modem access through your digital telephone, and the company will save a small fortune on telephone line charges. And just think of all the money they can recover through selling those used modems they confiscate!

Modem-pooling is a crock. I've been through it with dozens of client companies. It always sounds good when it's pitched to the telecom planning committee; it always looks good on paper; it's a telecom manager's dream.

And it never works right. *Ever.*

Do you have a spare serial port on your PC? I don't. Sure, you had to have a serial port available for your modem, but that was probably an internal modem that didn't need an external serial-port connector, and you (or your company's PC-support group) may well have played tricks with the PC's interrupts to share that communications port with another device.

Do you have a second, spare serial *connector* on the back of your PC? I don't. Many PCs come with just one parallel and one serial connector installed.

Has your telecom manager ever heard of things like mice and trackballs—which need a serial port? Or plotters, which usually require serial ports? Or digitizing tablets? For that matter, has your telecom manger ever actually *seen* a PC serial port . . . or has he only heard about them from the salesmen for the digital phone system he just bought?

It gets worse. Just getting your PC and communications software working with pooled modems takes forever. I know of one company where skilled PC support people took weeks to work out the bizarre, lengthy new character string PC users' communications software had to send just to grab a dial tone through the modem pool. (Naturally, the documentation for the digital phone system had the character-string wrong.) Some of the PC communications software packages in use in that company wouldn't support such a long character string. The lucky users of those packages also got the thrill of learning a new communications program, as they enjoyed the wonders of the modern all-digital telephone system.

Once you get the system up and running—if you do—you'll probably find that at least some of the features of your comm software no longer work properly. Users of *Lotus Express,* a sophisticated comm program that uses tight links with MCI Mail to provide powerful e-mail access and message-storage, will be tearing their hair out as they try to get it working with this swell new modem pool.

Thanks, But No Thanks

I'm hardly antitechnology, and I like wringing fat out of data-processing and telecommunications budgets as much as the next harried manager. And I'd love to enjoy the wonders of a modern all-digital telephone system. But watch out for that guy who wants to take your modem, and promises you you'll never know the difference.

Tell him sure, and your check's in the mail, too. And then tell him to get lost.

TIME OUT IV

Measuring Productivity:
You Don't Have to Lie
About the Numbers

The payback on PCs is incredibly fast. Even as the purchase price of top-of-the-line PCs has crept past $10,000, and now $20,000, the value the machines deliver has continued to outpace the increase in prices. The idea of depreciating PCs over three to five years is an accounting fiction fostered by the IRS's depreciation-guidelines schedule; if this were a sane and rational world, we'd expense 'em and be done with it.

But actually *measuring* that productivity is a lot harder than knowing in your bones that it exists. It isn't hard to see how an assistant is far more productive using a PC, Microsoft *Word*, and an H-P LaserJet than she was when she used a Correcting Selectric typewriter. If you're content with characters-per-second comparisons, or with "captured keystrokes" counts, then the calculations are easy. But obviously that assistant doesn't sit and type all the time. What about her productivity while she's searching through drawers for a file, making a couple of Xerox copies at the machine down the hall, picking up a fax, or sorting through a stack of the boss's unfiled expense-account receipts from last December? That PC didn't directly help with those things . . . and yet they're certainly important parts of her job.

How do you measure productivity increases if you're talking about *overall* productivity, not just specific-task productivity?

What about a draftsman who moves from Rapidograph pens and a T-square to *AutoCad* and a Compaq 486? Drawings aren't a whole lot faster to create under that new system, but they're enormously faster to *revise*—and revisions are the biggest cost in drafting. What about quality? The drawings that now roll off that big E-size plotter tied to the draftsman's Compaq are far more accurate, far more legible than the old pen-and-ink work on vellum or mylar. Measurements shown on the drawings are more precise. So there are fewer mistakes on job-sites, fewer change orders and remakes. Surely that kind of quality improvement is part of an increased-productivity calculation. But how do you run those numbers?

Weighing Paybacks

The really hard questions come when we start trying to measure the productivity improvements PCs can bring to professionals, managers, and technical and creative people. They don't get paid to do piecework; you can't measure keystrokes or square inches of base drawings or any other obvious measure. *Yet you know the payback from putting PCs on the desks of those professionals far outweighs the payback from helping secretaries type letters faster.* If only because making someone who takes home $50,000 or $75,000 a year more productive means a far faster payback than improving the productivity of someone making $17,500.

The first thing you can do is argue that this is like trying to count angels on the head of a pin. As useful and maybe important as quantifying productivity gains can be, if everyone involved can come to agreement that for a certain class of workers—say, your field salespeople, or your securities analysts, or your managers of departments with five or more workers—productivity, the quality of decision-making, personal growth, and job satisfaction have all increased substantially, and by a far greater amount than the cost of putting PCs on their desks, do you really need to attach a number?

If the purpose of such productivity-improvement assessments is to decide whether to spend the money to extend those improvements further throughout the company, isn't the certainty that the reward substantially exceeds the cost enough to justify the investment? Do you still need precise quantification?

Unfortunately, the answer may be yes. Meaningless quantification is still revered in some companies.

If Count You Must . . .

If you try to carry the day with the *"why do we need exact numbers?"* argument but fail, then let me suggest that you adopt a simple rule for the frustrating work that is going to follow: Don't lie.

Moreover, don't *appear* to lie.

I've spent thousands of hours working with clients on projects designed to measure real-world PC productivity gains. I can't recall a single case where I thought in the end that (a) the effort was worth the cost, or (b) the numbers were right. Start down that path, and you start down a road to frustration and, finally, very little satisfaction with what you've accomplished.

But at minimum, you can promise yourself that the results aren't going to make you look stupid. Even if the assignment itself was.

I've seen dozens of PC-productivity studies that reported results so far beyond the realm of probability that I wince at the thought of reading even one more of them. I have seen highly scientific studies—I should say, studies that were made to appear highly scientific, while having little basis in fact—that blithely reported such things as "average productivity gains for middle-managers over the first six months of PC use of 43 percent."

Think about that for a minute. Think about what a productivity gain of *43 percent* over six months would be. If you're really measuring productivity in an environment turned a hundred and eighty degrees away from piecework—and that's not a bad description, if certainly an incomplete one, of the typical manager's job—how can anyone with a straight face report a 43 percent average gain in productivity?

Who *are* these slugs who got 43 percent more productive? What were they doing before?

Did they even come to work?

When a report like that hits the desks of top managers (and assuming they get beyond the Executive Summary), it destroys the credibility of the people who worked on the report. You don't get to be a CEO by believing that your middle-level managers were suddenly 43 percent more productive than they were six months earlier. Ten percent, maybe. Twelve percent, possibly. And you'd *kill* for 15 percent greater productivity—over a year or two.

But 43 percent in six months?

Unfortunately, the same opprobrium that eventually attaches to the people who produce these hyperinflated studies also attaches to the whole notion of gaining productivity improvements by putting a PC on people's desktops. If these results, so laughably exaggerated, are the best we can come up with, maybe the whole idea that people are more productive when they get their hands on a PC is phony. Why else, the reader of the report soon comes to wonder, would these people have concocted this nonsense? What are they covering up?

"Have we spent $12 million-something over the last five years bringing PCs in here—and at least that much more on showing our employees how to use them effectively—in vain?"

You have at least two good reasons not to let your name appear on reports that indulge in such whimsy. First, to save your own hide; second, to save the credibility of the idea that PCs really are productivity tools.

Don't hang yourself. And please, don't hang the rest of us, either.

When Software
Upgrades Become
*Counter-*Productivity Steps

During the first few years that PCs were coming into wide use in business, most PC users looked forward with eager anticipation to the next releases of their favorite software programs. There were so many things missing, we complained, that no matter what they fixed in the next release, it *had* to be worth it. And the cost—in cash as well as in time and trouble—was small for the individual upgrader. Usually priced from $25–$75, next-release upgrades were a cheap way to keep up with the technology.

In corporations with large fleets of PCs, most of which ran the same suites of corporate-standard programs, regular upgrades to each succeeding release also kept users in sync, using the same versions of those programs, which made for easy personnel moves within the company, and also made life easier for the people who staffed the Help Desk in the PC-support department. And corporations could negotiate very favorable prices for upgrades—sometimes, in those days, *free* upgrades, if the account was large and important enough—that made upgrading a great bargain.

But a funny thing happened as the PC software business began to mature: a number of large PC-using companies started to question whether they needed to go through the upgrading process every time a supplier released a new version of one of the company's approved-and-adopted programs.

In part that was because the programs themselves had grown so much better and more stable. Software-induced crashes have become rare, indeed, with the mainstream business PC applications. And those programs' feature sets—

the range of things they can do—have grown so large that most users today use only a relatively small part of the programs' capabilities. Why, then, corporate PC managers began to ask, should they continue to upgrade hundreds or thousand of users to new versions of programs, when there was little of value for the great majority of those users in the new releases?

The second reason for the growing resistance to automatic upgrading was that companies began to realize just how much upgrades were really costing them. Say a company has 1,000 users of *WordWonder.* A new release comes along, and they can buy upgrades for all those users for $50 each. That's $50,000 just to start. But the internal costs of distributing the software and manuals, getting the program loaded onto users' computers—most PC users will require at least some assistance, and in many companies, the PC support group installs *all* new software on users' machines—and helping users make the transition to the new versions will cost at least twice, and probably three to four times, the amount spent on buying the upgrade itself.

All of a sudden our $50,000 investment—not a trivial figure, by any means—has blossomed into a $100,000–$200,000 event. And at every company I know, including the largest ones, $200,000 expenditures require substantial cost justification.

But wait: we decided few of our users would really get much out of this upgrade. So why spend the dough?

It's easy to see why that costly habit of automatically upgrading has gone out the window.

All this was brought home to me recently during a consulting visit to a Fortune 1000 company I've worked with for years. I was chatting with one of their information-systems managers, and asked how their upgrade from *Word-Perfect* 5.0 to the then-newly-released version 5.1 was going. He laughed. Not only, he told me, were they not upgrading from 5.0 to 5.1 . . . they were still using 4.2, and hadn't found a reason in any of *WordPerfect's* later releases to upgrade. Moreover, he didn't think they would be upgrading any time in the foreseeable future. *WordPerfect* 4.2 did everything they needed; their people knew how to use it; its cost had long since been recovered; they were now using, in effect, free software. So why change?

Why, indeed?

That principle applies equally to the individual user. We tend to ignore the costs of installing and learning those upgrades we load on the machine ourselves, then slog through the new manuals to learn. But these costs are real—and they come out of our pockets and out of time we could devote to other work . . . or to a few sets of tennis, or to reading a new book, or to a thousand other, better ways of spending the time.

I've come to look with a jaundiced eye at highly touted new releases of the software upon which I rely. I unabashedly use a two-year old version of *1-2-3,* for example, for much of my spreadsheet work. I've skipped the latest upgrade of my main word-processing program, and from what I've seen of its next release, I'll probably skip that one, too. Performance continues to improve with succeeding releases of the database program I use, but the point of diminishing returns seems pretty near there, too. My choice for desktop publishing, *PageMaker,* still has a lot of growing to do, so I do keep up with major (whole-number) upgrades there. I jumped at *Windows* 3.0, since I found previous versions almost unusable, but I'm not going to reflexively sign up for every new *Windows* upgrade.

In practice, many software upgrades have in fact become *counter*-productive steps for PC users and also for managers of huge fleets of PCs. I hardly think we're Luddites, ready to stab our wooden stakes into the gears of progress, simply because we examine critically the offerings of each new version of the software upon which we rely; and when we find little that applies to our work—when the gain falls short of the pain—we ought to say "thanks, but no thanks."

And go on happily using what we know well and find well suited to our needs.

Why Senior Management Doesn't Use PCs . . . Yet

It really galls a lot of PC buffs, power users, micro managers, and others that while the people in the trenches in their companies make such good use of PCs in their everyday routines, the people at the top don't much care for them.

Sure, the CEO and COO may have PCs on the credenzas behind their desks. They may even know where the power switches on those machines are. But those PCs don't get much of a workout. You can search their hard disks for file creation dates and not find one more than a day or two after the machine was installed . . . months or years ago.

This isn't, we should note, really a matter of whether top management uses PCs, but rather, whether they use computers at all. Certainly they appreciate the value of computers, and the contributions the machines make to running the company, to gaining strategic advantages, to making workers more productive. And certainly there are some business leaders who use computers themselves, and use them effectively. Ben Heinemann at Northwest Industries was one: a high-profile advocate for extending the power of the computer to the desk of every "knowledge worker."

But it's fair to say—and I generalize here, but I don't care, because the generalization is correct—that those in top management of American corporations don't use computers much. They have, as they'll tell you in a second, *people to do that for them.*

They see themselves as overseers, as managers of people and capital, but not of raw data. They move people and capital around, funding this venture in its formative stages by milking that one as a cash-cow. They haven't time or interest in wrestling with data themselves; they use their top managers as screens for that kind of data. They aren't much interested in seeing a computer's analysis of the company's present situation or prospects; they want to hear what their managers think about that position or those prospects.

And they're right.

None of that means that computers generally, and PCs specifically, haven't anything to contribute to helping top management do its job better. But until we accept the notions that top executives' jobs aren't like those of the people a few layers down, and these people at the top have a pretty good sense of what their needs and priorities are, we're not going to make much progress on supporting their decision-making processes with PCs.

Information to Manage By

The single most important thing PCs can do is deliver up-to-the-minute information about The State of The Corporation to its senior managers. Top executives can also use e-mail effectively; a CEO with a personal touch may want to write the occasional speech on his PC; a numbers guy may want to massage the figures on a big deal once more himself, in *1-2-3*, at his PC. But day-in, day-out, nothing a PC can deliver to a top-level executive is as valuable as up-to-date information.

The perverse thing about using PCs to get that information is that they've not been much better at the job than a simple terminal. Because information on that scale typically lives on the company's mainframes, or at least in its minicomputers, or in rare (but increasingly frequent) cases on the servers attached to its local area networks. And because he doesn't so much want to play what-if with the information at the computer as simply be able to get at that information on a moment's notice, PCs haven't brought much more to the executive's desk than decent terminals.

I can hear the moans and groans now from the PC Faithful: *Heresy! What is he saying?*

Stay with me.

What that small group of people at the top of a company really needs is quick access to a relatively small universe of linked data about the company's performance. The size of that group? Never more then 20, probably fewer than a dozen, usually no more than six or seven. The number of people who can really use this information varies, depending on corporate structure, but it's not a very long list. And it isn't strictly hierarchical.

One approach to delivering such information has been the traditional Executive Information Systems path. Someone, or more often several someones, in the MIS department are detailed to write routines that capture and present, often graphically, some basic information on the company: current ratios, actual-vs.-plan performance, sales histories and forecasts. Then someone writes, or buys, a presentation package for that data. Which, once installed, calls up the mainframes in the MIS department's Glass House, asks for the data, formats it graphically, and ships it back to the querying terminal or PC.

At the user end, the interface may be a series of boxes on-screen, each with a category shown in it. (The similarity to *Jeopardy* is at once hilarious and not at all unintentional.) The executive launches a query by hitting the function key for a certain report, or typing in the single letter shown for that report, or maybe moving a mouse's cursor to that box and clicking. On some EIS systems, he or she may just touch the screen. Before long, that report appears on-screen.

The usefulness of that kind of MIS system is tied closely to the degree of customization possible within it, and the willingness of the MIS group to make fast changes in the system, to accommodate executives' requests for new "screens" of data. Indeed, the frequency with which those executives ask for new features on the system is a good measure of the importance they attach to it. If people use the system heavily and come to rely on it, they're going to be demanding new reports, and new formats for existing reports, all the time. To use any system is to spot the gaps within it and want them to be filled; people on the level we're talking about have both the savvy to spot those gaps and the clout to get them filled fast.

If they use the system.

EIS: Flawed Designs

Executive Information Systems are nothing new. But despite a long history in the market, they've hardly taken over. Comshare and a few other old-time EIS outfits do OK, but they're not burning up the market. Metaphor Systems has great new ideas and good products, but not a very long customer list. Something's missing here; this idea is so good that it must be the implementation. Else *every* company of any size would have one of these systems installed.

In fact, the two things missing are the two missing links PCs can provide better than any other tools: transparent interconnectivity on the system level, and effortless interactivity on the user's level.

There have been two basic models for the management of data within EISs. In one, every query that comes through to the MIS department from an executive's EIS terminal is seen as a new job. The system runs around scooping up data, makes any necessary calculations, formats the data, and sends it back to the terminal. No computation capability (or only very little) is required at the terminal, so a dumb device (in the technical sense) is perfectly appropriate at the user's end.

This kind of system has the advantage of immediacy—the data shown is always the most recent data available—but it also takes a while for each of those queries to be answered. Which leads to a lot of drumming of fingers on the desktop, as busy, high-paid executives sit waiting for each screenful of information to be assembled and displayed. Systems using this model also typically support a wide range of possible queries, and it's a simple matter to add new queries to the system, since writing the code for that new query is a one-time job for an MIS programmer.

In the second model, a relatively small number of predefined reports are devised, each delivering one screenful of information. A decision is made as to how old the information can be and still be of value to management. The MIS department custom builds those screens at that interval—every day, every week, every month. Sometimes the predefined screens are literally rebuilt by hand by MIS staffers; more often, code is written to assemble and store them, usually in the early morning hours when few other demands are being made on the system. Information varies in the importance of its immediacy, of course; so the intervals at which the screens are updated usually vary from topic to topic.

The idea here is to give very fast answers: those prebuilt screens can be delivered to executives' terminals about as fast as they can hit the keys. But the system does so at considerable cost in the immediacy of the information shown; by definition, it's *always* old. "Old" may mean only a day or so, but if later information is available within the company, why can't these executives have that most recent, most up-to-date information? And why must they limit themselves to a short list of queries?

The Answer

I can hear what you're thinking.

Why, with fast PCs, fast local area networks, fast network servers, and fast bridges between networks to mainframes, can't a system like this be constructed that uses the best of three worlds: the mainframe as a central repository of data; the server as a constantly updated way station and formatter of that data; and the executive's PC as a retrieval system and manipulator of the data on his or her desk?

Why can't that system accommodate a huge range of queries, not just a few? And not just simple, canned queries, but cross-tabbed queries, and queries the users of connected PCs interactively change as they issue them—and still get nearly instant response?

Why can't a single additional server on the executives' LAN automatically and transparently gather the necessary information to service those queries, as often as new data is available on the mainframe, so every screen shown is *always* up to date?

Why can't the system resident on the individual PCs connected to this grid make certain kinds of what-if'ing easy, even semiautomatic—offering executives a range of options when they ask for some screens, including among those options local data-manipulation on the PC?

And why can't the system watch each executive's data-querying habits, "learn" those habits, and start *anticipating* requests—for example, constantly gathering, in the background, the information needed for the half-dozen or dozen queries he makes most often, so those are available, fully up-to-date, in a flash? And looking ahead every time a query is issued to the kind of query the executive usually goes to next after he's seen that set of data, so it can be displayed as soon as he hits a key?

There's no reason that couldn't be done today. It's a job only PCs and distributed processing built on a client-server network model can handle.

And it's what's going to put PCs on executives' desks around the world.

◆

IX

ON THE SYSTEM LEVEL

AUTOEXEC Savvy

One of the most basic files on your PC is the AUTOEXEC.BAT file. When you turn on the PC, the computer first loads DOS, then immediately looks for this file. If it finds an AUTOEXEC file—they're optional, but it's hard to imagine using a PC without one—it runs the series of commands included in that file before producing the familiar C> prompt, so you can begin working.

In the process, an AUTOEXEC file can completely reconfigure your PC. It will call programs that reorganize and assign memory, change video-display attributes, tell the PC how to find the application programs you use, and load any pop-up programs you may use. Finally, it can deliver you to either that C> prompt or to a shell program you've chosen to make using the PC easier.

Old hands in the PC business wind up with AUTOEXEC files 40 or 50 lines long—sometimes even longer. And tweaking their AUTOEXECs becomes almost a hobby with some power users: they keep seeking that elusive goal of a perfect AUTOEXEC file. Of course, their definition of "perfect" keeps changing, too, which keeps the game interesting for them.

If you've been using a PC for very long, all this is no doubt old hat to you. You probably have an AUTOEXEC file of a dozen or 20 lines, which does some pretty exotic things as it sets up your PC for your style of working. If you're a relative newcomer, or a more casual PC user who's not caught up in the technical aspects of computers, you'll be surprised at the things an AUTOEXEC file can do for you.

Either way, there are a few simple tricks even old-timers haven't yet caught on to that can make setting up and maintaining an AUTOEXEC file easier.

- **Don't try to use EDLIN to create or maintain an AUTOEXEC file.** EDLIN, the feeble line-editor included with DOS, is one of the crummiest programs ever written. It's clumsy, limited, and a nuisance to use—yet almost every PC's manual, and most PC books, begin by telling you how to use it to create and later modify AUTOEXEC files (and your CONFIG.SYS file, and other batch files).

It's better by far to use your word processor—any word processor, even the simplest ones—for that job. Just make sure you use the word processor in its plain ASCII text mode, so it doesn't add control characters, so it uses zero-width margins, and so it doesn't add a file-header that would confuse DOS.

- **Always save a copy of your current AUTOEXEC file on a floppy disk or in a subdirectory somewhere on your hard disk, before you start changing the file.** That gives you a fast, secure way to revert to the old version if a change you've made produces unexpected and unwelcome results. (See *Protecting Your Stash*, later in this section, for more on AUTOEXEC protection.)

- **As you modify your AUTOEXEC file, don't delete lines you aren't using any more.** Instead, add the letters REM at the beginning of the line, followed by a space. DOS interprets that as a "REMark," or nonexecutable line, and simply skips over it when running through the commands in your AUTOEXEC file.

  "REM'ming out" obsolete lines in your AUTOEXEC file is one of the most useful tricks you'll ever find for working with batch files; it makes it easy to reactivate those lines if you change your mind, by simply deleting the REM tag. This is especially important when there are a number of tricky-to-set parameters on the line; if you need to reactivate that command line you won't have to experiment to find the correct values, but instead can simply erase the REM and space at the head of the line.

- **Use a PROMPT command.** Your DOS manual explains the many uses of the PROMPT command. Simply put, it lets you change the C> prompt to whatever you wish. The most common change is to use PROMPT to reset the C> to a line that shows you the current path. That's done by adding a line to your AUTOEXEC that reads PROMPT pg. Thereafter, your C> prompt will appear instead as, say, C:\MSWORD50\CORRESP> if your current path is set for the CORRESP subdirectory in the MSWORD50 directory of drive C. (Though you could type that line manually every time your PC starts up, putting it in your AUTOEXEC.BAT file means the modified C> prompt is installed automatically for you. Which is what the "auto" in AUTOEXEC is all about.)

- **Consider using a sign-on message.** It's easy to build a simple screen that appears when the PC is booted up, and asks anyone into whose hands your PC falls to return it to you. This suggestion appears, in much more detail, in *Lost, Strayed, and Stolen PCs*, in the **On the Road** section of this book; but the idea is much more widely applicable.

A "please return me" message isn't a bad idea for desktop machines, which get stolen in office (and home) break-ins, and are unlikely to be turned on until they're fenced to a used-computer dealer or pawn shop. A screen with your name and telephone number may well bring that PC (and probably more importantly, the precious data on its hard disk) back to you.

But other sign-on messages can be helpful, too. For example, if your office has a shared PC, which rolls around on a cart to the desk of whomever needs it at the moment, a sign-on screen might alert users to its memory configuration, any special programs on its hard disk, or even a reminder to return it to its usual location when they're finished. I've also seen sign-on screens created by PC managers that included support information, such as the company's Help Desk telephone extension number, and a few 800 numbers for outside support for programs on the machine's hard disk.

It's easy to fall into the habit of frequent tinkering with your AUTOEXEC file. I try to avoid that, and you should, too. It's easy to lose an hour in Fritter Factor time fiddling with the file, without producing a detectable improvement. But it *is* worth going through that tweaking when you make a substantial change in your PC's working environment. Adding significantly more RAM, loading new versions of memory-management utilities, installing a new pop-up program—all require or at least suggest tuning up that critical AUTOEXEC start-up file.

These tricks can help you do that safely and easily.

❧

Cache Flow

Most worthwhile PC enhancements are pretty expensive, and most involve buying some hardware. Adding more memory can almost always speed up a PC's operations, as well as letting it tackle larger programs—but memory chips and SIMMs can cost a hundred dollars or more per megabyte. A math coprocessor chip can speed up calculations with programs designed to look for and use a numeric coprocessor—but math chips cost several hundred dollars. A bigger, faster hard disk can make a dramatic difference—but hard disks cost *thousands* of dollars.

There's one profound performance enhancement you can install on your PC, though, that doesn't involve buying new hardware, and will cost well under a hundred dollars. Just add a software-based disk-caching program, and the speed of your PC will increase dramatically. The process takes only a couple of minutes—you just copy the caching program to your hard disk, then add a line to your AUTOEXEC.BAT file to put it to work—but the payback in terms of perceived speed gain will knock you out.

Disk-cache programs work by trying to guess your next move. Every time a program you're running has to go to the hard disk to read more information into active memory, there's a delay while the hard disk finds that data, moves its heads into place to read it, intercepts the information as the disk comes spinning around to the heads, then sends that data to working memory. The other end of the process—writing new or changed data to the disk once the program has completed its work with the information—causes a delay as well, of course.

These are *tiny* delays, with today's speedy hard disks . . . but they're delays nonetheless. And their cumulative effect can be substantial, especially with programs that go to disk a great deal.

Caching programs try to reduce, and sometimes even almost eliminate, those delays, by setting aside a block of RAM to use as a kind of way station between the computer's working memory and the hard disk. When your application program first reads in data from the disk, the caching program watches that read, then tries to guess what you and the program will want to see next. As soon as that first batch of data is moved to memory, the caching program reads into its block of RAM the data it thinks you'll want next. Thereafter, on all disk-read requests, the caching program looks through the data it has already fetched, to see if the information you need is there. If so, it passes that data directly to memory—and looks to the hard disk again, guessing what you'll want next time and moving *that* data into the cache.

An Easy Speed-Up

Moving data from one block of RAM to another—from the cache's RAM to the PC's working RAM—is much faster than going through the electromechanical process of finding the data on disk, readying the disk to read it, retrieving the data, then sending it to working RAM. So the effective time required for the disk-read is much shorter. Which makes the PC seem to run *much* faster.

As you work, a disk cache continues this process, working invisibly in the background, trying to outguess you and your application program. Good caching programs are *very* good guessers; their "hit rate," or the number of times the data sought is already available in the RAM cache, is over 90 percent.

Caching programs not only cache disk reads, but also disk writes. Rather than waiting for the hard disk to completely store all the information sent to it, the caching program intercepts that data, fills the cache with it, then starts writing it to the disk. If the data sent is larger than the cache space, the caching program manages a constant process of refilling the cache at the top, so to speak, while draining off data at the bottom and writing it to the disk.

There is some very small risk of losing data with cached disk-writes—should you suffer a power failure during a cached disk-write-the information not yet stored on the disk would be lost—but in practice that same power loss might still lose some of the data, without a cache . . . and in any case, power failures are (or ought to be!) rare events.

If you're concerned about possible data loss with cached disk writes, you can turn off the write-caching process in your caching. I consider the risk of lost data extremely small, and leave write-caching turned on all the time.

The best disk-caching program I've used is *Super PC-Kwik.* It's available separately for under $100, or as part of a *Super PC-Kwik* "Power Pack," with a number of other utilities (none of which I use) for a little more.

On a raw-performance basis, *Super PC-Kwik* tops every other caching program I've tested. But beyond absolute performance, I like *Super PC-Kwik* because it offers so many controls to let me fine-tune it for my computing environment. Not only can you set the size of the cache—how much memory you're willing to surrender for the RAM cache—you can divide memory among standard, extended, and expanded RAM. You can also use a phenomenal variety of "soft switches"—letters and numbers added to the command line in your AUTOEXEC file that loads *Super PC-Kwik*—to control just how it does its job.

Caching Tips

If you decide to use a caching program, here are a few suggestions for maximizing the speed gain without using too much of that valuable RAM.

- **Use as much extended or expanded memory, as opposed to base 640 KB DOS memory, as possible for the cache.** Many caching programs (including *Super PC-Kwik*) allow you to use mostly high memory (that is, extended memory, or extended memory converted to expanded memory) for the cache, with only a small kernel of the caching code in base RAM. That works extremely well: while there is a tiny theoretical performance penalty to caching in high memory, in practice the overall speed gain is so great that you'll never notice that theoretical loss. (But if you don't have any extended or expanded memory available, don't forsake caching programs; just use as little DOS memory, probably 16 KB to 32 KB or so, as you can get away with. The benefits will still be evident the first time you boot up your newly cached PC.)

- **Don't go overboard on cache size.** As little as 8 KB of cache memory can make a noticeable difference in computing speed. I've found the optimum cache size—considering the other important uses contending for the RAM installed in our PCs!—is usually between 64 KB and 128 KB. A very large cache—say, 1 or 2 MB of RAM—can produce somewhat faster results, but not nearly the huge gain you'd expect from surrendering that much more memory to the caching function.

- **Don't cache floppies.** Unless you write a lot of data from within applications to floppy disks, it's probably better to turn off caching for your PC's floppy disk drives. Also, remember that caching programs expect to find the same disk in the same drive all the time. Removable media—floppy disks, for example—can cause problems. If you start a program while running a cache, save data once or twice through a write-cache, then swap floppy disks again and save again, you might wind up losing data.

- **Use caching on your lap-portable!** Too often even experienced PC power users associate such tricks as disk-caching only with their powerful desktop machines. In practice, the generally lower performance of portable PCs means they need even more of the speed gains possible with caching. If your portable has only floppy disk drives, ignore the advice in the preceding paragraph, and cache those drives. If you use a floppy-based portable, you need all the performance help you can get. Just develop good habits about disk-swapping.

Disk-caching programs are my favorite PC speed-up trick. They're inexpensive, easy to install, invisible in daily use—and provide more immediate payback than any other simple way I know to boost your PC's performance.

❧

The Magic F3 Key

If you use a PC very much, you use its function keys—that row of keys marked F1 through F12 (or higher), strung across the top of the keyboard, or those two odd vertical rows of keys, F1 through F10, at the keyboard's left edge—fairly often. In fact, if you run a PC program that is heavily function-key oriented—*WordPerfect* is the classic example—you use those keys a *lot*.

Did you know you can use them at the C> prompt, when you're in DOS, as well?

Probably you didn't: the DOS functions of those function keys are almost unknown. In a way that isn't so surprising, since when Microsoft developed the MS-DOS operating system upon which we rely, it made very poor use of those keys. Most of the functions they provide under DOS seem to have been intended more for programmers than for people using PCs for personal-productivity tasks—and even the ones intended for programmers aren't very well thought out. But there's one DOS function key assignment that is genuinely helpful.

To understand the DOS function-key operations, you need to know that DOS considers whatever you type in at the C> prompt a kind of reusable template. It not only executes that command—or tries to, fails, then reports your error, if you made a mistake—but it also stores a copy of that line you typed in a special memory area called the *template*. Because that line has been stored, the function keys can selectively retrieve all or part of it for you to reuse. That's helpful when, say, you discover a typing mistake near the very beginning of a long typed command . . . and you don't want to have to type in the whole command again.

Here's what those function keys can do under DOS:

The **F1** key will retype your previous command for you, one character at a time. I find that pretty useless; it's usually faster to manually retype the whole line, or use F3 (as below), then backspace in from the right end of the line.

The **F2** key copies a fragment of the previous command, up to a character you type after hitting the F2 key. (For example, if you typed ABCDEFG, and wanted the F2 key to automatically retype the first five characters of that line for you, up to the F, you'd hit F2, then F.)

F3 is the one really useful DOS function key: it simply repeats whole the last command you typed.

The **F4** and **F5** keys are essentially useless.

The **F6** key inserts a CTRL + Z character, which is needed to close a file such as an AUTOEXEC.BAT batch file, so it can be executed. (But you probably edit your AUTOEXEC in your word processor, so this one's not very helpful, either.)

The **F7** and higher keys are not used under DOS.

Finally, the ESC key will wipe out a mistaken line you've just typed (before you hit ENTER to try to execute it), drop down a line, and let you begin again without having to backspace over that bad line.

There now. Don't you feel virtuous for knowing about those DOS function keys? Seriously, you can forget about all of them except F3. You'll find it handy when you're issuing a directory-listing command, or a format command, or another DOS command-line entry . . . and make a mistake.

❧

A Better DIRectory
Command

One of the most common instructions PC users type into their machines is the DIRectory command, which displays a listing of the files stored in the default directory on the logged disk. Type DIR and hit ENTER, and a long list of filenames scrolls right down your screen—and down, and down, and down, right off the bottom of the display. So fast, usually, that you won't be able to read a one of them.

Savvy PC users know that you can use the CTRL + S keystroke combination as a kind of toggle switch, to stop and restart again and again that inscrutable list of files as it races by. That's always good fun, too: trying to time your CTRL + S's so that you get a whole new screen of files displayed between each use of the command—but don't miss any filenames that scroll off before you can stop the list. (PC purists also know that you can get the same result by banging away at the CTRL + NUMLOCK keystroke combination, which is even less convenient.)

There are better ways to look at a directory of your files.

The first brings some sanity to that scrolling process, by grouping filename displays into clusters of 23 files each. Just add a space, a slash, and the letter p (for "pause," in upper- or lowercase—it doesn't matter) after the letters DIR, as

C>DIR /p

and then hit ENTER to execute the command. This time, notice that the PC scrolls through just one screenful of filenames, then politely stops and asks you to strike any key when you're ready to continue. It will then show you one more screenful, and stop again until you hit a key.

Nice, huh?

There's another better-DIR trick. Since DOS filenames can only include a maximum of 12 characters (eight letters or numbers, a period, and three more letters or numbers), the standard DIR command, whether stopped with a /p addition or not, wastes a lot of your screen. DOS also displays file sizes and the time and date each file was created or last changed, but even with that information, the standard DIR command still uses only about half your screen.

If you're willing to give up that file size, date, and time information, you can get five times as many files listed on-screen at once. Just type a space, a slash, and a w (for "wide") after the DIR command, as

    C>DIR /w

and now DOS will show you five neat columns of filenames across the screen.

I can hear your next question: can you combine the two command extensions? Sure. Just type

    C>DIR /p /w

and DOS will show you 23 rows by 5 columns of filenames—115 in all—and then (assuming the directory you're examining has still more files) invite you to tap a key to see the next five-column screenful.

These tricks are useful any time you're looking through directory listings. They can be absolutely indispensable when you're in a hurry.

❧

VERsions of DOS

Quick: which version of DOS do you have on your PC?

If you don't know, or if you're not certain, you're not alone. Even computer-savvy PC users can find it hard to remember which version of DOS is loaded on their PCs. Especially since many serious PC users began avoiding IBM and Microsoft's buggy DOS upgrades somewhere around DOS 4.0, it's no longer safe to assume the most recent version has been installed on your machine.

Yet when you're talking with telephone-support people about software or hardware problems, one of the first questions they ask is usually "Which version of DOS are you using?"

One of DOS's least-known commands will tell you in an instant which version is running on your PC. At the C> prompt, just type VER, and DOS will immediately respond with your version number.

The VER command is one of a group of so-called "internal" DOS commands —that is, commands that are hidden away inside the COMMAND.COM file DOS installs on your disk, rather than those more familiar commands that exist as separate (and visible) DOS files, such as FORMAT.COM, CHKDSK.COM, or XCOPY.EXE.

Knowing which version of DOS is controlling your machine may not be a very interesting factoid—but it can be extremely useful in tracking down problems.

❧

Stupid RAM Tricks

If you've been using a PC for some time—maybe since those early, heady days not long after the IBM PC was introduced, when those of us who dragged them into our offices felt like guerrilla fighters—you may still be using some tricks you learned long ago. Especially with the RAM installed in your PC.

One of the oldest PC-user tricks is to set aside part of the computer's block of memory as a "RAM disk," a disk-simulator into which you can load and from which you can run programs that repeatedly return to the disk to swap into the rest of the PC's memory little modules, or overlays, of program code.

That's one example of a category of holdovers from the early days, which I suspect David Letterman would call "stupid RAM tricks."

We used RAM disks mainly because the software we used hadn't been written to run on IBM PCs. Programs like *Wordstar* came from a different environment—not to mention a different age!—in which computers had so little memory that they couldn't hold a whole application in RAM at once. So the programmers worked around those other machines' limitations by breaking up their programs into small chunks of code, which were repeatedly read from disk into memory, used, then overwritten in RAM (or overlaid, hence the term "overlays") by the next module of code, as it was called in.

That was an effective work-around for another generation of computing . . . but it came at a price. The process of constantly reloading pieces of code into memory one after another, with a trip to the floppy disk for every new module, was incredibly slow. Floppy disk drives are slow, and all those trips to disk meant users were often left waiting while the computer searched for, found, and read into memory the next piece of the program.

Smart users instead created a simulated floppy disk out of RAM. That imaginary disk could be formatted and then used just as if it were a real one; transfers from it were almost instantaneous. Programs that used a lot of overlays could be loaded onto that simulated disk, from which they could then be run many times faster.

RAM disks were a clever idea, and made a big difference for some PC users.

Today, however, there are at least two good reasons to avoid wasting memory on RAM disks. First, relatively few programs in wide use today use extensive overlays. Some that do, such as Borland's *Quattro Pro*, use a newer software technology (which Borland calls *VROOM!*), to speed up necessary code-swaps. You needn't worry about overlay problems with most of today's PC software.

Second, we have better things to do with RAM than sacrificing it for needless RAM disks. Using a large disk cache, for example (see *Cache Flow*, in this section), can speed up overall operation of your computer more effectively than a RAM disk can.

To be sure, there are some situations today where RAM disks make sense. Users of *Ventura Desktop Publisher, Professional Edition,* for example, soon learn the benefits of using a RAM disk. And *Windows* users may be using a RAM disk without realizing it, depending on how they have set up their PCs.

But for most mainstream PC work, RAM disks are a relic from the past, an outdated idea that can now be safely retired.

❧

A Little Privacy,
Please

Funny, sometimes, how we misuse PC products. By which I mean turning them to ends other than—sometimes, almost opposite to—those intended by their developers.

Revolution Software's *VGA Dimmer* is a good example. There are scores of little screen-dimming utilities available from shareware public-domain and commercial sources. Most work pretty well, though few handle reliably all of the odd video standards in place today. Screen-blanking programs are less important now than in the days when monochrome displays were dominant —burned-in characters on a color screen are much less likely than with a green or amber-phosphor monochrome display—but they're still popular.

And of all the screen blankers I know for PCs, *VGA Dimmer* is the best. It works with *everything:* monochrome, color, Hercules, CGA, EGA, VGA, etc.

Which hasn't got much to do with why I use it.

One of the more irritating things in life is the rube who wanders into your office to chat for a minute, then spends most of his time looking over your shoulder, reading what you have on-screen on your PC. Even when what you're working on is hardly confidential, there's a principle being violated here: Don't snoop. And it's worse with computer displays than with the random piece of paper on your desk . . . for while few visitors would try to read that piece of paper *while you're talking with them,* an amazing number of otherwise polite and decent people find they simply cannot keep their eyes off that glowing computer screen while they talk with you.

Which is, beyond questions of privacy and good manners, *extremely* distracting.

I used to think I was nearly alone in being bothered by people who succumb to the temptation to read a PC display over my shoulder. But when I began joking about it in speeches to corporate PC users, I got a lot of knowing laughter, sometimes robust applause when I said "Don't do it!" . . . , and a lot of people came up afterwards to tell me they wished people wouldn't do that to *them*.

That's easy to fix. Put *VGA Dimmer*—a simple $30 utility—on your PC. It does all the usual screen-dimming tricks, and it will prolong the life of the PC's display.

But what *VGA Dimmer* does that really counts is let you instantly and discreetly blank that screen when someone walks in and you turn to greet them. Just three quick taps on either SHIFT key, and your screen is blank. It'll stay that way until you next hit a key—any key, though I use the "5" on the numeric keypad, since it doesn't change the cursor position from where I left it.

It's easy to get into the habit of using those three key flicks when someone walks in. And while *VGA Dimmer* may not break them of trying to read others' PC screens, I can guarantee they won't be reading *your* screen any more.

The Computerized
Phone Book

Sometimes the most amazing contributions personal computers can make to personal productivity come from obscure hardware gizmos and offbeat software packages that hardly qualify as mainstream tools.

For example, the single most-used, won't-do-without-it program running on my PCs is General Information's $99 telephone dialer, *Hot Line II*. It's actually a complete database system for managing the names, addresses, telephone numbers, and other details of your contacts. But its telephone-management tricks are so nifty that if you buy it to do nothing more than place your calls, you'll probably find *Hot Line's* payback faster than that of any tool—computerized or not—that you've ever used.

I take, and make, a lot of calls in the course of a day. The incoming calls are screened, which saves a lot of time. But that's only half the problem. I could let my secretary place outgoing calls for me, make sure Mr. or Ms. So-and-So is on the line, then pass the call along to me. But I find the presumptuousness and bad manners of that approach unacceptable; I keep imagining self-important Hollywood moguls screaming "Calls! Get me some calls!" at their teams of secretaries. And I know how much I'm put off when someone's secretary calls *me* then puts me on hold until she can find Mr. Big.

(OK, I confess: I do use that system once in a great while: when I'm in a meeting, when I'm rushing off to the airport, when I have to return 10 calls in six or seven minutes. I hope the people I reach will understand the circumstances, and will know that I don't make it a routine. And I fear they often don't understand.)

Besides, I like doing things myself. But I'm not crazy, either: I don't want to have to look up everyone's telephone number, or dig through several Rolodexes, or call my secretary to find a number.

Phone Power

So I rely on *Hot Line*. I just tap ALT + 2 on my PC's keyboard, and *Hot Line* pops up. I type the first few characters of the name of the person or business I want to call, hit ENTER, and *bam!* the number is on the screen, along with the local time in that person's area, popped up in a *Hot Line* display over whatever I had on-screen before. I hit F2 and up comes a screen with the background information I might need on that person or company: secondary contacts, additional telephone numbers, fax and telex numbers, addresses, names of secretaries and spouses and kids, and so on. I hit F2 once again, and the call is placed. When I hear the phone ringing, I just pick up the handset, tap the PC's space bar—and I'm talking, with the PC out of the loop.

While I'm talking, I can if I wish add notes on the person or on the specifics of this call in a Notes field in the *Hot Line* record. (I could have several thousand words of annotation per listing, but I've never needed that much.) When I finish, I tap the ESC key, *Hot Line* disappears, and I'm back in the spreadsheet or word-processing document or whatever I was working on before I placed the call.

Like many things with PCs, it takes a lot longer to describe that process than to simply *do* it. I usually get calls through in about five seconds from the time I hit *Hot Line's* hot key. That's far faster than any other system I know—and certainly faster than asking someone else to put the call through for me, then call me so I can pick up.

The program does much more than just auto-dial. It can search your entire database in a couple of seconds by a name, or a fragment of a name, or any other bit of data buried in a record somewhere in that database. Give it an area code and it will tell you where in the world that area code is used, and the local time there. Give it a city name and it will tell you the area code—then, with one more keystroke, call information for that area, so you can get an unknown telephone number. *Hot Line* lets you manually dial numbers from your PC's numeric keypad; or dial a number it finds on-screen in a letter or other document; and it times and logs your calls by date, duration, party called, and destination. You can set it up to fight through almost any switchboard, handle oddball LATA and inter-LATA routings, and choose among several long-distance services.

When you buy *Hot Line,* you'll find General Information throws in a 10,000-entry directory of US businesses. You can also buy separate "InfoPacks" of thousands of names, addresses, and telephone numbers in many fields: advertising/media/PR, high-tech, toll-free, travel, financial, colleges and universities, and more. Once loaded on your PC's hard disk, those directories are available just like your own personal directory, at the touch of a couple of keys.

Personalized Phone Books

I keep *Hot Line* on the portable PCs I use, too—actually, it's the first program that goes on the hard disk of *any* new PC I use, installed right after I've formatted the disk and put DOS on the machine. But when I'm traveling, I don't always have a PC with me—and when I do, it may not be sitting open, turned on, and ready to use. For those occasions, I use a customized "phone book" printed from *Hot Line's* listings. Our *Hot Line* database now has something over 3,000 listings in it; the resulting minitelephone book is 5 × 8 inches and 128 pages long.

That phone book has virtually every number I need, no matter where I am, from local airline reservations numbers around the world, to home numbers for my staff, to the numbers to call if I lose a credit card.

We print out new phone books for everyone here every quarter; before each printing we gather all the old books and make sure the inevitable handwritten additions and corrections in them are folded into our master electronic *Hot Line* database. The day-to-day updates are automatically written into that master copy, of course, as we work.

Hot Line stores its files in standard *dBASE* .DBF format, and thus you can use any database program that reads *dBASE* files to format and print those phone books. I prefer, though, to use a clever little database-printing utility, *Books, Cards & Labels,* which produces these phone-book booklets, printed front and back and with full imposition—a printer's term for making sure the printed pages of multipage booklets come out in the right order.

Corporate Directories

One of the most interesting larger-scale uses of *Hot Line* is to produce and distribute throughout a company customized electronic telephone directories. By giving each employee a copy of *Hot Line* and a disk with a company's internal phone directory—or a directory of customers, or suppliers, or any other group—firms can assure that all their employees are dealing with current, accurate data. Updating those directories is as easy as simply distributing the updated file on floppy disks.

This idea of distributing customized directories has been given another twist in the Seattle area, where General Information is based. In cooperation with USWest, the local phone company, the company sells a special *Hot Line II* package that includes a Seattle-area electronic phone-book file. That file lists 90,000 Seattle-area business numbers, with company data, addresses, and even SIC codes. Since *Hot Line* files are easily searched with any database program that handles *dBASE* files, it's a snap to search the Seattle file for prospects by SIC, then start calling them. (Of course, those bound to more traditional approaches could print address labels from the file, for a promotional mailing.)

General Information says the Seattle directory experiment may lead to other, similar local or regional business directories on disk soon.

You can also access *Hot Line* on a file server on a local area network, of course . . . though current versions leave something to be desired when it comes to network management tools.

You may think I'm exaggerating when I say *Hot Line* is the most important, most-used program on my PC. I'm not: I sometimes use it 50 or 60 times a day. Nothing—not *1-2-3*, or *Excel*, or *Word*, or *Paradox*, or any of another dozen favorite programs of mine—contributes so directly to making my business day go smoothly.

Simply put, *Hot Line II* has become my most important PC productivity tool.

I Remember *Exactly*
Where I Put That File . . .

No matter how cleverly you construct a naming convention for your files, and how wisely you organize those files into directories and subdirectories, you're still going to lose files. Not by inadvertently erasing them, but by not being able to remember where on your hard disk you stashed them.

In the days when floppy disks were our primary means of data storage for PCs, it was hard to lose a file on a disk; there just wasn't room for that many files on a floppy. (The problem then, of course, wasn't on the file level, but on the *disk* level: Which disk was the file on . . . and where was that disk?) Even when those first huge 5MB and 10MB hard disks appeared for PCs, losing a file wasn't much of a problem. As capacious as five or ten megabytes seemed then, there still wasn't that much electronic real estate in which to misplace files.

But now, with 20MB to 40MB hard disks the smallest in common use, the standard disk pushing 80MB, and plenty of 150MB to 600MB disks around, it's become incredibly easy to lose files.

I know all too well: I do it all the time.

But I find those files very quickly, thanks to two clever utilities. Though there's a bit of overlap in their functions, there's also a huge difference in the scope of the services they offer, and I find I can't do without either of them. I think you'll find at least one or the other of great value—and perhaps, like me, you'll come to think of both of them as indispensable.

Quick and Easy

The first is Microlytics' *GoFER*. It can run either as a pop-up or a stand-alone program. Give it a couple of words from the document you want to find, the degree of exactness it should use in looking for those words (for example, whether the combination of capital and lowercase letters you used when you entered the search criteria is critical), and the name of the directory or directories you want searched, and *GoFER* goes off looking for files it thinks may be the ones you want.

It will stop at each file, and show you the relevant passage. You can skip to the next file, or print that one, or get a printed list of all the files in which *GoFER* believes it may have found matches for your specifications.

Often that kind of *ad hoc* searching is just what I need: a quick zip through a limited universe of possibilities, with no added bells and whistles. *GoFER* is intentionally limited to the kinds of file-searching many of us need to do every day—for example, searching through a welter of old electronic-mail messages you've saved to disk, to find the one with the phone number for the audio-visual service in Sacramento.

GoFER is reasonably fast, cheap ($50) and very useful. If I'm fairly sure I know where a file is, and very sure I know some of the words or phrases used in it—even though I can't remember the filename I gave it—I turn first to *GoFER*.

The Great Explorer

Sometimes I've not only forgotten the name of the file, but also exactly the words I used in it; I know in a general sense what I'm looking for, but not the specifics. I may remember, for example, that the file dealt with a sailboat docked in St. Pete—or was it Tampa?—and as for where it is on the hard disk, I haven't a clue. At that point I've usually looked through all of what I considered the obvious places, haven't found the file, and am not in a very good mood.

With a scowl on my face, I turn to Lotus's *Magellan*. When I first saw *Magellan* in a very rough prerelease version, I told the developers I thought it was the most useful new program I'd seen in two or three years. Experience using the program through its first two releases has done nothing to change my mind.

Magellan is hard to define: It's sort of a DOS shell, sort of a hard-disk manager, sort of a file-finder, sort of a file-compression utility, sort of . . . an all-purpose toolkit. But what it does absolutely best is search through the files on your hard disk for documents you can't find.

Magellan takes a different approach than *GoFER* to looking for strayed files. *GoFER* needs no indexing; it simply opens every file, looks through it, and either shows you part of the file or closes it and goes on to look in the next file in that directory. That makes *GoFER* too slow, for my taste, in searching through several directories, or across several partitions on a very large hard disk. It also means that *GoFER* insists on stopping and showing you every file it thinks may be the one you're looking for. When *GoFER* finds two or three files that meet your specs, that's great; when it finds a hundred files, and stops at each one, things get tedious.

Magellan, on the other hand, requires you to run an indexing routine on your hard disk when you first install it, and then to run an index-update routine from time to time. It records the location of every word on the disk in an astonishingly compact index—typically less than five percent the size of the material indexed. In return for that help, and for the space on your disk to store that index, *Magellan* can do astonishingly fast searches, even across very large disks.

And even better, it first builds a list of possible "found" files for you, then shows you one after another, with literally instant switching from one to the next. That's a lot more convenient than GoFER's approach of asking you to wait while it examines and then shows you each file.

Both programs have smart "viewers" that show you the contents of each file without loading the application that created that file. *Magellan* has more (and more sophisticated) viewers than *GoFER,* but if the programs you usually use are on *GoFER's* list, *Magellan's* greater reach may be academic.

A Matter of Style

If you have a modest-size hard disk, use only a few applications programs, usually have a fairly good idea where a file may be lurking, and simply don't want to go through those files manually looking for your missing gem, I'd recommend *GoFER.* If on the other hand you use a large hard disk, use many applications, and often haven't the slightest idea where to start, *Magellan* is the better choice.

You may also prefer *Magellan's* style of searching, though remember: You buy the convenience of examining files in a batch at the cost of running indexing updates from time to time. If the file hasn't been indexed, *Magellan* isn't going to find it. And *Magellan's* other features, from making hard disk backups to compressing files to save disk space or for archiving, are useful tools, too, making it a great bargain at a typical price of $99 or so.

Either way, you won't have to sit there at your PC, glumly loading file after file, staring at the screen and cursing under your breath, vowing never to use obscure filenames again.

Memory-Management
To the MAX

When the 80386 microprocessor first appeared, Intel engineers loved to brag about all the clever things it could do, especially in managing the memory installed in a personal computer. We could create multiple concurrent virtual DOS PCs in a single '386-equipped machine, they said—each with access to its own 640 KB of memory. We could load memory-gobbling terminate-and-stay-resident programs in that maze of underused memory between 640 KB and 1 MB. We could move part of DOS's structure, such as device drivers, up into that memory range. We could . . . they went on and on.

Unfortunately, few '386 PC users found they actually used the chip's memory-management capabilities. It turned out you needed some very smart system-level software—code far beyond PC users' ability to create—to gain access to that valuable bag of tricks. Quarterdeck's *Desqview 386* and *QEMM* were one answer: they managed '386 PCs' memory in a way that let users jump among several windows, each with a program running in it. Microsoft's *Windows/386* tried the same thing with a graphical interface, and largely flopped. *Windows* 3.0 does much better, and in fact works so well that if you really want to multitask several programs at once, you probably should use it even if you don't care for its graphical approach to computing.

But throughout the '386 mania, one company introduced, then kept improving, what I'm convinced is the most useful memory-management system of all. Now in Version 5.0, Qualitas' *386*^{MAX} (often written and called "386 to the Max," or "386^Max") won't give you icons, windows, or multitasking. What it will give you is very intelligent management of all the memory you have in your PC—in a way that frees up more of that precious first 640 KB of RAM than any other program available.

A full recounting of *386*^MAX^'s tricks would be a long read. Instead, let me tell you what it does, and how simple it can be to use.

Your '386 PC can directly address up to four *gigabytes* of memory. I don't know anyone who has that much RAM installed (nor for that matter, how you'd shoehorn it into your PC, given present RAM-chip capacities); most '386 machines have 1 MB, though increasingly businesses are equipping '386 PCs with 2 to 4 MB of memory. *386*^MAX^ can make good use of whatever it finds in your PC, but it really shines when you have just 1 MB of RAM installed. DOS knows how to use the first 640 KB of that 1 MB memory minimum; anything above 640 KB requires special handling.

Though we've long said PCs can only address 640 KB of memory, that isn't really true. From the very first IBM PC, all PCs and PC compatibles have used the full 1 MB of RAM the Intel 8088 chip knew how to address. The space between 640 KB and 1 MB, however—a region generally known as "high memory"—wasn't available to us. The PC's ROM BIOS used it for such system-management tasks as video-display management. No PC used *all* that high memory, though, so there were typically several ragged little chunks distributed between 640 KB and 1 MB that went unused.

Meanwhile, DOS got bigger; we learned about the glories of TSR programs, and started loading up on them; and local area networks came along, with their requirement for network-driver software. All that had to come out of our 640 KB of "base" or "user" RAM. Even if you had the full 640 KB installed, you might find yourself with only 500 KB or so of memory left for your programs— often, especially in the case of networked PCs, even less. That made it impossible to use such programs as *Paradox,* for example, which require a minimum of 512 KB of free RAM to load.

Clearly all those '386 memory-management tricks the Intel guys liked to talk about offered hope for solving this "RAM Cram" crisis . . . but how to use those tricks?

Qualitas' *386*^MAX^ shows how. The program first "organizes" your memory, looking for little chunks of lost RAM above 640 KB and below 1 MB. It gathers those into a pseudo-contiguous block of memory. Finally, using a clever utility, *Maximize,* included with *386*^MAX^, it goes through your CONFIG.SYS and AUTOEXEC.BAT files, looking for pieces of code it can relocate into that reclaimed high memory.

The results can be astonishing. I've found PCs that with as little as 500 KB of available RAM before running *386*^MAX^ can wind up with 570 KB, 580 KB, and even more available after it's been installed.

If you had to work out which pieces of code could be loaded into high memory, and write the instructions to do so yourself, *386*^MAX^ would still be worth the trouble. That is, in fact, exactly how *386*^MAX^ was used before Version 5.0. Now, however, *Maximize* does all that work for you. You simply keep rebooting the machine as you install *386*^{MAX}; *Maximize* works out another little move on each pass, until finally—perhaps five minutes after you start the process—it decides it can do no more.

And then, after you reboot once more, you discover you have 50 KB or 75 KB more available memory than when you began. Thereafter, *386*^{MAX}'s work is completely transparent: you'll never know it's there.

Few under-$100 programs can deliver so much value to the PC user as *386*^{MAX}. It works equally well on 80486-based machines, of course (because the '486 chip is basically a faster '386 with some external support chips brought onboard). Either way, *386*^{MAX}'s uncanny ability to rebuild the memory in your PC is the key to putting the full power of '386- and '486-based PCs to work.

LapLink Again

I know: you heard about *LapLink* in **On the Road,** where I described how useful this speedy file-transfer utility is for moving files between diskless portable PCs and desktop machines. But there's a lesser known use of *LapLink* that can be even more valuable when you're upgrading from an old PC to a new one—or if you have to set up the hard disks of several PCs with identical software kits.

Normally, of course, *LapLink* is used to transfer files from a traveling PC to one kept at a fixed location. It does that quickly and easily, by revving up the two machines' serial ports to 115,000 bps—about six times their usual speed for data-transfer—then pumping perfect, error-free copies of selected files on Machine A through that hyper-speed serial connection to Machine B. When you use a notebook-size lap portable, without a floppy disk, that kind of *LapLink* data transfer becomes a part of your everyday routine.

But there are sneakier uses for *LapLink*—uses its creators no doubt never intended.

My favorite is to use *LapLink* to set up a new PC from an existing one. If, say, you need to set up several new PCs your company has just bought so that the software on their hard disks matches exactly the software on the company's standard-issue PCs, *LapLink* makes the job incredibly easy. Normally you'd have to go through a tedious routine of setting up all the directories and sub-directories needed on each new machine, then copying each program from its master floppy disks to each of the new machines' hard disks. That can take *days* . . . and of course, you need to sit there and endlessly shuffle those floppies in and out of the drives on each new computer.

Or you could do a full backup of the master PC's hard disk, then run a re-store routine with those backup disks onto each new machine. Which would take even *longer.*

Instead, you could just connect a serial cable between the master PC and, in turn, each new PC, then install a copy of *LapLink* on each computer—*LapLink* will even copy itself automatically onto each machine, as it's connected to the master PC, if you wish—and let it set up the new machine for you. It will copy the complete directory and subdirectory structure of the master PC, all the programs, and even any data files (such as word-processing templates) you may have on the main machine. You don't need to sit there throughout the routine, either: *LapLink* runs the entire transfer routine by itself. And if there are some directories or subdirectories you don't want copied, *LapLink* lets you exempt them from the transfer.

(You could also do this with the XCOPY command, added by Microsoft and IBM in DOS 3.2. But I still prefer the convenience of *LapLink*, because it allows me to exclude items I don't want copied; XCOPY copies everything.)

That kind of convenience is priceless for managers of PC support departments. But even if you're never called on to set up a fleet of new computers to match a standard configuration, you may find this trick handy.

Say you're upgrading to a new PC. You don't want to leave all your old programs and files behind, of course. Before *LapLink*, the only way to transfer that data was to make a full backup of your current PC, then tediously restore all that data to the hard disk in the new machine. You'd have had to use the same backup medium and mechanism on both machines, of course, which usually meant running that backup/restore from floppies. Have you ever done a backup of an 80 MB hard disk, and then a restore to a second hard disk, on floppy disks? It takes about 70 disks, and several hours . . . for each half of the backup/restore process.

LapLink makes upgrading incredibly easy. The total set-up time might be five minutes; then you can walk away while *LapLink* completes the job faster than you ever could with floppies. All by itself.

You don't have to be a PC manager to find *LapLink*ing two desktop PCs a useful trick. You *do* have to hate wasting time.

I can't leave this point without bringing up the issue of the legal ownership of all those programs you're going to be shipping back and forth. When you or your company buy a PC software package, you only buy a license to use it under the terms established by the software publisher and printed in the dense, tiny-print license found inside the box. (If this sounds awfully one-sided, you're right: the publisher gets to make up the rules, and you don't have any legal say-so in the matter.)

Those licenses typically allow you to use one copy of a program, on one machine, at a time. Some software houses, notably Borland *(Paradox, Quattro Pro, Sidekick),* are civilized enough to state clearly in the license that as long as it's only possible for you to use one copy of the program at a time, it's OK if you have a second copy loaded on another machine—one copy, say, on your desk-top PC at the office, plus another on your traveling laptop, or on a second PC at home. Others leave that in doubt, though my experience is that software publishers aren't much disturbed by the finer legal distinctions, so long as that one-user-at-a-time rule is followed.

But if you copy all your existing software from the hard disk in your old PC to the hard disk in your new one, and then your old machine is passed along by your company to a coworker . . . you are suddenly very much in violation of the licenses for every program you copied. Of course this applies on an even larger scale to PC managers who may install a copy of a program on a master PC, then endlessly copy the contents of that PC's hard disk to new machines to be distributed in the firm.

The point here is that you should possess a full, legal copy of each program installed on each PC in the office. Software publishers won't bother you if they find that you replicated one copy of *WhizCalc* a hundred times onto a hundred more PCs . . . if you can show you also provided a separate, legal copy of the program and its documentation to each of those hundred users. (It's OK if those copies sit unopened; the software people just want to make sure you bought as many copies as you have users of the program.)

The extraordinary convenience of setting up PCs through utilities such as *LapLink* can easily draw us into innocent and quite inadvertent violation of software licenses. Once, that was only a moral lapse, and you weren't likely to get tagged for the transgression. But today, the Software Publishers Association is swooping down on companies every week, demanding the right to do a "software audit" to make sure there are as many purchased copies of member companies' programs as there are users of those programs. If that happens in your office, and there's a discrepancy, your company will wind up in an expensive settlement with the SPA—and your stock is not going to be very high with your boss.

Even if you're not swayed by the moral-justice argument—that programmers and their software-publishing patrons deserve to get paid for their work—keeping your own hide intact ought to be motivation enough to avoid illegal software copying.

✎

System Snoops

Given enough time, savvy, and tools, it's not hard to find out what's gone wrong when a PC begins to behave oddly. Just run the right diagnostics programs, use logic testers, an oscilloscope, and some other fancy instrumentation, and apply a large dose of experience. But what if you're a PC *user*, not a PC technician? Can you get a quick diagnosis when things start to go awry?

There are at least four widely distributed diagnostic and check-up programs available for PCs. Each will let you snoop around inside your machine without ever opening the case. No more screwdrivers, static-grounding wrist loops, and chip testers: these programs sniff around for you in your PC's innards, test such components as memory chips, printer ports, and video cards, and give you a diagnostic report on-screen, or send it to your printer.

While this kind of hardware analysis without tools is extremely useful for the individual PC user who must, in effect, become his own support department, it's also important in corporate settings where a help desk may be only a quick call away. Increasingly, those help desks are off-site, making it impossible, or at least very expensive, for a technician to come calling desk-side.

But no matter how far away they are, if one or more of these packages is installed on your PC, you'll be able to give the technician at the other end of that phone line fast, authoritative answers to his most important questions: the amount of memory in your machine, how it is allocated, the entries in your AUTOEXEC.BAT and CONFIG.SYS files, a list of interrupts and their assignments, and so on. Indeed, these programs are becoming popular in some corporations, and are installed on every PC in the company for just that reason.

Each of the four programs works in a different way, and each is successful to a different degree in meeting various kinds of users' needs. Here's a quick rundown on each, and some pointers on how to match your own needs to one of these programs. The four: *System Sleuth, CheckIt, Manifest,* and *Control Room.*

An All-Purpose Tool?

At the low end of that list in terms of technical sophistication, Ashton-Tate's *Control Room* is, at first glance, the most comprehensive of the four. But in its attempt to be "all the utility you'll ever need," it becomes too broad and un-focused, and also too underpowered for the needs of most readers of this book. *Control Room* is not only a system snoop, but also a disk manager and a caching utility, and it performs many more PC-*management*, rather than PC-diagnostic, jobs. (Indeed, *Control Room's* developers do not consider the pro-gram primarily a diagnostic package, but rather a central control station for your PC. I include it here only because so many PC users consider it a diagnos-tic toolkit, despite Ashton-Tate's positioning efforts.)

While *Control Room* can perform some low-level system-snooping jobs, such as checking a BIOS-creation date or reporting on a PC's memory configu-ration, it only scratches the surface of what most of us need when we're poking around deep inside our computers. *Control Room* is probably a good choice for the PC neophyte, who isn't so much interested in (or ready for) system-diagnostics expeditions as he is eager to learn more about how his PC works. *Control Room's* long, verbose descriptions—screen after screen of clumsy, wordy description of such things as memory caches—turn out to be very use-ful for the new PC user interested in a once-over-lightly, one-topic-at-a-time course in basic PC operations. And it's nice to get all those performance-boosting utilities in one box—and to be able to set them up from a "control room"-style central panel.

But for the modestly experienced to very experienced PC user, *Control Room* is likely to be both too broad and too shallow to answer most questions.

Digging Into Memory Usage

Manifest, published by Quarterdeck Systems, is a big jump up from *Control Room* in technical savvy—but it's even easier to use. It has one of the most attractive and intuitive interfaces ever developed. *Manifest* pokes into system configuration, BIOS dates and makers, memory speeds, interrupts, and other arcane matters, and can be a godsend when you need a quick answer in any of those areas.

Manifest organizes its view of your PC into several areas: System, First Meg of Memory, Expanded Memory, Extended Memory, and DOS. Each is directly accessible from a menu-item devoted to that area. If *Manifest* finds Quarter-deck's *QEMM/386* memory manager or its *Desqview* multitasking utility load-ed in your system, it automatically adds those categories to the menu, as well.

As you'd expect, since *Manifest* comes from a company with extensive ex-perience in analyzing, allocating, and managing memory, the program con-centrates on your PC's RAM resources. It can show you which parts of DOS, and which parts of every other program you're using, are loaded, and where. It can tell you which interrupts are being used—invaluable information when you're trying to get a new peripheral, such as a CD-ROM drive, running.

Manifest will give you a quick peek at your AUTOEXEC.BAT and CONFIG.SYS files, without having to load a text editor or word processor first. It can report the size of the DOS "Environment" space on your PC, to see if it should be increased in order to accommodate a longer PATH statement or additional SET entries in your AUTOEXEC file.

Manifest will also run memory-performance timing loops, which can be a great help when you're trying to see which memory in your system is fast and which is slow. That's a big help when you're trying to figure out where to load things such as remapped video ROM code, which always needs the fastest possible execution.

Finally, *Manifest* will prowl through your system and your way of setting up the system, and if it finds areas where it believes trouble is brewing—or where you could simply make better use of the system's resources—it makes specific suggestions for changes.

Manifest is so quick and simple to use that even if you choose another of these utilities as well—as I think many power users will—you'll find it worthwhile keeping on your hard disk all the time.

The Heavyweights

If *Control Room* is a first step towards a system-examination and diagnostic toolkit, and *Manifest* another step along that path—and each is better-suited for one kind of PC user or another—then the last two snoop utilities on my list, *System Sleuth* and *CheckIt,* are positioned head-to-head and are intended for the PC user willing to invest a little time digging around in his machine's hidden regions in the course of diagnosing problems.

System Sleuth was the first product of its kind on the market, and it got a lot of attention. A second, substantially improved Version 2.0 established it as the early leader in snoop utilities. Succeeding versions have added features and improved reliability; Dariana Technology, publishers of *Sleuth,* also produce *WinSleuth,* a special *Windows* version of the program.

CheckIt is a newer entry, now in its third major version. It is probably the market leader (sales are notoriously hard to track in software-utility markets), and offers the most useful set of tests of any of these programs.

If I had to choose between the two, I'd pick *CheckIt.* Its information is often presented graphically, instead of in a numeric/tabular form, which makes it faster and sometimes easier to find what you're looking for. It includes very good system benchmarks, with bar-graph read-outs, which exercise the PC's processor, video display, hard disk, and math coprocessor (if present).

But I refuse to choose. Every time I decide I can really live with only one or the other, I find myself tracking down a problem that can only be answered by combining the test suites and system probes of both packages. Each of these programs costs under $100, so it's not a financial burden to keep both of them —along with *Manifest*, which costs just $50 or so—available for both day-to-day "confidence" tests as well as for those harried moments when things go Seriously Wrong, and I start sweating.

I think almost every savvy PC user could benefit from having *Manifest* on hand; and for the slightly more technically inclined, the combination of *CheckIt* and *System Sleuth* rounds out an unbeatable diagnostic toolkit.

All without ever turning a screw, popping the lid off your PC, or pulling a card. Impressive.

Protecting Your Stash

For experienced PC users, the AUTOEXEC.BAT and CONFIG.SYS files often represent not only a finely tuned path to setting up their PCs the way they want them, but also a big investment of time in fiddling and tweaking, to get those files just right.

Which makes it all the more irritating when the installation routine for a new program modifies those files, as part of its job of moving the new program onto your PC's hard disk. Even when installation programs ask for permission to make those changes before actually doing so, it's the rare PC user who hits *Y* for Yes without a wince and a few minutes' concern over whether he's about to lose something.

Sometimes installation programs are written as simple .BAT batch files, making it easy to snoop around in the file before running it, to make sure it isn't about to do violence to your precious AUTOEXEC and CONFIG files. But increasingly, installation routines are .EXE or .COM files, which means the only way to find out what they'll do is to actually run them . . . and suffer the consequences.

PC users have developed all sorts of little tricks to protect their AUTOEXEC and CONFIG files. The most common is to keep an extra copy of each, but with a different filename extension, such as AUTOEXEC.XTR or CONFIG.BAK. But semi-well-behaved installation routines often save your current AUTOEXEC and CONFIG files with extensions such as .BAK before modifying them; install a couple of programs that work that way and you'll find that your original, prized, unaltered, safety-net copies have been overwritten by those .BAKs.

Though there are more devious tricks to avoid losing these two critical files in the form you prefer, my favorite is simply to create a directory called STASH on the hard disk, and copy the current, tested-and-proven AUTOEXEC and CONFIG files to that directory. Installation programs always look for these two files in the root directory of your hard disk (since neither can be found and run when your PC boots up unless it's in the root directory) so putting extra copies away in another directory keeps them out of harm's way.

Once you've created that STASH directory, consider moving copies of any configuration files created by your applications there, as well. That way, if you make a change you later regret, you won't have to tediously track back through those changes, but can instead simply copy the spare, unchanged configuration file from STASH back into the program directory, and you're back in business.

❧

Where's Your Boot Floppy?

Quick: where's your boot floppy? In the bottom drawer of your desk? Tucked away with your most important data disks? Stashed with your most recent backup disks or tapes?

What? You don't *have* a boot-up floppy . . . ?!?

The voice of experience: one fine day you're going to turn on your PC, and listen to the hard disk's whine as it comes up to speed. And then you're going to get a very nasty prompt on-screen, something like

General failure reading drive C:

Your disk may or may not have gone south. But that's OK—you have all those wonderful disk-fixing utilities right there on your hard disk, right? So you can probably diagnose and maybe even fix it yourself, right?

Sure. But if you have to boot off the hard disk, how are you going to bring the PC up in the first place so you can load those swell toolkit programs . . . when the hard disk isn't working?

At that point, one of two things will happen. Either you'll reach in the drawer for your trusty boot-up floppy, put it in drive A, reboot, watch the system come up, then go to work figuring out what's wrong (perhaps using the original floppies of those disk-fixing programs). OR, you'll curse and scream, and slip into the despair of someone who knows he could have avoided a lot of trouble with one very simple trick.

But you never got around to making that boot-up floppy you know you should have made, eh . . . ?

Boot-up floppies are nothing new, of course: we all used them in the days before hard disks. A boot-up floppy needs only the DOS system files (the hidden IBMBIO.COM and IBMDOS.COM files, and the visible COMMAND.COM file). If you're smart you'll also put on that floppy your AUTOEXEC.BAT and CONFIG.SYS files, and also any files they call (such as memory-managers, DOS shells, etc.), so the boot disk can set up your PC exactly the way you're used to using it.

I keep a couple of copies of my boot-up floppy. Both are bright-red—finally, a use for colored floppy disks!—and are kept in separate places, as extra protection against damaging or misplacing one.

It's *so* easy to make a boot-up floppy and keep it nearby. But so few PC users do it. . . .

The Hotshot Backup Disk

This is one for those among you—you know who you are—who love to talk about the importance of backups, but hardly ever make one. Or maybe, have *never* made one. I'm going to try to save you from yourself, but I can't do it without your help.

When the IBM PC-AT was introduced in September of 1984, it brought to market the brand-new 1.2 megabyte 5¼ inch floppy disk. Those of us who had been using PCs for years marveled at the huge capacity of that disk: almost four times that of the 360KB floppies we'd gotten used to with the PC-XT and DOS 2.1. *Wow!* What would we ever *do* with all that space on a floppy?!?!?

Since those 1.2MB floppy disk drives invariably appeared only in machines that also included hard disks, there was little interest in running programs from disks in that floppy drive, nor in writing data to floppies there. Before long, we came to see floppy disks as backup media, as distribution media for new software, and as a medium for exchanging files with others. Which meant that 99 percent of the time, that new, gee-whiz 1.2MB floppy drive was going to waste.

I began showing friends at client companies a little trick for using that high-density floppy-disk drive productively. It caught on, and when I wrote about the trick in a computer magazine, a steady stream of letters began to arrive from readers who'd tried it and loved it. Been *saved* by it, they often said. Those letters continued for years; I still get one every now and then.

The trick is simple: keep a formatted high-density floppy disk in drive A. When you're working on really important projects, from time to time tell your application program to make an extra copy of the current version of the file onto that floppy disk. Don't let these copies take the place of the usual, working copy of the file on your hard disk; just make and keep them as hot-shot, *ad hoc* backups.

Because some afternoon you're going to be working on a presentation due the next morning, or on a proposal that has to go out by FedEx in an hour. And something's going to go wrong with your PC. Maybe a power failure takes the system down, and when you boot up, the PC can't find your hard disk. Maybe the hard disk simply gives up the ghost. Maybe the problem isn't related to the hard disk at all, but, say, the power supply in your PC goes out.

It doesn't matter where the problem is, nor even that you may be able to get the PC fixed pretty quickly the next day, or the next week: *What are you going to do in the interim?* It's easy to borrow or rent another PC . . . but when the file or files you need are on that hard disk in your broken PC, you're still up the creek.

Unfortunately, most PC applications make it a nuisance to save these extra copies on a floppy. You'll have to save the regular, hard-disk copy first, then do a second save—and for that second save to the floppy, you'll wind up typing in the whole new path. In other words, instead of just hitting the ENTER key to save the file XERR04.DOC once again in the subdirectory ANNLMEET, under the directory MSWORD50, on hard disk C, you'll have to erase the file-saving path that appears on-screen in that application (in this case, `C:\MSWORD-50\ANNLMEET\XERR04.DOC`) and type in the new path

      `A:\XERRO4.DOC`

Then to return to saving your regular stream of incremental working copies on the hard disk, the next time you save you'll have to type that whole `C:\MS-WORD50\ANNLMEET\XERR05.DOC` string in again.

I know: it's a nuisance.

But it's not one-twentieth, or one-hundredth, or maybe even not one-thousandth the nuisance of losing the work, just when you need to finish it.

The large capacity of those 1.2MB floppy disks—and their 1.44MB counterparts in the 3.5 inch disk world—means you can stack up "protection" copies of files on one disk for months. When that disk gets up to about 1MB or so of files, swap it for a new one.

This is an absolutely no-tech way of making quick, emergency backups. It's no substitute for real backups of everything on your PC's hard disk; the last thing I want to do is persuade you that you don't really need to make backups of that hard disk.

But this trick can save your bacon when something goes wrong between those full backups, and it also helps you finally get some mileage out of those otherwise little-used floppy drive you paid a hundred bucks for.

☙

SOURCES

Though it's easy enough to find IBM PCs, Lotus 1-2-3, and Hayes modems almost anywhere computer equipment is sold, the distribution of thousands of other important PC hardware and software tools is woefully uneven. Bad distribution is endemic to the PC business; that a product may be difficult to find should never be seen as an indication of its quality or usefulness.

The extraordinary rise of national direct-marketers—especially those that sell not only house-brand equipment and software, but also long lists of products from many other companies—gives hope that before long it will be possible to order almost any worthwhile computer product with a single 800-line telephone call.

Until that nirvana is reached, here are the manufacturers and their primary telephone numbers for the products mentioned in this book; a call to any of these companies will usually produce the name and telephone number of a dealer near you.

1-2-3
Lotus Development Corp.
617-693-8500

25-in-1 Font Cartridge
Pacific Data Products
619-552-0880

386^{MAX}
Qualitas, Inc.
302-469-8848

Allways
Funk Software, Inc.
617-497-6339

Baler, Baler XE
Baler Software, Inc.
312-490-5325

Calendar Creator Plus
PowerUp! Software
415-345-5900

Cambridge Spreadsheet Auditor
Cambridge Software
617-576-5744

Carbon Copy Plus
Microcom
203-798-3800

Charisma
Micrografx, Inc.
214-234-1769

CheckIt
Touchstone Software
213-598-4446

Close-Up
Norton-Lambert
805-964-6767

Co-Session
Triton Technology
201-855-9608

Control Room
Ashton-Tate
800-437-4329

Diconix printers
Eastman Kodak
312-218-5305

Expert Mouse
Kensington Microware
212-475-5500

GoFER
Microlytics, Inc.
716-248-9150

GrandView
Symantec, Inc.
408-253-9600

GraphWriter II
Lotus Development Corp.
617-693-8500

Harvard Graphics
Software Publishing Corp.
800-345-2888

Headlines in a Cartridge
Pacific Data Products
619-552-0880

Hot Line II
General Information
206-483-4555

HotShot Graphics
Symsoft, Inc.
702-332-4200

Impress
PC Publishing
213-556-3630

JetWare
Computer Peripherals
800-854-7600

LapLink
Travelling Software
206-483-8088

LaserJet printers
Hewlett-Packard
619-487-4100

LocalUnion 41, 81
Laser Tools, Inc.
415-420-8777

Magellan
Lotus Development Corp.
617-693-8500

Manifest
Quarterdeck Software
212-392-9701

MemoryMate
Broderbund Software
800-527-6263

Microsoft Excel
Microsoft Corp.
206-882-8080

Microsoft Windows
Microsoft Corp.
206-882-8080

Microsoft Word
Microsoft Corp.
206-882-8080

Norton Utilities
Symantec Corp.
408-253-9600

P.D.Queue
Funk Software
800-822-3865

PageMaker
Aldus Corp.
206-662-5500

pcANYWHERE
DMA, Inc.
516-426-0440

Persuasion
Aldus Corp.
206-662-5500

Pizazz Plus
Application Techniques
508-433-5201

Practical Peripherals buffers
Practical Peripherals
818-991-2200

PrintCache
Laser Tools, Inc.
415-420-8777

Professional File
Software Publishing Co.
415-962-9100

Professional Write
Software Publishing Co.
415-962-9100

Q&A
Symantec, Inc.
408-253-9600

QMS printers
QMS, Inc.
205-633-4300

Quattro Professional
Borland, Inc.
408-438-8400

Remote2
DCA, Inc.
404-442-4930

SatisFAXtion card
Intel PCEO
800-874-6835

ShareSpool units
Extended Systems, Inc.
208-322-7575

Sideways
Funk Software, Inc.
617-497-6339

Smart Cable
IQ Technologies
800-227-2817

Software Bridge
Systems Compatibility Corp.
800-333-1395

Spreadsheet Auditor
Computer Associates
408-942-1747

Super PC-Kwik
Multisoft Corp.
503-642-7108

SuperCartridge 1, 2
IQ Engineering, Inc.
800-765-3668

System Sleuth
Dariana Technology
714-994-7400

TCI phone-line managers
TCI, Inc.
415-349-0900

Top Priority
PowerUp! Software
415-345-5900

VGA Dimmer
Revolution Software
201-366-4445

Word for Word
Design Software, Inc.
312-231-4540

WordPerfect
WordPerfect Corp.
901-225-5000

XYZ Consolidate
Intex Solutions
617-431-1063

Index

About the Author

A former magazine photographer, award-winning film producer, and professional jazz drummer, Jim Seymour began working with PCs in the early days of the business. Through the years, his work as a consultant, writer, and speaker on PCs and productivity has brought him worldwide recognition. Seymour is a life-long resident of Texas and a graduate of the University of Texas. He lives in Austin with his wife and son.

"*PC Productivity Bible* takes the refreshing perspective of a business book that deals with computers, rather than a computer book that deals with business. The result is one of the most helpful books on computing I've seen . . . "

—Peter H. Lewis, *New York Times*

"The computer book of the month is *Jim Seymour's PC Productivity Bible*, which is the first of the new line of Seymour imprints from Brady Books. The book is filled with tips and tricks, some of which I use already, and some that I was pleased to learn about; and its written in Seymour's enviable style. This is definitely recommended."

—Jerry Pournelle, *BYTE Magazine*

"The 'good book' of personal computer productivity."

—John Woram, *PC Magazine*

"If you want to increase your PC Productivity and take advantage of techniques that can take years to learn, this book is just the ticket. The trouble and expense you will avoid by following Seymour's tips and advice will save you much more than the book's modest cover price, and you'll even have fun reading it."

—Nick Anis, *Computer Currents*

"Enhance your computing power by turning the doggone thing off and reading a couple of books . . . one of the best is Seymour's *PC Productivity Bible.*

—Larry Blasko, *Associated Press*

"Readable, humorous . . . Magnificent!"

—Sam Whitmore, Editor in Chief, *PC Week*